WAKE UP YOUR FAITH

365 daily encounters with Jesus

JEN LILLEY

BroadStreet

BroadStreet Publishing® Group, LLC
Savage, Minnesota, USA
BroadStreetPublishing.com

Wake Up Your Faith: 365 Daily Encounters with Jesus
Copyright © 2025 Jen Lilley

9781424570652 (faux leather)
9781424570669 (ebook)

All rights reserved. No part of this publication may be reproduced, distributed, or transmitted in any form or by any means, including photocopying, recording, or other electronic or mechanical methods, without the prior written permission of the publisher, except in the case of brief quotations embodied in critical reviews and certain other noncommercial uses permitted by copyright law. No portion of this book may be used or reproduced in any way for the purpose of training artificial intelligence technologies. As per Article 4(3) of the Digital Single Market Directive 2019/790, BroadStreet Publishing reserves this work from the text and data mining exception.

Scripture quotations marked TPT are from The Passion Translation®. Copyright © 2017, 2018, 2020 by Passion & Fire Ministries, Inc. Used by permission. All rights reserved. ThePassionTranslation.com. Scripture quotations marked NKJV are taken from the New King James Version®. Copyright © 1982 by Thomas Nelson. Used by permission. All rights reserved. Scripture quotations marked NLT are taken from the Holy Bible, New Living Translation. Copyright © 1996, 2004, 2015 by Tyndale House Foundation. Used by permission of Tyndale House Publishers, Carol Stream, Illinois 60188. All rights reserved. Scripture quotations marked NIV are taken from The Holy Bible, New International Version® NIV®. Copyright © 1973, 1978, 1984, 2011 by Biblica, Inc.™ Used by permission. All rights reserved worldwide. Scripture quotations marked ESV are taken from the ESV® Bible (The Holy Bible, English Standard Version®). Copyright © 2001 by Crossway, a publishing ministry of Good News Publishers. Used by permission. All rights reserved. Scripture quotations marked NASB are taken from the New American Standard Bible® (NASB). Copyright © 1960, 1962, 1963, 1968, 1971, 1972, 1973, 1975, 1977, 1995, 2020 by The Lockman Foundation. Used by permission. www.Lockman.org. Scripture quotations marked MSG are taken from *THE MESSAGE*. Copyright © 1993, 2002, 2018 by Eugene H. Peterson. Used by permission of NavPress. All rights reserved. Represented by Tyndale House Publishers, a division of Tyndale House Ministries. Scripture quotations marked NCV are taken from the New Century Version®. Copyright © 2005 by Thomas Nelson. Used by permission. All rights reserved. Scripture quotations marked NET are taken from the NET Bible®. Copyright © 1996–2016 by Biblical Studies Press, LLC. http://netbible.com. Quoted by permission. All rights reserved. Scripture quotations marked CEB are taken from the Common English Bible. Copyright © 2011 by Common English Bible. Scripture quotations marked CEV are taken from the Contemporary English Version. Copyright © 1991, 1992, 1995 by American Bible Society. Used by permission. Scripture quotations marked CSB are taken from the Christian Standard Bible®. Copyright © 2017 by Holman Bible Publishers. Used by permission. Christian Standard Bible® and CSB® are federally registered trademarks of Holman Bible Publishers. All rights reserved. Scripture quotations marked CJB are taken from the Complete Jewish Bible. Copyright © 1998 by David H. Stern. All rights reserved. Used by permission of Messianic Jewish Publishers. www.messianicjewish.net. Scripture quotations marked TLV are taken from the Holy Scriptures, Tree of Life Version. Copyright © 2014, 2016 by the Tree of Life Bible Society. Used by permission of the Tree of Life Bible Society. Scripture quotations marked EHV are from the Holy Bible, Evangelical Heritage Version® (EHV®). Copyright © 2017 Wartburg Project, Inc. All rights reserved. Used by permission.

Cover and interior by Garborg Design Works | garborgdesign.com

Printed in China

25 26 27 28 29 5 4 3 2 1

To my best friend, the Holy Spirit, whose wisdom, kindness, provision, humility, and love are inexhaustible. May this devotional bring You glory and wake up Your beautiful bride.

INTRODUCTION

It's such an honor to write this devotional and be invited into your faith journey. The profound eternal consequences of what may transpire in your life as the result of working through this book each day bring me to humble tears. I know I may never meet you on this side of eternity, but I love you, and I'm so honored to be called your sister in Christ.

I pray that this devotional allows the Holy Spirit to draw nearer to you than ever before and that He will sweetly and gently convict you as much as He convicted me while writing it. Please remember, guilt and conviction are entirely different concepts. Guilt seeks to shame while conviction seeks to discipline. The word *disciple* comes from the same root word as *discipline*. Maybe reading the word *discipline* stirs up some very negative reactions and emotions from your childhood, but godly discipline is meant to create disciples, not to punish. Oh, how deep is the Father's love for us! How indescribable is Jesus' desire to transform you from merely a follower in the crowd listening to His teachings to a close friend and disciple!

I pray that this book stirs your heart and faith in a way you've never experienced. I pray it calls you to greater depths and understanding and ignites you with a passion and deep yearning to love God and people more sincerely than ever before. I was very intentional about clearing the deck at the beginning of the devotional year to make room for faith to grow as the year progresses. If you feel convicted, take a breath and welcome the Holy Spirit as He prunes your heart. I promise He is cultivating the most fruitful year of your life if you just hang in there.

And I promise once we clear the deck, we're going to build you up and ensure you're equipped with unshakable faith from the Holy Spirit. Each devotion ends with a *Today I…* prompt, designed to help you actively live out what you've just read. Faith without works is dead, so we activate our faith by putting it into action. These declarations and steps of obedience—no matter how small—will strengthen your walk with Christ and allow you to experience His presence in a deeper way. I am here to love and encourage you every day of this year, and I hope I do get to meet you this side of eternity to give you a very tight bear hug and remind you once again how deeply loved and valued you are in the kingdom of our amazing God.

Love,

Jen Lilley

JANUARY

Clearing the Deck:
The Art of Surrender

JANUARY 1

A NEW THING

"Behold, I am doing a new thing; now it springs forth, do you not perceive it? I will make a way in the wilderness and rivers in the desert."

ISAIAH 43:19 ESV

As we step into a new year, it's natural to reflect on the past and look ahead to the future. Perhaps you're entering this year feeling like your relationship with the Lord has lost some of its spark. Maybe the busyness of life or last year's challenges have left you feeling spiritually dry. But take heart, because God's promise in Isaiah 43:19 is for you today.

God declares that He is doing a new thing. He is ready to breathe new life into your bones, revive your spiritual walk, and make a way where there seems to be no way. This new year can be a season of reawakening your faith and rediscovering the joy and passion you once had in your relationship with Him. Are you ready?

Ask God to revive your spirit and guide you in areas He has prepared for you. Write down one specific area where you desire God to work in your life this year.

Today I…

JANUARY 2

BE STILL

"Be still, and know that I am God; I will be exalted among the nations, I will be exalted in the earth."

PSALM 46:10 NIV

This year, I'm going to help you activate your faith and learn how to encounter Jesus every single day. But first, I want to invite you to be still. Stillness is not something I'm good at, but it's profoundly necessary in order to live a life of faith and to truly encounter Jesus each day.

Quiet your heart and mind and remember that He is God. He is sovereign over all the earth, and His plans will prevail. Pause from your worries and fears and let His peace fill your soul. Acknowledge His lordship over your life and trust in His perfect timing and ways.

Spend a few minutes in quiet reflection, focusing on God's presence and sovereignty. Sit with your palms open and facing upward and give God permission to take out of your hands anything you're holding on to or to put into your hands anything you'll need this year. Write down any thoughts or feelings that come to mind during this time.

Today I…

JANUARY 3

WITH, NOT FOR

"Come to me, all of you who are struggling and burdened, and I will give you rest. Take my yoke upon you and learn from me, because I am gentle and humble in heart, and you will find rest for your souls."

MATTHEW 11:28–29 CJB

In the agricultural context of Jesus' time, a yoke was a wooden beam used to join two animals, like a young calf and a strong cow, for plowing. It was a tool of guidance and shared labor, where the stronger animal led and supported the weaker one. Similarly, Jesus desires you to do things *with* Him, not *for* Him. He invites you to take His yoke upon you and offers a partnership in your daily tasks. Jesus invites you to pair your weaknesses with His strengths, to find rest in Him, and to learn from His gentle and humble heart.

As you start your day, invite Jesus into each task, big or small. Let Him lead you and bring His perspective to your work. You'll find rest and peace, knowing that He is with you in every moment.

Choose one task or responsibility for today. Before you start, invite Jesus into that task. Ask Him to guide you and change your perspective as you work.

Today I…

JANUARY 4

REDEFINED

Anything not based on trust is a sin.

ROMANS 14:23 CJB

If we're going to wake up our faith, we need to start with repentance. For fifteen years, I struggled with an eating disorder, relying on my own strength instead of trusting in God. I battled with shame and turned to food for solace, seeking quick fixes instead of facing my problems. I believed God was a healer, but I didn't believe He would heal *me*. I believed that since I had gotten myself into my addiction, I deserved the consequences of it. I took God off the throne and judged myself.

Romans 14:23 transformed my perspective about everything. Suddenly, it was like God shined a light and exposed all my deepest parts. I had hidden sins that I didn't even realize were sins because there was so much I was trusting more than I trusted God. As soon as I yielded to God my fears and need for control and chose to trust Him more than anything else, He healed me completely.

This is a year of freedom. Identify areas where you are worrying instead of trusting in God's power. Repent. Ask Jesus to help you trust Him, knowing that He is an overcomer by nature, and He is with you. Again, let Him carry your burdens.

Today I…

JANUARY 5

ENTIRELY NEW

If anyone is in Christ, he is a new creation. The old has passed away; behold, the new has come.

2 CORINTHIANS 5:17 ESV

When we come into a relationship with Jesus, we are not merely improved or modified; we are made *entirely* new. There is transformative power through unity with Christ. Through Christ, we are made righteous in God's eyes. This righteousness is not based on our own works but on the finished work of Jesus on the cross (Colossians 1:19–22). As we grasp this truth, it empowers us to live as new creations, confidently walking in the freedom and victory that Christ has secured for us.

Satan is a liar and the Father of Lies (John 8:44). Stop believing what he says about you. You are a new creation. Don't forget that to trust in anything more than God is a sin (Romans 14:23). So trust in what the Word of God, who is Jesus (John 1:1), says about you. When we really get this, it changes everything. We can live each day knowing we're loved, accepted, and set free by Jesus.

Write down a lie you have been believing about yourself. Now write the opposite, the truth.

Today I…

JANUARY 6

NATURAL OUTCOMES

The fruit of the Spirit is love, joy, peace, patience, kindness, goodness, faithfulness, humility, self control. Nothing in the Torah stands against such things.

GALATIANS 5:22–23 CJB

The fruit of the Spirit is not something you have to strive to achieve through your own effort. Remember, you're a new creation! Just as a fruit tree naturally produces fruit, so, too, as a Christian born of the Holy Spirit, the fruit of the Spirit is a natural outcome of Christ's transformative power in your life.

Faith is about *being*. As you abide in Christ, allowing His Spirit to work in you, His love, joy, peace, patience, kindness, goodness, faithfulness, humility, and self-control become evident in your life. These aren't manufactured qualities; they're fruits of the Spirit that flow organically from a heart transformed by the power of God.

Choose one of the fruits of the Spirit to focus on today. Ask God to help you cultivate this quality in your life and use it to bless others. Look for opportunities to practice this fruit in your interactions with others, remembering that it's not about striving but about surrendering to the work of the Spirit within you.

Today I…

JANUARY 7

DIVINE GUIDANCE

Your word is a lamp for my foot and a light on my path.
PSALM 119:105 CJB

It's natural to wonder if you're on the right path. I have good news! God's Word isn't just a guide; it's the light illuminating every step of the story God has written just for you. As you begin this new year, trust Him to lead you by using His Word to guide you. Let's start with two verses that can guide you through life.

First Corinthians 16:14 says, *"Let love and kindness be the motivation behind all that you do"* (TPT). When your motivation is love and kindness, you're on the right path and positioned to be led by God. Next, Ephesians 2:10 says, *"We are God's accomplishment, created in Christ Jesus to do good things. God planned for these good things to be the way that we live our lives"* (CEB). God cares so deeply for those around you. Every moment of your life has the potential to be a divine appointment, filled with people you're meant to cross paths with and love on today.

> Remember, we are the hands and feet of Jesus. Pay attention to those around you today and look for opportunities to encourage or love someone.

Today I…

JANUARY 8

RESTORATIVE LAWS

The Torah of Adonai is perfect, restoring the inner person. The instruction of Adonai is sure, making wise the thoughtless.

PSALM 19:8(7) CJB

Torah means "instruction" and refers to the first five books of the Bible. Psalm 19 reveals that it's God's teachings that restore our inner person—emotions, heart, and mind. God sets boundaries to protect and restore us, not to limit us or tear us apart.

The more I study God's Word, the more I'm in awe of His precision and intentionality. Rabbi Abraham Joshua Heschel said this of the Torah: "Every letter, every word, whether expanded or limiting a subject, is intended to teach a lesson."[1] One stunning example is found in the genealogy of Genesis 5. Dr. Chuck Missler explained how the meanings of the names from Adam to Noah form a hidden message that tells the gospel story—declaring God's plan of redemption long before Jesus walked the earth. God's wisdom far exceeds the world's most prestigious degrees, and His Word makes us wise.

Ask God to reveal all He's saying through the Bible. Spend six minutes watching Chuck Missler's "Hidden Codes—Torah Points to YHWH."[2]

Today I…

---

1 Abraham Joshua Heschel, *Heavenly Torah: As Refracted Through the Generations*, ed. and trans. Gordon Tucker (Continuum, 2007), 56.
2 Chuck Missler, "Hidden Codes—Torah Points to YHWH," posted November 4, 2012, by Tim Starz, YouTube, youtube.com. Please note this is not numerology.

JANUARY 9

SEEING CLEARLY

The precepts of the LORD are right, rejoicing the heart; the commandment of the LORD is pure, enlightening the eyes.

PSALM 19:8 ESV

Yes, we're looking at Psalm 19:8 again today. Sometimes, the best way to study Scripture is to slow down and ask the Lord to reveal Himself verse by verse. There's an important distinction between precepts and commandments. Commandments are absolute directives from God that must be obeyed while precepts are guiding principles designed to lead believers toward righteousness. Obedience to God's commandments keeps us on the narrow path, but walking in His precepts helps us stay in step with His heart. When we align our lives with both, our hearts rejoice because our consciences are clean.

Jesus summarized the entire Torah when He said, "'*Love the Lord your God with all your heart and with all your soul and with all your mind and with all your strength.' The second is this: 'Love your neighbor as yourself.' There is no commandment greater than these.*" (Mark 12:30–31 NIV). God's commandments enlighten our eyes—clarifying our perspective so we can view others through the lens of heaven and discern what is truly right and wrong in a world that calls evil good and darkness light (Isaiah 5:20).

Embrace God's precepts and look for ways to love your neighbor. Notice how it makes your heart feel.

Today I...

JANUARY 10

FEAR OF THE LORD

The fear of A‍donai is clean, enduring forever. The rulings of A‍donai are true, they are righteous altogether, more desirable than gold,…also sweeter than honey.…Through them your servant is warned; in obeying them there is great reward.

Psalm 19:10–12(9–11) cjb

We need a healthy fear of the Lord. In his books and sermons, author and pastor John Bevere teaches that the fear of the Lord is a holy reverence and awe of God, coupled with a fear of being separated from Him. Jesus warned us of eternal death, where unholy fear and darkness are indescribably multiplied because hell is absolutely void of God's light and love. This fear keeps us clean by compelling us to draw close to God and remain in His presence through the blood of Jesus. But how do we do this?

We should deeply desire God's judgment or rulings because they're perfect. When we accept Jesus as our Lord and Savior, we're covered by His blood. In other words, when God sees us, He sees the blood of Jesus instead of our sin, and He judges us as righteous and worthy of eternal life. That is surely sweeter than honey and more desirable than gold!

Ask the Lord to give you a healthy fear and awe of Him, for this is the beginning of wisdom.

Today I…

JANUARY 11

UNINTENTIONAL SIN

Who can discern unintentional sins? Cleanse me from hidden faults. Also keep your servant from presumptuous sins, so that they won't control me. Then I will be blameless and free of great offense.

PSALM 19:13–14(12–13) CJB

Sometimes we judge others or get offended without even realizing it. John Bevere's book *The Bait of Satan* highlights how offense is a major snare that leads us away from God's purpose.[3] When we harbor offenses, even unknowingly, they can control us and hinder our spiritual growth. This is why David's prayer in Psalm 19 is so crucial; he was asking God to reveal hidden sins and keep him from presumptuous sins that could dominate his life.

In *The Fear of the Lord*, Bevere explained that a healthy fear of God drives us to seek His will and live righteously.[4] Again, this fear isn't about being scared of God but about being deeply aware of His holiness and desiring to stay in His presence. By constantly seeking the Holy Spirit's guidance, we can identify and lay down sins as they happen, ensuring they don't take root and control us.

Ask the Holy Spirit to reveal and remove any hidden sins.

Today I…

---

[3] John Bevere, *The Bait of Satan: Living Free from the Deadly Trap of Offense* (Charisma House, 2014).

[4] John Bevere, *The Fear of the Lord: Discovering the Key to Intimately Knowing God* (Charisma House, 2006), 4, 137.

JANUARY 12

HEART THOUGHTS

May the words of my mouth and the thoughts of my heart be acceptable in your presence, ADONAI, my Rock and Redeemer.

PSALM 19:15(14) CJB

Notice how David wrote the phrase *"the thoughts of my heart."* The heart and the mind are deeply connected. What we think takes root in our hearts and informs our perspective. Consider salvation: First we mentally accept our need for Jesus, and then we invite the Holy Spirit into our hearts to transform us. Jesus said, *"The mouth speaks what the heart is full of"* (Matthew 12:34 NIV), meaning that our words are a reflection of our inner thoughts and heart condition.

In Romans 12:2, you're called to *"be transformed by the renewing of your mind."* When our minds are renewed by God's truth, our hearts follow suit, allowing us to reflect His love more fully. Proverbs 4:23 reminds us to guard our heart because *"from it flow the springs of life"* (ESV). We must be careful about what we allow to influence our thoughts. If we want to encounter Jesus, we need to allow the Holy Spirit to search our hearts and minds (Romans 8:27) and replace our perspective with His.

Pray Psalm 19. Invite the Holy Spirit to transform your heart and mind to align yourself with God's will.

Today I…

JANUARY 13

ON PURPOSE, FOR A PURPOSE

"I know the plans I have for you," declares the Lord, "plans to prosper you and not to harm you, plans to give you hope and a future."

JEREMIAH 29:11 NIV

There has never been anyone in all of history exactly like you—and there never will be. Even your fingerprints are a testament to that truth. No one has ever had the same design as you. God wove every detail of your being with a specific purpose in mind. He uniquely crafted your appearance, personality, and gifts for this exact moment in time (Esther 4:14). You are not a mistake. You were born on purpose and for a purpose.

In a culture constantly telling us to measure our worth by social media likes and comparisons, it's easy to feel like we don't measure up. But beloved, your value doesn't come from fleeting opinions or societal standards—it comes from God Himself. Your Creator has plans just for you, plans to prosper you, give you hope, and secure your future. The plans He designed for your life are unique, and no one can fulfill them but you. It's time to stop looking outward for validation.

Today, spend time in prayer asking God to reveal His plans for your life. Write down any dreams or passions He has placed on your heart.

Today I…

JANUARY 14

SUPER(NATURAL) GLUE

He is before all things, and in him all things hold together.
COLOSSIANS 1:17 NIV

I want to build on yesterday's devotion and talk about how even your genetic makeup reflects the nature of God. Have you ever heard of laminin? It's a family of proteins that play a crucial role in biology, particularly in holding tissues and organs together. What's fascinating about laminin is its structure—it has been described as having a shape resembling a cross. Louie Giglio gave a famous sermon discussing laminin, highlighting how even at a molecular level God has left His mark and reminding us that *"in him all things hold together"* (Colossians 1:17).[5]

Just as laminin is the "glue" that holds our physical bodies together, Jesus is the supernatural glue that holds our spirits together. Without His presence, everything would unravel. In Him, we find not just cohesion but also strength to hold together through life's challenges. He knits us together in a divine tapestry of faith, creating a community bound by love and grace.

Where are the places in your life where it feels like things are falling apart? Invite Him into those spaces. Then, think of someone you know who might also feel like their world is unraveling and extend the love of Christ to them in a tangible way.

Today I…

---

[5] Louie Giglio, "How Great Is Our God | Pastor Louie Giglio," posted April 12, 2021, by Louie Giglio, YouTube, youtube.com.

JANUARY 15

YOU ARE MINE

I praise you because I am fearfully and wonderfully made; your works are wonderful, I know that full well.

PSALM 139:14 NIV

It can be tough to love our bodies, especially with the modern pressures of a curated and filtered social media. Our bodies are intricate masterpieces, designed with extraordinary precision to reflect the image of God: *"God said, 'Let us make humankind in our image, in the likeness of ourselves'"* (Genesis 1:26 CJB).

We see divine order in nature, such as the Golden Ratio (1.618) found in galaxies, flowers, and even the proportions of the human body. As I was considering this, I realized that in Hebrew, the letters corresponding to 1 (*aleph*, א), 6 (*waw*, ו), and 8 (*heth*, ח) tell a powerful story. *Aleph* represents God and unity, *waw* symbolizes connection, and *heth* signifies life. Since Hebrew is read from right to left, 1.618 can reflect this idea: "Life from God, united with God." God has set His mark upon us, linking us to Himself with His divine breath and life. We are fearfully and wonderfully made—not random or forgotten but deeply known and loved by our Creator.

Stand in front of a mirror and declare Psalm 139:14 over yourself.

Today I…

JANUARY 16

BUILD UP

Do not let any unwholesome talk come out of your mouths, but only what is helpful for building others up according to their needs, that it may benefit those who listen.

EPHESIANS 4:29 NIV

The Bible clearly says your words carry immense power. The New Age movement teaches the concept of "manifesting," which essentially means that if you say positive words, positive things will happen to you. They believe this is their idea, but its principles can actually be found in Scripture. We know as believers that Satan is constantly perverting biblical principles meant to glorify God and serve others by tempting us to use them to serve ourselves.

Remember, the power of life and death is in the tongue (Proverbs 18:21); your words can build others up or tear them down. So choose to speak words of encouragement, kindness, and love, uplifting those around you and bringing glory to God.

Be intentional about your words today. Before speaking, ask yourself if your words will build others up and benefit them. Encourage at least one person today with words of life and encouragement, letting them know how much you appreciate and value them.

Today I…

JANUARY 17

PROMISE KEEPER

"God is not a human who lies or a mortal who changes his mind. When he says something, he will do it; when he makes a promise, he will fulfill it."

NUMBERS 23:19 CJB

I'm so grateful that God is completely faithful and unchanging, unlike humans who may lie or change their minds. His promises are unbreakable and trustworthy because they're rooted in His very nature. When we're facing doubt, we need to take the Romans 14:23 test—*"anything not based on trust is a sin"*—and ask ourselves, *What am I trusting more than I trust God in this moment?* As Numbers 23:19 points out, when our God makes a promise, He will fulfill it.

Consider the power of His assurances: God promises to never leave you nor forsake you (Deuteronomy 31:6), to provide for your needs (Philippians 4:19), to give you peace that guards your heart and mind (v. 7), to grant wisdom to those who ask (James 1:5), to make us new creations in Christ (2 Corinthians 5:17), and to give us eternal life through Jesus (John 3:16). God's promises are all anchored in His character and nature.

What's a specific promise God has made that you need to cling to today?

Today I…

JANUARY 18

DIE DAILY

"If anyone would come after me, let him deny himself and take up his cross daily and follow me."

Luke 9:23 ESV

When you accept Jesus as your Lord and Savior, you're choosing to live a life fully surrendered to God. It's human nature to want to resurrect our flesh, but Jesus said we should take up our cross daily. Every action and every word we speak should be an expression of love and obedience to Him: *"Whatever you do, whether in word or deed, do it all in the name of the Lord Jesus, giving thanks to God the Father through him"* (Colossians 3:17 NIV). We should fear God more than man's opinion and obey His Word.

This mindset transforms the mundane obligations of life into opportunities to glorify God and serve others with gratitude.

Today, purpose in your heart to take up your cross and live out Colossians 3:17 by doing everything as unto the Lord. Whatever tasks or conversations come your way, do them with excellence and gratitude, knowing that you are representing Christ in all that you do. Take a moment to thank God for His presence in your life and ask Him to help you live in a way that honors Him.

Today I…

JANUARY 19

WHITEWASHED TOMBS

"Woe to you, teachers of the law and Pharisees, you hypocrites! You are like whitewashed tombs, which look beautiful on the outside but on the inside are full of the bones of the dead and everything unclean. In the same way, on the outside you appear to people as righteous but on the inside you are full of hypocrisy and wickedness."

MATTHEW 23:27–28 NIV

Religious hypocrisy and corruption can deeply impact one's faith journey. Many encounter judgmental attitudes within religious institutions, leading them to associate the flaws of others with God's character. However, Jesus had significant issues with hypocrites who prioritized rules over genuine faith and love. He called them *"whitewashed tombs,"* criticizing their outward appearances of righteousness by exposing their inner corruption. With righteous anger, He condemned those who misrepresented God's character and led others astray through their actions.

When you encounter hypocrisy, it's vital to separate the failures of individuals from the essence of God. While people may fail, God remains steadfast in His goodness and love. Jesus invites you into a relationship that transcends organized religion. Rather than allowing others' actions to deter your faith, turn to Christ, who embodies perfect love and grace.

Forgive the Christians who have wounded you and remember that Jesus is perfect and will never fail you.

Today I…

JANUARY 20

CHURCH HURT

Be kind to one another, tenderhearted, forgiving one another, as God in Christ forgave you.

EPHESIANS 4:32 ESV

Forgiveness is a cornerstone of our faith and a reflection of God's grace in our lives. It's also a commandment with a condition: If we don't forgive others, God will not forgive us (Matthew 6:14–15). So how do we forgive, especially when the damage comes from other Christians? Ephesians 4 specifically addresses conflict within the church, which is not a new phenomenon. Church hurt is particularly painful because it often carries the implication that "they should know better" or "if they really loved Jesus, then…"

When I was a teenager, I experienced intense church drama. Despite my continual efforts to resolve the issue or love my enemies, I was met with stonewalling and hostility. It felt hopeless until my mentor advised, "Pray for them. Don't pray for judgment. Pray for blessings. I know you don't want to, but you must." As I surrendered to this biblical principle, I experienced profound healing. My heart overflowed with love for those who hurt me. When we pray for people who have hurt us, God softens our hearts, making room for forgiveness and healing and ultimately making us stronger than before.

Pray for your enemies and ask God to bless them.

Today I…

JANUARY 21

BE TEACHABLE

Live in harmony with one another. Do not be haughty, but associate with the lowly. Never be wise in your own sight.

ROMANS 12:16 ESV

In Romans 12:16, Paul gave us a powerful key to living in unity: having a humble, teachable spirit. Living in harmony with others, especially within the body of Christ, requires a willingness to learn from each other, no matter our position, background, or experience. It challenges us to not think too highly of ourselves but to associate with those whom others may overlook or consider lowly.

Unity in the church is only possible when we resist the temptation to be prideful and wise in our own eyes. A teachable spirit means recognizing that we don't know everything and that God can use anyone to teach us— sometimes in ways we least expect. When we allow ourselves to be humble, we become more open to correction, growth, and deeper relationships with those around us. And it's our unity that will reveal Christ as the Messiah (John 17:21).

Ask God to reveal any areas of pride in your heart and pray for a teachable spirit today. Seek opportunities to learn from others, especially those whom you may not usually look to for insight.

Today I…

JANUARY 22

UNITY

> "I pray also for those who will believe in me through their message, that all of them may be one, Father, just as you are in me and I am in you. May they also be in us so that the world may believe that you have sent me.…Then the world will know that you sent me and have loved them even as you have loved me."
>
> JOHN 17:20–21, 23 NIV

The unity Jesus prayed for isn't a superficial agreement but a deep, intimate oneness that reflects the unity of the Trinity itself. We're not just saved by Jesus—we're united with Him. Scripture says that we are seated with Christ in heavenly places (Ephesians 2:6) and that He didn't just die for us but *as* us (Romans 6:6–8).

This unity isn't just relational—it's supernatural. Jesus said, *"These signs will follow those who believe"* (Mark 16:17 NKJV). The same power that raised Christ from the dead now lives in us (Ephesians 1:19–20), equipping us to bring healing, deliverance, and the reality of His kingdom on earth. Jesus wants us to be so united with Him and with one another that the world will marvel and believe in Him.

Reflect on your relationships with other believers. Are there any divisions or conflicts that you need to resolve?

Today I…

JANUARY 23

SPUR EACH OTHER ON

Let us keep paying attention to one another, in order to spur each other on to love and good deeds, not neglecting our own congregational meetings, as some have made a practice of doing, but, rather, encouraging each other.

HEBREWS 10:24–25 CJB

God created us for community. We're called to uplift and encourage one another in our faith journeys. In a culture that feels isolated, divided, and competitive, we must prioritize fellowship with other believers. The book of Hebrews encourages us to gather regularly, to spur each other on toward love and good deeds.

Meeting together isn't just a suggestion; it's a command with a purpose. When we gather, we're not just filling seats. We're also fulfilling God's plan for us. We're meant to challenge and inspire one another to love and good deeds.

Send a text, make a call, or write a note of encouragement to another believer today. Let them know you're thinking of them and praying for them. Consider inviting them to join you for a time of fellowship and prayer even if it's virtual. Together, we can strengthen each other in our faith and walk closer with God.

Today I…

JANUARY 24

LESS SELF

In humility, regard each other as better than yourselves—look out for each other's interests and not just for your own.

PHILIPPIANS 2:3–4 CJB

True love, what C. S. Lewis called "charity" in *The Four Loves*, is selfless and sacrificial, seeking the good of others above our own desires.[6] Jesus, the ultimate example of love, demonstrated this by washing His disciples' feet—a task reserved for the lowliest servants—in order to teach us that greatness in God's kingdom is measured by our willingness to serve others.

When we step out in love and serve others, we not only reflect the character of Christ but also experience a deep sense of joy and fulfillment. It's in losing ourselves in service to others that we find our true purpose and identity as children of God. James 4:14 reminds us that our life is but a vapor, here today and gone tomorrow. While we still have the opportunity, we should live each day with a sense of urgency, seeking to love and serve others as Christ did.

Take a bold step in serving others today. Sign up to volunteer at a local soup kitchen or shelter.

Today I…

---

6 C. S. Lewis, "Charity," *The Four Loves* (Harcourt, 1960), 128–29.

JANUARY 25

NAME BEARERS

"You shall not take the name of the Lord your God in vain, for the Lord will not hold him guiltless who takes his name in vain."

Exodus 20:7; Deuteronomy 5:11 ESV

Until recently, I didn't understand the profound depths of the first commandment. In Hebrew culture, a name is more than a label. It represents the essence and authority of the person. Invoking a name in ancient Hebrew culture was invoking the presence and power of the one named. Misusing God's name was a severe offense because it meant misrepresenting His essence and authority.

Furthermore, the original Hebrew word translated as "take" in these verses is תִּשָּׂא (*nasa'*), which more accurately means "bear" or "carry." In other words, you should not say you're a follower of Christ (bearing His name) and then act in a way that would dishonor or profane His name. As Christians, we are called to bear God's name with reverence, reflecting His character in our actions and words.

Consider how you represent God's name in your daily life. Are your actions and words honoring to Him? Today, make a conscious effort to embody His love, grace, and truth in all you do, showing the world the true nature of our God.

Today I…

JANUARY 26

NO WORRIES

"Can any one of you by worrying add a single hour to your life?"

MATTHEW 6:27 NIV

Life has wilderness seasons, those times when it's easy to get caught up in worry and anxiety. We fixate on the future, our families, our jobs—the list goes on. We stress over things we can't control, hoping that our concerns will somehow change the outcome. Yet Jesus asks us a profound question: *Can all your worrying actually add a single moment to your life?*

Worrying doesn't change our circumstances; it only robs us of peace and joy. Instead of focusing on our problems, Jesus encourages us to focus on Him. He reminds us to ask ourselves this: If God cares for the birds of the air and the flowers of the field, how much more will He care for us, His beloved children (Matthew 6:26–30)?

Today, when worry knocks at the door of your heart, choose to trust in the Lord instead. He is still the author of your story (Hebrews 12:2). He will not forget you (Isaiah 49:15). Take a deep breath, say a prayer, and release your burdens to Him. Tell Him you trust Him.

Today I…

JANUARY 27

FIX YOUR EYES ON JESUS

[Let us fix] our eyes on Jesus, the pioneer and perfecter of faith. For the joy set before him he endured the cross, scorning its shame, and sat down at the right hand of the throne of God.

HEBREWS 12:2 NIV

In our journey of faith, we encounter challenges and obstacles that can distract us from our true purpose. Hebrews 12:2 calls us to fix our eyes on Jesus, the perfecter of our faith. Jesus, who endured the agony of the cross, did so because of the joy set before Him. That joy was us!

Jesus looked beyond the pain to the glory of bringing us back into a relationship with God. When we focus on Jesus, we find the strength to persevere. By keeping our eyes on Him, we're reminded of His love, His sacrifice, and the victory He achieved for us. This perspective both transforms our trials into opportunities to grow closer to Him and strengthens our faith.

Today, make a conscious effort to fix your eyes on Jesus. When you face difficulties, take a moment to pray and remember His sacrifice and victory. Reflect on how *you* were the joy set before Him, motivating Him to endure the cross.

Today I…

JANUARY 28

GOD OUR WARRIOR

"The LORD will fight for you; you need only to be still."
EXODUS 14:14 NIV

When our circumstances seem impossible, the Lord Himself fights for us. We need only to be still and trust Him. We often think miracles were commonplace in biblical times, so it was easier for people to have faith then. But that is not what Scripture says. When the Israelites were trapped between the Red Sea and the pursuing Egyptian army, they were terrified.

But Moses spoke these words of faith. The Israelites obeyed, despite the coming terror they saw with their eyes, and they put their trust in God. That was the exact moment that God miraculously parted the sea, delivering His people from their enemies. Whatever you're facing, stop trying to fight your battles on your own. Surrender them to God and be still. He is your Defender and Protector. His power is unmatched, and He is faithful.

Today, identify a specific battle you are facing and give this battle over to the Lord. Trust that He will fight for you and then be still in His presence. Throughout the day, remind yourself that the battle belongs to the Lord.

Today I...

JANUARY 29

PRIORITIES

"Seek first the kingdom of God and his righteousness, and all these things will be added to you."

MATTHEW 6:33 ESV

Life is short. Seeking God's kingdom and prioritizing a relationship with Him matters most. Jesus promises that when you focus on Him, your needs will be met. Daily responsibilities are overwhelming. It's human nature to prioritize your to-do list over your devotions when pressed for time. Remember, human nature is at odds with your spiritual nature (Galatians 5:17). Likewise, human logic is often contrary to God's wisdom (1 Corinthians 1:20–25; 3:18–20; James 3:13–18).

Paul and James said that human wisdom stems from selfish ambition. Fear and busyness are two of Satan's best-laid traps. Satan's goal is to keep you from knowing Jesus and your identity in Jesus. By prioritizing your to-do list over time with Jesus, you're relying on human wisdom and strength to achieve something that serves you instead of trusting God to provide. Working hard is godly, but it is not as important as intimacy with Jesus.

God can do more for you in a moment than you can do in ten years of striving. Resolve to prioritize God and then look at your to-do list and ask God to supernaturally accelerate your ability to accomplish your tasks.

Today I…

JANUARY 30

IDENTITY

Think of what you were when you were called. Not many of you were wise by human standards....But God chose the foolish things of the world to shame the wise; God chose the weak things of the world to shame the strong. God chose the lowly things of this world and the despised things—and the things that are not—to nullify the things that are, so that no one may boast before him. It is because of him that you are in Christ Jesus, who has become for us wisdom from God.

1 Corinthians 1:26–30 NIV

God's kingdom operates on principles that sometimes contradict human logic. Society values academics, influence, and wealth, but God delights in using what the world considers foolish and weak to accomplish His purposes. God's call is not based on our qualifications but on His grace.

God uses our weaknesses to display His strength and glory. Stop striving for worldly approval and instead rest in the knowledge that your value and effectiveness come from God. Jesus is our wisdom, righteousness, holiness, and redemption. We find our identity and worth in Him alone.

Reflect on your weaknesses and surrender them to God, trusting that He will work through you to demonstrate His love.

Today I…

JANUARY 31

FOR HIS GLORY

"In the same way, let your light shine before others, that they may see your good deeds and glorify your Father in heaven."

MATTHEW 5:16 NIV

This verse seems to contradict Matthew 6:1: *"Be careful not to practice your righteousness in front of others to be seen by them. If you do, you will have no reward from your Father in heaven."* However, both these verses are from the same teaching of Jesus. Matthew 5:16 emphasizes doing good deeds to glorify God while Matthew 6:1 warns against doing good deeds to glorify yourself.

Your light is supposed to point those in darkness to Jesus, who is the Light of the World. Remember, your human nature is always at odds with your spiritual nature, so you must die to yourself daily, stand firm, and not allow yourself to be tied up again to sin (Galatians 5). I find it so comforting that even the early believers who walked with Jesus and witnessed so many miracles needed this reminder.

Reflect on your motives. Are you seeking to glorify God or yourself? Ask God to reveal any pride in you and then surrender it to Him. Perform one act of service today to point others to Jesus.

Today I…

FEBRUARY

Living Out Love

FEBRUARY 1

REAL FAITH

What good is it, my brothers, if someone claims to have faith but has no actions to prove it? Is such "faith" able to save him? Suppose a brother or sister is without clothes and daily food, and someone says to him, "Shalom! Keep warm and eat hearty!" without giving him what he needs, what good does it do? Thus, faith by itself, unaccompanied by actions, is dead.

JAMES 2:14–17 CJB

All right! We did a lot of work in January clearing the deck. Now it's time to wake up our faith. Each day presents us with opportunities to encounter Jesus in the midst of our routines, but we also have to pause and pay attention to those around us.

In the hustle and bustle of life, it's easy to overlook the needs of others. Yet James reminds us that we demonstrate true faith through our actions. We are called not only to believe in Jesus but also to live out our faith by loving and serving those around us.

Today, consider putting an extra coat or some non-perishable food in your car to give to a person experiencing homelessness. Such kindness meets a physical need and reflects the love of Jesus in a tangible way.

Today I…

FEBRUARY 2

EVERYTHING IN LOVE

Do everything in love.
1 Corinthians 16:14 niv

To do everything in love means to approach every task, no matter how mundane, with a heart that seeks to honor God and serve others. It means treating people with kindness even when they don't deserve it, being patient when it's easier to be frustrated, and showing compassion even when it requires sacrifice. This kind of love is not self-seeking. It's a love that mirrors the selfless, sacrificial love of Christ.

This verse also challenges you to examine your motives. Are you acting out of love, or are other factors driving your behavior? It's easy to let pride, anger, or selfishness influence your actions, but 1 Corinthians 16:14 reminds you to realign your heart with God's. When love becomes your guiding principle, it transforms how you approach every aspect of your life.

Commit to making love the foundation of all you do. Let this verse guide your actions, decisions, and interactions. Ask God to help you see opportunities to show His love in practical ways. As you do, you'll be living out the heart of the gospel, bringing God's love into every corner of your life.

Today I…

FEBRUARY 3

A NEW COMMAND

"I am giving you a new command: that you keep on loving each other. In the same way that I have loved you, you are also to keep on loving each other. Everyone will know that you are my talmidim by the fact that you have love for each other."

JOHN 13:34–35 CJB

I prefer the Complete Jewish Bible translation because it provides a valuable Jewish perspective and historical context since the Bible was mostly written by Jewish believers. The word *talmidim* in today's passage simply means "disciple." This translation of John 13 makes me laugh because it emphasizes that we should *"keep on loving each other"* even after Jesus ascended to heaven. It reminds me of siblings who fight the minute their parents leave the room. Children who continue to treat their siblings with kindness when the authority figure isn't watching are truly absorbing their parents' teachings.

Similarly, it's easy to get into disagreements with other believers, our spiritual brothers and sisters. But Jesus commanded us to let our love surpass our preferences and differences with others. When we can agree to disagree on small theological interpretations that are not a matter of salvation, the world will know we truly are disciples of God and mature Christians.

Reach out to a fellow believer with whom you've had a disagreement and seek reconciliation. Show kindness and understanding, reflecting Jesus' love.

Today I…

FEBRUARY 4

THE NAME TEST

Love is patient and kind, not jealous, not boastful, not proud, rude or selfish, not easily angered, and it keeps no record of wrongs. Love does not gloat over other people's sins but takes its delight in the truth. Love always bears up, always trusts, always hopes, always endures.

1 Corinthians 13:4–7 CJB

Rabbi Julius Gordon is commonly thought to have said, "Love is not blind—it sees more, not less. But because it sees more, it is willing to see less." This beautifully encapsulates the essence of 1 Corinthians 13:4–7, where Paul described the true nature of love. Christian love is a love that goes beyond feelings and emotions, a love that reflects the character of Christ.

If we're continually running the race to reflect the nature of Christ, here's a simple test: Replace the word "love" in 1 Corinthians 13 with your name. Can you honestly say these qualities describe you? If not, write down the phrases where you fall short. This isn't about self-criticism. It's about growth. Becoming a disciple involves disciplining yourself to align your actions and preferences with those of Jesus.

Identify the areas where you struggle and ask God for the strength and guidance to improve. Commit to working on one specific trait this week and ask a friend or family member to hold you accountable in your journey to become more like Jesus.

Today I…

FEBRUARY 5

LENS OF LOVE

Don't let love be a mere outward show. Recoil from what is evil, and cling to what is good. Love each other devotedly and with brotherly love; and set examples for each other in showing respect.

ROMANS 12:9–10 CJB

When Paul urged us to *"love each other devotedly and with brotherly love,"* he was calling us to form deep, meaningful connections with our fellow believers, showing respect and honor to one another.

Genuine love has the power to transform lives. When we see others through the lens of Christ's love, we no longer define them by their past or shortcomings but by their God-given value and potential. When we truly understand that everyone is valued and loved by God, our interactions with others are transformed. We are called to be examples of Christ's love, not just in grand gestures but in everyday acts of kindness and respect. This involves turning away from evil, rejecting behaviors and attitudes that harm others, and clinging to what is good. All these things reflect God's character.

Identify one way you can demonstrate respect and kindness to someone in your life today, whether through a kind word, a thoughtful gesture, or the gift of listening. Remember, true love is not just an outward show but a reflection of God's love working through you.

Today I…

FEBRUARY 6

PURSUE LOVE

Pursue love, and earnestly desire the spiritual gifts, especially that you may prophesy.

1 Corinthians 14:1 ESV

It's important to seek the fullness of God's Holy Spirit and His gifts, but we often invert today's Scripture by prioritizing spiritual gifts over God's love. While it's exciting to witness miracles and the prophetic (not to be confused with demonic practices, which are condemned in Deuteronomy 18), we must remember that order matters to the Lord. Love must come first and be the foundation for operating in spiritual gifts. Without love, as Paul said in 1 Corinthians 13:1–2, even the most impressive gifts are meaningless.

True Christianity is about becoming love itself, not just performing miracles. Our identity in Christ is rooted in His love, which should flow through us in all we do. Pursuing love is essential, and those who perform miraculous signs without love await the terrible judgment described in Matthew 7:21–23. Let's strive to be vessels of God's love, allowing love to be the driving force behind our desire for spiritual gifts.

Spend some time today evaluating your motives. Have you been seeking spiritual gifts over godly love? Ask the Lord to convict you of any selfishness and to fill you with His love.

Today I…

HUMILITY

Always be humble, gentle and patient, bearing with one another in love.

EPHESIANS 4:2 CJB

Author and pastor Rick Warren wrote that humility isn't "thinking less of ourselves but thinking of ourselves *less*."[7] It means putting others first, being gentle and patient, and bearing with one another in love. When we approach others with a humble heart, we break down barriers and build bridges. This gentleness and patience can soften even the hardest of hearts, allowing God's love to flow through us and touch the lives of those around us.

Accessing others' hearts is easiest when we are humble because humility reflects the character of Christ. It shows that we value others and are willing to listen, learn, and grow together. By being humble, we create a safe space where others feel valued and understood, and we foster an environment of love and unity.

Today, seek out an opportunity to serve someone in humility. It could be a simple act of kindness, offering a listening ear, or helping someone in need. Let your actions reflect the gentle, patient love of Christ, and watch how that love opens hearts and builds stronger relationships.

Today I…

---

[7] Rick Warren, *The Purpose-Driven Life* (Zondervan, 2002), 265.

FEBRUARY 8

LOVE COVERS

Above all, love each other deeply, because love covers over a multitude of sins.

1 Peter 4:8 niv

As Christians, we are commanded to love others with the love of Christ. This kind of love isn't superficial; it requires a genuine commitment to others, forgiving and overlooking faults. When we love deeply, we reflect God's love, which is patient, kind, and enduring. In our daily interactions, we encounter people who may wrong us or disappoint us. It's easy to hold grudges or become bitter, but in today's verse, Peter called us to rise above these reactions.

Love has the power to heal wounds and mend broken relationships. By choosing to love deeply, we embody the grace and mercy that God shows us every day. This deep love fosters a forgiving heart and a willingness to see past imperfections, recognizing that we, too, are recipients of God's boundless love and forgiveness. Let's strive to let this profound love guide our actions and interactions.

Today, make a conscious effort to love someone deeply, especially someone who may have wronged you. Remember, hurting people hurt people. Extend forgiveness and understanding in your heart, letting your love reflect the love of Christ.

Today I…

FEBRUARY 9

LOVE BINDS

Above all these, clothe yourselves with love, which binds everything together perfectly.

COLOSSIANS 3:14 CJB

Love is the supreme virtue that binds together all other virtues in perfect unity. Paul's message to the Colossians highlights the importance of love as the glue that holds our Christian walk together. Without love, even our best efforts fall short. Think of love as a garment we put on daily. Just as we dress ourselves each morning, we should also clothe ourselves with love, intentionally choosing to act with compassion, kindness, humility, gentleness, and patience. This love transcends personal preferences and prejudices, creating harmony in our relationships and communities.

When we clothe ourselves with love, we reflect God's nature and create an environment where peace and unity can flourish. This kind of love is not passive; it actively seeks the good of others, promoting understanding and forgiveness. It's the love that Jesus demonstrated, a love that sacrifices and serves. By making love our highest priority, we align ourselves with God's heart and become instruments of His grace in a broken world.

Today, make a deliberate choice to wear love as your garment. Do something to tangibly show someone kindness and observe how God's love brings everything together.

Today I…

FEBRUARY 10

YOU'RE ALREADY SENT

The whole law is fulfilled in one word: "You shall love your neighbor as yourself."

GALATIANS 5:14 ESV

When many of us think of Isaiah's response to God's call—*"Here I am. Send me!"* (Isaiah 6:8 EHV)—we dream of being sent by God to far-off lands, envisioning grand missions and exotic locations. However, God has already placed us exactly where we need to be, with a divine purpose and assignment. Your neighborhood is no accident. You live among these specific people for a reason. Each interaction with a neighbor is an opportunity to fulfill God's command to love your neighbor as yourself.

Loving our neighbors means more than being polite. It involves intentional acts of kindness, genuine concern for their well-being, and a willingness to serve. Small acts of kindness prepare hearts and cultivate meaningful relationships, allowing us to witness to our neighbors effectively and organically. Instead of a one-off evangelism approach, we can help our neighbors open their minds and hearts to Jesus through ongoing discipleship rooted in love.

Today, take a step to connect with your neighbors. Introduce yourself if you haven't met or offer to help with a task. Show God's love through a kind gesture, cultivating a relationship that allows you to effectively and organically share His love over time.

Today I…

FEBRUARY 11

WALK THE WALK

Children, let us love not with words and talk, but with actions and in reality!

1 JOHN 3:18 CJB

It's easy to profess love with words, but we demonstrate true love through actions. The apostle John urged us not to love in mere words but to show love through tangible deeds. This aligns with Jesus' teachings, which emphasize the importance of love in action. Our lives should be a reflection of God's love, not just in what we say but in how we live. This requires us to be intentional in our actions, showing kindness, compassion, and generosity to those around us.

When we love in action, we embody the love of Christ, making a tangible difference in the lives of others. Let's challenge ourselves to go beyond words of love and demonstrate love through our actions. Whether it's a simple act of kindness, a helping hand, or a word of encouragement, our actions speak volumes about the love of God in our hearts.

Today, choose one person to whom you can show love through your actions. Whether it's a family member, friend, colleague, or stranger, find a way to demonstrate God's love in a practical and meaningful way.

Today I…

FEBRUARY 12

LOVE'S COVERING

Hate stirs up disputes, but love covers all kinds of transgressions.

PROVERBS 10:12 CJB

The wisdom of Proverbs is pivotal amid political and ideological division. While it's natural to have differing opinions, it's essential to approach these differences with love and respect. Love doesn't mean agreement; it means seeking understanding and finding common ground. Hate darkens our spiritual eyes, informing our perspective in a way that leads to division through fruitless disputes. On the other hand, love has the power to bridge even the deepest divides. When we choose love over hate, we pave the way for reconciliation and understanding.

As followers of Christ, we're called to be peacemakers and agents of reconciliation. This doesn't mean we ignore injustices or compromise our values. Instead, it means we engage with others in a spirit of love, seeking to build bridges and foster understanding. Let's be mindful of our words and actions, especially in the midst of political discussions. Instead of stirring up hate and division, let's choose to cover transgressions with love, promoting unity and peace in our families and in our world.

Today, reflect on how you can respond to political differences with love and understanding. Seek to understand other perspectives and find common ground, demonstrating the transformative power of love in the midst of disagreements.

Today I…

FEBRUARY 13

NO FEAR IN LOVE

There is no fear in love. On the contrary, love that has achieved its goal gets rid of fear, because fear has to do with punishment; the person who keeps fearing has not been brought to maturity in regard to love.

1 JOHN 4:18 CJB

In the journey of faith, we often encounter moments when fear threatens to overshadow our trust in God's love. Fear is faith in reverse, pulling us away from God's promises and purposes. Dan Mohler emphasizes that fear stems from a lack of understanding of God's love for us.[8]

God's love is not a fleeting emotion; it is a steadfast, unwavering force. As we grow in our understanding of this love, fear loses its grip on us. Today, meditate on the vastness of God's love for you. Remember you can and must trust Him. Allow His love to replace any fear lingering in your heart. Embrace the truth that you are deeply, intimately, and personally loved by the creator of the universe.

Take a moment to reflect on any areas of your life where fear may be causing you to not trust the Lord. Recall Romans 14:23. Surrender those fears to God and ask Him to fill you with His perfect love.

Today I…

---

[8] Dan Mohler, "Understanding the Nature and Love of God—Dan Mohler," posted October 7, 2023, by Dan Mohler, YouTube, youtube.com.

FEBRUARY 14

GOD IS LOVE

> Beloved friends, let us love one another; because love is from God; and everyone who loves has God as his Father and knows God. Those who do not love, do not know God; because God is love.
>
> 1 John 4:7–8 cjb

Love is not just something God does; it's who He is. When we truly grasp this truth, it changes everything. Our ability to love others is not dependent on our own efforts or emotions but on our connection to God, who is the source of all love.

Love is not just a feeling or an action but a core part of our nature as His children. You are loved by God, and His love flows through you to others. Every interaction is an opportunity to demonstrate God's love, not out of duty but out of the overflow of His love in you.

This Valentine's Day, show a stranger a tangible act of love. It could be a kind word, a small gift, or a helping hand. Let your actions reflect the love of God that is within you. Then watch as His love transforms not only their heart but yours as well.

Today I…

FEBRUARY 15

A LIFE OF LOVE

Live a life of love, just as also the Messiah loved us, indeed, on our behalf gave himself up as an offering, as a slaughtered sacrifice to God with a pleasing fragrance.

EPHESIANS 5:2 CJB

The depth of Christ's sacrifice, vividly portrayed in Ephesians 5:2, is humbling. Jesus didn't just give a token gesture; He offered His very life as a fragrant offering to God to redeem us from the fall and curse of sin. John Bevere often speaks about how the profound love Jesus demonstrated through His sacrifice shows us the true nature of servanthood.

Christ's sacrificial love should be the hallmark of our lives as believers. We are called to mirror Christ's love not just in our words but in our actions, even to the point of sacrificial giving. As we meditate on the sacrificial love of Christ, let it challenge us to live lives of love. Let's not just speak about love but embody it, sacrificially giving of ourselves for the sake of others. When we do, our lives become a fragrant offering to God, pleasing in His sight.

Ask God to show you how to love as Christ loved—fully, unconditionally, and sacrificially. Then step out in obedience, knowing that your love, when offered with a pure heart, is a pleasing fragrance to Him.

Today I…

FEBRUARY 16

PRITORITIZE LOVE

The Messiah's love has hold of us, because we are convinced that one man died on behalf of all mankind (which implies that all mankind was already dead) and that he died on behalf of all in order that those who live should not live any longer for themselves but for the one who on their behalf died and was raised.

2 CORINTHIANS 5:14–15 CJB

When we truly grasp the magnitude of Christ's sacrifice, it fundamentally alters our perspective. No longer can we live for ourselves; we're compelled to live for Jesus. This transformation isn't about mere obligation but about a profound shift in our hearts and minds.

C. S. Lewis likened this shift to moving from a "toy world" to the real world—understanding that our temporary desires and ambitions pale in comparison to the eternal reality of living for Christ.[9] Our actions, decisions, and interactions are no longer centered on self but on the one who gave everything for us.

When we prioritize love, it emboldens us to share Christ's message. Show kindness to someone, knowing that seeds sown in love will produce a harvest. That harvest could be meaningful conversations about faith with that person or a complete change of their heart.

Today I…

---

[9] C. S. Lewis, "The Obstinate Toy Soldiers," *Mere Christianity* (HarperCollins, 2001), 178–82.

FEBRUARY 17

OVERFLOWING WITH LOVE

As for you, may the Lord make you increase and overflow in love toward each other, indeed, toward everyone, just as we do toward you.

1 Thessalonians 3:12 CJB

Paul's heartfelt prayer for the Thessalonians is a beautiful reminder of our calling to love. He prayed that their love would not just grow but overflow toward one another and everyone they encountered. This overflowing love isn't limited to those we find easy to love; it extends to everyone, reflecting God's boundless love for us.

True love is not passive but actively seeks the best for others even when it's difficult. Remember, our capacity to love comes from understanding how deeply and sacrificially Jesus loves us. When we grasp this, our love for others naturally increases, breaking barriers and building bridges. Paul's prayer for overflowing love is especially relevant in today's world, where divisions and conflicts are rampant. As followers of Christ, we are called to rise above these divides and be vessels of God's love, spreading kindness, understanding, and grace in every interaction.

Identify one person you find difficult to love. Pray for God to increase and overflow your love toward them.

Today I…

FEBRUARY 18

WHILE WE WERE STILL SINNERS

God demonstrates his own love for us in that the Messiah died on our behalf while we were still sinners.

ROMANS 5:8 CJB

This verse reminds me of the most profound encounter I've ever had with God. When I refused to audition for the role of Theresa on *Days of Our Lives* because I thought she was devoid of morals, I heard the Holy Spirit say, *This is your role.*

Deciding to test the Spirit, I asked why, assuming there was no way this was God's voice. He replied instantly, *Because Theresa is the exact condition the world was in when I sent My Son to die for them, and the audience needs to know there is no pit so deep that my love cannot find them still. And when the guy leaves or the drugs wear off, you'll play the reality of what that girl is feeling. Emptiness and dissatisfaction because only I can fill her void.* I am still undone by God's love and convicted by my harsh judgment. We are called not to judge but to love. In fact, Jesus said, *"The way you judge others is how you will be judged"* (Matthew 7:2).

The moment you find yourself judging anyone today, stop and show that person the tangible love of Jesus.

Today I…

FEBRUARY 19

LAY IT ALL DOWN

The way that we have come to know love is through his having laid down his life for us. And we ought to lay down our lives for the brothers!

1 JOHN 3:16 CJB

True love is costly. It goes beyond convenience and comfort, demanding selflessness and sacrifice. When we lay down our lives for our brothers and sisters, we reflect the love Christ showed us. Laying down our lives doesn't necessarily mean physical death; it can mean putting others' needs above our own or offering our time, resources, and support.

Dan Mohler often teaches that love transforms us to see others through God's eyes, leading us to act compassionately. When we lay down our lives for others, we testify to the transformative power of Christ's love in our lives. Because the world is focused on self-interest, embodying sacrificial love becomes a powerful testimony of God's love. It's a radical way to live that stands out and speaks volumes about our faith.

Ask yourself, *Where have I chosen comfort over love? Is there a situation where I've held back because it was inconvenient or required sacrifice?* Today, take a step beyond your comfort zone—offer your time, resources, or encouragement to someone in need. Let your love be more than words—let it cost you something just as Christ's love did for us.

Today I…

FEBRUARY 20

A DIRECT CORRELATION

We ourselves love now because he loved us first.

1 John 4:19 CJB

First John 4:19 reminds us that our capacity to love others is directly linked to our understanding of God's love for us. Grasping the depth of His immense love and compassion for us, despite all our flaws, shifts our perspective, enabling us to see others through God's eyes. It's like a key that opens our hearts. Paul prayed in Ephesians 1:18 that *"the eyes of [our] heart[s] may be enlightened"* (NIV), highlighting the transformative power of God's love. When we allow God's love to illuminate our hearts, we begin to view others not as obstacles or enemies but as fellow recipients of God's love and grace.

This shift in perspective is profound. It moves us from a self-centered view to a God-centered view, where our love for others mirrors God's profound love for us. We begin to see beyond outward appearances and behaviors, recognizing the intrinsic value and worth of every individual. This is the essence of Christian love: seeing others as God sees them and loving them accordingly.

Today, ask God to enlighten the eyes of your heart. Pray for the ability to see others through His eyes, with love and compassion. Look for opportunities to demonstrate this love in practical ways.

Today I…

FEBRUARY 21

INNER CIRCLE

*A friend shows his friendship at all times—
it is for adversity that [such] a brother is born.*

PROVERBS 17:17 CJB

In high school, I earned the superlative of "friendliest freshman" because I genuinely loved making everyone around me feel seen and heard. Plus, it was the WWJD bracelet era, and that's what Jesus would do. However, the older I get, the more selective I am about my deep friendships. I strive to be kind to everyone, but I'm more reserved with my deepest thoughts and struggles. Figuring this out has taken me decades and began years ago when I heard Lisa Bevere speak about Jesus making a distinction between the crowd and His disciples, even having an inner circle. He shared the deepest moments and revelations with Peter, James, and John, most notably, in the garden of Gethsemane and during the transfiguration.

Jesus demonstrated that while we should love all, we can have close, trusted relationships with a few. These friends are those who truly support us in adversity. This isn't about exclusion but about wisely investing in relationships that nurture and sustain us both emotionally and spiritually.

Reflect on your friendships. Ask God both to strengthen the bonds in those relationships He intends for you to nurture and also to organically transition you away from friendships that are meant to be seasonal.

Today I…

FEBRUARY 22

SACRIFICIAL RELATIONSHIPS

"No one has greater love than a person who lays down his life for his friends."

JOHN 15:13 CJB

The Bible repeats the idea of laying down your life many times, so though we've already explored this, it clearly bears repeating. God's love is radical and countercultural. It puts others first even when it costs us something significant. True love calls us to move beyond superficial interactions into genuine, sacrificial relationships that reflect Christ's heart. It's more than words—it requires stepping into others' lives with compassion, bearing their burdens, and sharing their struggles. It means standing with them in their darkest moments, offering support, and walking alongside them in faith.

Sacrificial love isn't about convenience or comfort. It's about commitment. It's choosing to love when it's hard, to serve when it's inconvenient, and to stay when walking away would be easier. Christ's love requires us to step into meaningful relationships, share burdens, and intentionally seek to serve.

Reflect on one relationship where you can practice sacrificial love. How can you intentionally put others first today even when it costs you something? Make that choice and see how God deepens your love for Him and others.

Today I…

ABIDE IN HIS LOVE

We have come to know and to believe the love that God has for us. God is love, and whoever abides in love abides in God, and God abides in him.

1 JOHN 4:16 ESV

To truly know God, we must abide in His love. This means more than just acknowledging God's love intellectually; it requires us to live out love daily. To abide in love means to stay connected to God, letting His love flow through us and influence every aspect of our being. This connection transforms our hearts and minds, aligning our desires with God's will. Jesus deeply desires a relationship with every person, no matter how lost or broken they seem.

Living in God's love inspires us to extend His love to others. It challenges us to act and react with the fruit of the Spirit when we face challenges. Our love for others is a testament to our relationship with God, drawing them to experience His love for themselves.

Invite the Holy Spirit to lead and guide you each day. Though He is always with us, He often waits for our invitation to work actively in our lives.

Today I…

FEBRUARY 24

HIS GREAT LOVE

I pray that you will be rooted and founded in love, so that you, with all God's people, will be given strength to grasp the breadth, length, height and depth of the Messiah's love, yes, to know it, even though it is beyond all knowing, so that you will be filled with all the fullness of God.

EPHESIANS 3:17–19 CJB

Grasping God's love seems unfathomable. Author and speaker Graham Cooke wrote that God's love is "high enough to lift us above everything, deep enough to rescue anyone from anything, long enough to last for eternity and broad enough to cover every failure."[10]

Jesus removed our sins *"as far as the east is from the west"* (Psalm 103:12 NIV). He's committed to us forever. His love is so deep that there is no pit we could ever find ourselves in where His love cannot still find us (Psalm 139). His love lifts us up, giving us a heavenly perspective and filling us with joy and peace. His love sustains us when we feel weak, comforts us in our grief, and reassures us in our doubts. It never wavers, never runs out, and never gives up—because it's who He is.

Pray for God's love to fill the areas in your life where you feel broken.

Today I…

---

[10] Graham Cooke, "Making the Most of Failure," Lutheran Renewal, January 2005, lutheranrenewal.org.

FEBRUARY 25

LOVE VERSUS TOLERANCE

Speaking the truth in love, we are to grow up in every way into him who is the head, into Christ.

EPHESIANS 4:15 ESV

In today's society, tolerance is often celebrated as the highest virtue. However, the Bible calls us to a higher standard: love. Tolerance may avoid conflict, but it often fails to address deeper issues. True love, as modeled by Christ, speaks truth with compassion and seeks the well-being of others even when it's uncomfortable.

God's commandments are not restrictive but protective. God's hatred of sin is rooted in His love for us. Sin begins small but quickly grows until it burdens and controls us (Galatians 5:9), preventing us from experiencing God's grace and freedom. Tolerance ignores sin, leaving a person captive, while love sets captives free. We are called to mirror Jesus' selfless love by addressing sin with compassion. Tolerance might encourage us to overlook sin to keep the peace, but true love compels us to gently speak the truth and offer support for change. True love is transformative.

Reflect on areas where you might be practicing tolerance instead of true love. Pray for the courage and wisdom to speak the truth in love, reflecting God's heart and desire for freedom.

Today I…

FEBRUARY 26

GOD'S INVISIBLE SOUND BATH

> "Adonai your God is in your midst—a mighty Savior! He will delight over you with joy. He will quiet you with His love. He will dance for joy over you with singing."
>
> ZEPHANIAH 3:17 TLV

There are several verses that describe God singing over us. Imagine the creator of the universe singing over you with joy. Zephaniah 3:17 paints a vivid picture of God's deep, personal love for each of us. He's not a distant deity but a mighty Savior who's actively involved in our lives. God rejoices over us with gladness, delighting in who we are. His love quiets our fears and anxieties, bringing peace to our hearts when everything around us is chaos.

The image of God encircling us with dance and loud singing is a powerful reminder of His exuberant, unwavering love—a love that celebrates, heals, and renews us. God used sound waves to create the universe, and He can heal and reorder chaos. Imagine God hovering over you with songs and healing words. Your worth isn't based on your achievements but on God's delight in you.

Listen to the song "Amazed" by Steffany Gretzinger. Remember that He dances over you while you are unaware.

Today I…

THE POWER OF LOVE

Set me like a seal on your heart, like a seal on your arm; for love is as strong as death, passion as cruel as Sh'ol; its flashes are flashes of fire, [as fierce as the] flame of Yah. No amount of water can quench love, torrents cannot drown it. If someone gave all the wealth in his house for love, he would gain only utter contempt.

SONG OF SOLOMON 8:6–7 CJB

The vivid imagery in Song of Solomon 8:6–7 portrays the intensity and unquenchable nature of true love. This passage describes love as strong as death and as fierce as the flames of Yahweh. It is a powerful force that cannot be extinguished by any amount of water or adversity. This divine love is a reflection of God's love for us, passionate and relentless.

God's love is not just passionate; it is also fiercely protective. In ancient times, a seal represented ownership and protection. To be set as a seal on the heart and arm signifies a deep, unbreakable bond. This is the kind of relationship God seeks with us.

Show someone God's protective love today by standing up for them, offering support, or simply being a listening ear. Let them know that they are cherished and safe in God's love.

Today I…

FEBRUARY 28

THE GOOD LIFE

Human being, you have already been told what is good, what Adonai demands of you—no more than to act justly, love grace and walk in purity with your God.

MICAH 6:8 CJB

This verse serves as a timeless reminder of what it means to live a life pleasing to God. Acting justly involves making fair and righteous decisions and treating others with equity and integrity. It means standing up for what is right even when it is difficult or unpopular. Justice reflects God's own nature, which we're called to mirror as His disciples.

Loving grace encompasses both extending kindness and receiving God's empowerment. Grace goes beyond justice, offering compassion and forgiveness where it is undeserved. It also includes God's empowerment, enabling us to live out His commands, which creates a ripple effect of kindness and mercy in our communities. Walking in purity with God speaks to our relationship with Him. It calls us to live authentically and transparently before Him, free from hypocrisy and hidden sin. Walking in purity means staying close to God, seeking His guidance, and striving to live a life that reflects His holiness.

Ask God to reveal any areas where you need to grow in justice, grace, and purity. Write down what He reveals and make a plan to address these areas.

Today I…

FEBRUARY 29

PERMISSION TO LOVE YOURSELF

If you really fulfill the royal law according to the Scripture, "You shall love your neighbor as yourself," you are doing well.

JAMES 2:8 ESV

There's something radical hidden in this familiar passage: *"Love your neighbor as yourself."* To love others well, you must also care for yourself. If you don't take the time to rest and reconnect with God, you'll burn out, and your ability to love others well will suffer because it will be depleted by exhaustion. Even Jesus, who *is* love, took time to retreat and recharge. After hearing about John the Baptist's death, He withdrew to a solitary place (Matthew 14:13). Luke 5:16 tells us that Jesus *"often withdrew to lonely places and prayed"* (NIV). Before major decisions, like choosing His disciples (Luke 6:12–13), and before going to the cross, Jesus withdrew to seek the Father.

So while loving your neighbor is essential, so is taking the time to rest, recharge, and care for your own heart and spirit. When you do, you'll find that your ability to love others will deepen, your patience will grow, and your compassion will flow more freely.

Today, pause to reconnect with God. Let Him fill you up so you can love others from a place of strength, not weariness.

Today I…

MARCH

In Like a Lion, out Like a Lamb:
A Call to Boldness

MARCH 1

WHOSE APPROVAL?

Am I now trying to win the approval of human beings, or of God? Or am I trying to please people? If I were still trying to please people, I would not be a servant of Christ.

GALATIANS 1:10 NIV

Living boldly for God means standing firm in our faith and values even when they contradict societal norms. It requires courage to speak the truth in love and to act according to God's will, regardless of potential backlash or disapproval from others. This boldness isn't about being confrontational but about being steadfast in our commitment to Christ.

True boldness is rooted in love. When our actions are motivated by genuine love for God and others, we naturally become more courageous. Love empowers us to live authentically and selflessly, reflecting Jesus in our words and deeds. It's through this love that we find the strength to be bold, knowing that our ultimate goal is to honor God and share His love with the world.

Identify one area where you've been seeking human approval over God's. Take a bold step in love to align that area with God's will, whether by sharing your faith or standing up for a godly principle. Let your actions reflect your commitment to pleasing God above all else.

Today I…

MARCH 2

CARPE DIEM

You don't even know if you will be alive tomorrow! For all you are is a mist that appears for a little while and then disappears.

JAMES 4:14 CJB

John Burke's research into near-death experiences brings me to tears. Hearing and reading people describe God and heaven fills me with awe at God's majesty and reminds me how fleeting life on earth is. Our time on earth is just the beginning—like a baby in the womb, we can't yet grasp the vastness of eternal life.

In *Imagine Heaven*, Burke shares stories of breathtaking heavenly landscapes—pristine beaches, majestic peaks.[11] Knowing that earth's most beautiful scenery exists in heaven yet is indescribably more wonderful shifts my focus. Instead of chasing my travel bucket list, I now prioritize building God's kingdom. These near-death testimonies echo Paul's words: "*Forgetting what lies behind and straining forward to what lies ahead, I press on toward the goal for the prize of the upward call of God in Christ Jesus*" (Philippians 3:13–14 ESV).

Be bold today—seize every opportunity to share Jesus, love fearlessly, and make an eternal impact.

Today I…

---

[11] John Burke, *Imagine Heaven: Near-Death Experiences, God's Promises, and the Exhilarating Future That Awaits You* (Baker Books, 2015), 75, 93, 107, 113–14, 303.

MARCH 3

BOLD

*The wicked flee when no one pursues,
but the righteous are bold as a lion.*

PROVERBS 28:1 ESV

We must stand firm on what the Bible says is true. I believe we're where we are culturally today because we've reversed Proverbs 28:1. I have seen the church forget who she is and retreat in fear of being "canceled." I've been guilty of this, too, by allowing a spirit of intimidation to silence me when I should speak. It's time to get bold! The boldness of a lion is rooted in its confidence and strength. Similarly, our boldness as believers comes from our confidence in God's strength and our identity in Him. We're called to stand firm and unafraid, ready to act in faith, knowing that God is our strength and shield.

In *Lioness Arising*, Lisa Bevere called upon women to rise up like lionesses to protect, provide, and be proactive in their faith. This boldness isn't about being loud or aggressive. It's about being courageous and standing firm in the truth with love.[12]

Reflect on an area in your life where you need to be bolder. Pray for God's strength and courage to face it with the boldness of a lion.

Today I…

---

12 Lisa Bevere, *Lioness Arising: Wake Up and Change Your World* (Random House Publishing Group, 2010), 153–54.

MARCH 4

FULLY CONVINCED

He was fully convinced that what God had promised he could also accomplish.

ROMANS 4:21 CJB

Abraham is known as the father of faith not because of what God promised him but because he was fully convinced that God could and would fulfill His promises even when circumstances seemed impossible. When Abraham believed God for descendants, he and Sarah's bodies were as good as dead. Yet Abraham didn't waver. He chose to believe that God could bring life out of a barren situation.

It's not faith if we only believe when things seem possible. Faith is stepping out when everything tells us it's impossible, when our logic says it can't be done. Abraham wasn't just hoping that God might come through—he was certain. He acted on a promise before seeing it fulfilled. Being fully convinced requires us to silence doubts, fears, and unbelief. When we're faced with challenges, we can either magnify the problem or magnify God. Bold faith chooses to fix its eyes on God's Word, not our circumstances. God's ability to accomplish His will does not depend on human limitations. Pastor and evangelist Lester Sumrall once said, "Faith is a life that you live.…Faith is an act."[13]

Consider fasting to strengthen your spirit over your flesh.

Today I…

---

13 Lester Sumrall, "Dr. Lester Sumrall—The Greatest Message on Faith Ever Preached!" posted March 5, 2019, by Encounter Today, YouTube, youtube.com.

MARCH 5

WHO IS THE HOLY SPIRIT?

After they prayed, the place where they were meeting was shaken. And they were all filled with the Holy Spirit and spoke the word of God boldly.

ACTS 4:31 NIV

The Bible talks about the Holy Spirit a lot, and yet He's the most misunderstood person of the Godhead. So who is the Holy Spirit? First, the Holy Spirit is not an "it" but a He. The fullness of God the Father and God the Son resides in Him. He is omnipresent (always present), omnipotent (all-powerful), and omniscient (all-knowing). He is our great Counselor and Comforter. He is very real and very active.

Jesus Himself said He had to go back to the Father so that one just like Him—the Holy Spirit—could come. Jesus chose to humble Himself and leave His glory to be bound by flesh and walk among us in a specific historical time and place. The Holy Spirit now continues His transforming work in every believer's heart. The Holy Spirit is my best friend, and I pray He becomes yours as well if He's not already.

Spend time learning more about the Holy Spirit from the Word, trusted mentors, and theologically sound books. I highly recommend the book The Holy Spirit: An Introduction *by John Bevere.*

Today I…

MARCH 6

BE FILLED WITH THE HOLY SPIRIT

After they prayed, the place where they were meeting was shaken. And they were all filled with the Holy Spirit and spoke the word of God boldly.

ACTS 4:31 NIV

Let's continue to consider what it means to be *filled with* the Holy Spirit. I recently heard an incredibly simple analogy. Think of a plain glass of milk, representing us, and delicious chocolate syrup, representing the Holy Spirit. When you become born again, the Holy Spirit is deposited inside of you. When you deposit chocolate syrup into milk, it sinks to the bottom. It's there, but if you sip the milk, it will taste like plain milk because all the chocolate is at the bottom until you stir the milk.

When you receive the baptism of the Holy Spirit, it's like a spoon is inserted into the glass, stirring up the chocolate syrup until all the milk is transformed into chocolate milk. However, chocolate milk left untouched will start to separate and settle, and when left for too long, it spoils. Friends, we need a daily infilling of the Holy Spirit so we can pour out what He's putting inside of us.

If you're not already baptized in the Holy Spirit, ask God about it. Don't be afraid! He's a good Father (Matthew 7:9).

Today I…

MARCH 7

BOLDNESS COMES FROM INTIMACY

After they prayed, the place where they were meeting was shaken. And they were all filled with the Holy Spirit and spoke the word of God boldly.

ACTS 4:31 NIV

Okay, I promise this is the last day I'll spend on this verse. Forgive me, I just love the Holy Spirit so much! When we're filled with the Holy Spirit, He empowers and emboldens us to fulfill God's purposes and share the gospel fearlessly. If Jesus Himself needed to be filled with the Holy Spirit, how much more so do we need to be filled with the Holy Spirit?

Throughout *The Holy Spirit: An Introduction*, John Bevere explained that being filled with the Holy Spirit is about surrendering to God's will and allowing His Spirit to work through us, breaking down barriers and empowering us to speak truth with conviction.[14] Boldness is necessary in a world that often opposes God's truth. The early believers' boldness came from their intimate relationship with God and their reliance on the Holy Spirit. This same boldness is available to us today when we prioritize prayer and seek the infilling of the Holy Spirit.

Ask the Holy Spirit to fill you afresh today and open your heart to those around you so you can accomplish His will.

Today I…

---

14 John Bevere and Addison Bevere, *The Holy Spirit: An Introduction* (Messenger International, 2013).

MARCH 8

FEAR IS A SPIRIT

God has not given us a spirit of fear, but of power and of love and of a sound mind.

2 Timothy 1:7 NKJV

Fear is *not* an emotion but a spirit—and not one sent from God. Pay close attention to biblical exchanges. What does God give us instead of fear? Love, power, and self-discipline. That means the opposite of these gifts is the spirit of fear. If you're struggling with your mental health, it could be that the spirit of fear holds authority over an area of your mind. Dear brother or sister, I am not accusing you or trying to shame you; instead, I am offering you spiritual eyes to address and take authority over that spirit so you may live in bold freedom.

Many translations of today's verse say *"self-discipline"* in place of *"sound mind."* Both deal with operating in God's grace to overcome our flesh. Contrary to what the world preaches, we are not animals that have no control over our fleshly desires and appetites or that lack the ability to understand consequences. Jesus overcame our sin, so our sin does not have to overpower us. Exercise self-discipline and reclaim a sound mind.

Identify any areas you've given over to a spirit of fear. Tell the spirit of fear to go in Jesus' name. Trust God and stand firm.

Today I…

MARCH 9

PRAY LIKE A BRIDE

Let us then approach God's throne of grace with confidence, so that we may receive mercy and find grace to help us in our time of need.

HEBREWS 4:16 NIV

God's throne is a place of grace and empowerment where we find the help we need in every situation. Whether we're facing trials, temptations, or uncertainties, we are assured that we can come to God openly and honestly, a profound privilege made possible through Jesus Christ. God welcomes us with open arms, ready to provide the mercy and grace we need.

Author and speaker Graham Cooke encouraged us to "pray as a bride instead of praying as a widow."[15] A bride approaches her beloved with trust, confidence, and the expectation of good things. A widow prays out of desperation and lack. By praying as the bride of Christ, we align ourselves with the truth of our identity in Him and of His loving provision. Evangelist Smith Wigglesworth often emphasized the power of approaching God with bold faith, believing that He is both willing and able to meet our needs. This confidence is not arrogance but a deep trust in God's character and promises.

Approach God's throne of grace with confidence as you pray today. Bring your needs, concerns, and fears to Him.

Today I…

---

15 Graham Cooke, "The Building Blocks of Prayer," *Thinking the Way God Thinks* (podcast), Brilliant Perspectives, June 22, 2023, brilliantperspectives.com.

MARCH 10

THE RIGHT WORDS

Pray also for me, that whenever I speak, words may be given me so that I will fearlessly make known the mystery of the gospel.

EPHESIANS 6:19 NIV

We need divine assistance in effectively proclaiming the gospel. Paul asked for prayers not only for courage but also for the right words to communicate the profound mysteries of the gospel fearlessly. This teaches us that boldness in sharing our faith comes from reliance on God's strength and wisdom.

The Holy Spirit plays a crucial role in this process. His intimate knowledge of each individual we encounter allows us to connect with them on a deeper level, speaking directly to their hearts. The Holy Spirit can guide our conversations in organic ways, opening opportunities to witness without it feeling forced or awkward. He knows the struggles and questions of the people we encounter, and He loves to provide comfort and counsel. He often moves in unexpected ways when we're willing and obedient vessels, sometimes giving us divine words of knowledge and insight, which in turn encourage us to speak effectively and boldly.

Identify someone in your life who needs to hear the gospel. Pray for the Holy Spirit to guide your conversations in an organic way and to open up opportunities for you to witness effectively.

Today I…

MARCH 11

MAGNIFY GOD

"Have I not commanded you? Be strong and courageous. Do not be afraid; do not be discouraged, for the LORD your God will be with you wherever you go."

JOSHUA 1:9 NIV

In Joshua 1:9, God commanded Joshua to be strong and courageous as Joshua prepared to lead the Israelites into the promised land. This was not just a suggestion but a divine imperative rooted in God's promise to be with him always. While this verse can stand alone, it's even more profound in context.

Earlier, when Moses sent twelve spies to scout the land of Canaan, only Joshua and Caleb returned with a positive report. The other ten spies were overwhelmed by fear, seeing themselves as grasshoppers compared to the giants who inhabited the land. They relied on their physical sight and natural abilities, which led to a lack of faith and courage. Joshua and Caleb, however, trusted in God's faithfulness and power more than their own natural abilities and circumstances. They believed that God, who had promised them the land, was more than able to deliver it into their hands. Their courage stemmed from their unwavering faith in God's promises.

Whatever "giants" you're facing, choose today to magnify God and not the problem. When we focus on God's greatness, our insurmountable mountains become molehills.

Today I…

MARCH 12

UNASHAMED

"If anyone is ashamed of me and my words in this adulterous and sinful generation, the Son of Man will be ashamed of them when he comes in his Father's glory with the holy angels."

MARK 8:38 NIV

Jesus' words in Mark 8:38 are a sobering reminder of the importance of boldly standing for our faith. The world always has and will oppose God's truth and glorify sin, making it intimidating to share our faith. Yet Jesus calls us to live unashamedly even when it's difficult. Being ashamed of Jesus and His words means shrinking back, hiding our faith, or compromising our beliefs to fit in with the world. Jesus warned that such actions have eternal consequences.

However, this message is not just a warning but an invitation to live courageously for Christ. Jesus endured the cross for us and calls us to take up our cross daily and follow Him. When we stand firm in our faith, we honor Him and reflect His love and truth to those around us. Jesus' words are a call to live with integrity, letting our actions and words consistently reflect our devotion to Christ.

Examine your life and identify areas where you might be tempted to hide your faith. Pray for the courage to stand boldly for Jesus.

Today I…

MARCH 13

THE GOD WHO HEARS

*When I called, you answered me;
you greatly emboldened me.*

PSALM 138:3 NIV

God is faithful, and prayer is powerful. When we call out to God, He hears us and responds. He is not deaf that He cannot hear us, nor is His arm too short that He cannot save us (Isaiah 59:1). David, the psalmist, experienced many trials and tribulations. Yet in his distress, he turned to God in prayer, finding not only answers but also the boldness to persevere. This kind of boldness comes from knowing that we are not alone, that the Almighty God is with us, listening to our cries and providing strength and guidance.

When we face situations that seem overwhelming or daunting, we must remember to call upon the Lord instead of trying to solve them alone. His response may not always be immediate or given in the way we expect, but we can have total peace knowing that He is still in control and that He is with us. When we calm our anxious thoughts and make room to experience God's faithfulness, our faith grows stronger, and we become more confident in His promises.

Call out to God in prayer about a specific challenge you are facing. Trust that He hears you and will respond. Allow His presence to envelop you.

Today I...

MARCH 14

STAND GUARD

Be on your guard; stand firm in the faith; be courageous; be strong.

1 CORINTHIANS 16:13 NIV

Paul's exhortation to the Corinthians to be vigilant, strong, and courageous is as relevant today as it was then. The world is full of distractions and things that challenge our faith, so we must stay alert and rooted in our beliefs. To *"be on your guard"* means to be watchful, aware of spiritual dangers, and ready to stand against them. Standing firm in the faith requires a deep trust in God's promises and a commitment to living out His truth even when it's difficult.

Being courageous and strong are qualities that God instills in us through His Spirit. Courage is not the absence of fear but the resolve to act in faith despite our fear. Strength comes from relying on God's power rather than our own. These attributes enable us to face adversities with unwavering confidence in God's support.

Reflect on an area in your life where you need to be more vigilant, firm, courageous, or strong. Pray for God's help to embody those qualities in your daily walk.

Today I…

MARCH 15

ORDINARY PEOPLE

When they saw the courage of Peter and John and realized that they were unschooled, ordinary men, they were astonished and they took note that these men had been with Jesus.

Acts 4:13 NIV

Peter and John, though unschooled and ordinary, displayed remarkable courage that astonished even the religious leaders. Their boldness and authority were the natural fruit of their intimacy with Jesus. God can use anyone, regardless of background or qualifications. The key is spending time with Jesus. When we invest in our relationship with Him, His presence transforms us, and His courage naturally flows through us.

We cannot help but be bold and effective in God's kingdom because operating in authority is a natural byproduct of being filled with the Holy Spirit. We don't have to muster up our own courage in our own strength. All we have to do is come to Christ. Our time with Him equips us with the courage to stand firm and speak boldly, no matter the circumstances.

Spend extra time with Jesus today, whether in prayer, Scripture reading, or worship. Focus on Him. That's all you need to do for His transformative love and power to work in your life.

Today I…

MARCH 16

GOSPEL POWER

I am not ashamed of the gospel, because it is the power of God that brings salvation to everyone who believes: first to the Jew, then to the Gentile.

ROMANS 1:16 NIV

The Roman government was one of the most tyrannical in all of history. Yet Paul boldly and unapologetically proclaimed the gospel because he understood that the power of God is what brings salvation from eternal death for everyone who believes. Salvation is the greatest miracle. It's a deep spiritual transaction that supernaturally translates us from slavery in the kingdom of darkness to complete freedom and adoption as sons or daughters in the kingdom of light (Colossians 1:13; Romans 8:15).

Understanding this divine rescue should ignite a passionate desire to share the gospel with others. When we grasp the reality that everyone around us who does not know Jesus is destined for eternal separation from God, sharing His love becomes urgent. Jesus, in His infinite love, desires to save everyone from this fate, and He proved it by laying down His life to erase our sin debt (Colossians 2:14).

Reflect on the power of the gospel in your own life and then ask the Holy Spirit to give you the spiritual urgency to share your testimony with others.

Today I…

MARCH 17

BOLD RESOLVE

I can do all things through him who strengthens me.
PHILIPPIANS 4:13 ESV

Saint Patrick's Day commemorates the life and mission of Saint Patrick, the patron saint of Ireland. Born in Roman Britain in the late fourth century, Patrick was captured by Irish pirates at the age of sixteen and taken to Ireland as a slave. During his six years in captivity, he turned to God in prayer, finding strength and comfort in his faith. After escaping and returning to his family, Patrick felt a divine calling to return to Ireland—not as a slave but as a missionary. Despite the dangers and hardships he knew he would face, Patrick trusted in God's strength to guide and sustain him.

This remarkable resolve echoes the sentiment found in Philippians 4:13: *"I can do all things through him who strengthens me."* Patrick's mission in Ireland was fraught with challenges. The Irish were primarily pagan, with deep Druidic traditions. Patrick encountered life-threatening resistance and hostility, yet his unwavering faith in God's power and love enabled him to persevere, ultimately converting most of the nation to Christianity.

Reflect on the unwavering faith of Saint Patrick in the face of adversity. Consider the challenges you are facing today. How can you rely more on God's strength to persevere and overcome these obstacles?

Today I…

MARCH 18

BOLDNESS DESPITE CULTURE

He proclaimed the kingdom of God and taught about the Lord Jesus Christ—with all boldness and without hindrance!

ACTS 28:31 NIV

We often put the disciples on a pedestal, thinking it was easier to be an effective Christian back then. However, the challenges they faced were immense. Under the rule of Emperor Nero and the pervasive, ruthless, and sexually idolatrous culture of the Roman Empire, proclaiming the gospel was incredibly difficult and often led to death. Despite these harsh conditions, Paul proclaimed the kingdom of God and taught about Jesus with boldness and without hesitation. His courage and unwavering commitment to the gospel serve as a powerful example for us today.

Paul's boldness came from his deep relationship with Jesus, which resulted in the empowering presence of the Holy Spirit in his life. Purpose to grow in intimacy with Jesus so you can effectively share the gospel with boldness and love. Remember, your effectiveness depends on your reliance on God and intimacy with Jesus.

Reflect on Paul's boldness and pray for the Holy Spirit to empower you to share the gospel without fear. Ask Him to set up opportunities for you to share the love of Jesus today.

Today I…

MARCH 19

WE DARED

We had previously suffered and been treated outrageously in Philippi, as you know, but with the help of our God we dared to tell you his gospel in the face of strong opposition.

1 Thessalonians 2:2 NIV

We must constantly choose building God's kingdom over a spirit of fear of retribution. While the Bible discusses being as wise as a serpent but as gentle as a dove, I don't think that's an invitation to shrink back but rather to prayerfully partner and collaborate with the Holy Spirit to expand God's kingdom.

We must constantly seek His guidance so that we know what to do and what to say or not say. Part of having boldness is being tuned in to the Holy Spirit and choosing to be obedient to whatever He asks in the moment. If the Holy Spirit asks you to do something and you have tested the Spirit (1 John 4:1), then be obedient to God, trusting that whatever repercussions come, God is still steps ahead of you and knows what He's doing. God is faithful. He will not mislead you.

Invite the Holy Spirit to lead and guide you today. Ask Him to loudly direct your steps. Then be obedient.

Today I…

MARCH 20

PREACH TO YOUR SOUL

The Lord is my light and my salvation—whom shall I fear?
The Lord is the stronghold of my life—
of whom shall I be afraid?

Psalm 27:1 niv

I love how David preached to his own soul constantly throughout the book of Psalms. When he faced trials and even murderous attempts on his life, he would quiet his soul and proclaim God's protection over himself as more powerful than his circumstances. Just as David did, we can and should preach to our own souls, reaffirming our trust in the Lord. Remember, there is power in our words (Proverbs 18:21). So follow David's example and preach to your own soul when you're feeling dismayed.

David's statement *"The Lord is the stronghold of my life"* reminds me of the strong-man lesson Jesus taught in Luke 11:21–26. There will always be a stronghold in your life, but it's our decision whether that stronghold is God or something else. Choosing God as our stronghold protects us and empowers us to overcome our circumstances. Dan Mohler often emphasizes the importance of allowing God to be our stronghold. He teaches that when we surrender our lives to God, we open ourselves to His protection and strength, enabling us to live victoriously.[16]

Today, preach to your own soul and declare God's promises over yourself.

Today I…

---

16 Dan Mohler, "'Becoming Love' by Dan Mohler," posted July 17, 2020, by All Things Are Possible, YouTube, youtube.com.

MARCH 21

TRANSPARENT RELATIONSHIPS

I have spoken to you with great frankness; I take great pride in you. I am greatly encouraged; in all our troubles my joy knows no bounds.

2 Corinthians 7:4 NIV

Paul's honesty and openness with the Corinthians show the importance of genuine, transparent relationships within the body of Christ. He didn't hide his feelings or struggles but communicated them openly, which led to a deep repentance, resulting in a stronger and closer community. This kind of transparency encourages others and fosters deeper connections and spiritual growth.

Paul was particularly encouraged by the Corinthians' reaction to his bold and frank speech. Rather than being offended or hard-hearted, they received Paul's rebuke and encouragement, demonstrating that God's transformative love was at work in their lives. This response showed their willingness to yield to the Holy Spirit over their flesh, resulting in supernatural growth and strength. Such a response greatly encouraged Paul because it further proved that the gospel he was preaching was worth all the persecution and suffering he was experiencing. Their salvation and growth made his trials worth it because Paul lived with an eternal perspective.

Reflect on moments when you've been offended or resisted spiritual growth. Ask God to help you release those offenses and embrace the necessary growth in your walk with Him.

Today I…

MARCH 22

FILLED WITH POWER

As for me, I am filled with power, with the Spirit of the Lord, and with justice and might, to declare to Jacob his transgression, to Israel his sin.

MICAH 3:8 NIV

Micah stood for justice because of the widespread injustice around him. His rebuke came out of love for the captives, showing a deep concern for those being oppressed. Micah moved in the power of God's Spirit even before Jesus came to earth. How much more should we, as believers, move in the power of God now that we have direct access to His throne through the blood and body of Jesus and the gift of the Holy Spirit?

Jesus' sacrifice opened the way for us to approach God boldly and receive His Spirit fully. We are not only recipients of God's grace and salvation, but we are also empowered to act with His authority and might. When we speak boldly, we should be motivated by love for those who are being oppressed and by a desire to see God's justice prevail.

Reflect on how you can move in the power of the Holy Spirit in your daily life. Seek opportunities to demonstrate God's justice and might, and boldly declare His truth to those around you, motivated by love for the oppressed.

Today I…

MARCH 23

OUR HIGH PRIEST

In him and through faith in him we may approach God with freedom and confidence.

EPHESIANS 3:12 NIV

The freedom and confidence we have in approaching God is a profound privilege in Jesus. Historically, only the high priest could enter the Holy of Holies, the innermost part of the temple where God's presence dwelled. This event occurred once a year on the Day of Atonement, and the high priest had to perform specific rituals to cleanse himself of sin. It is thought that a rope was tied around his ankle so that if he died in God's presence because of any sin in his life, others could pull him out without entering the sacred space.

This strict access highlighted the severity of sin and the holiness of God. The high priest acted as a mediator between God and the people, and the entire process underscored the separation caused by sin. However, Jesus, our High Priest, changed everything (Hebrews 4:14–16). His perfect sacrifice on the cross tore the veil separating us from God, symbolizing that the barrier of sin was removed. Now we can come boldly before the throne of God—not because of our own righteousness but because of Jesus' righteousness imputed to us.

Boldly bring one need or praise to God in prayer.

Today I…

MARCH 24

BE LIKE JESUS

This is how love is made complete among us so that we will have confidence on the day of judgment: In this world we are like Jesus.

1 JOHN 4:17 NIV

First John 4:17 speaks to the transformative power of God's love. When love is made complete in us, we can have confidence on the day of judgment. This completeness comes from living like Jesus, reflecting His character and love. Being like Jesus means embodying His love, compassion, and truth. Jesus lived a life of selfless love, always putting others first and doing His Father's will. As His followers, we are called to emulate this love. When we do, God's love is perfected in us, giving us confidence and removing fear of judgment.

This love not only changes us but also impacts those around us. When we love others as Jesus did, we become a living testimony of His grace. Our lives reflect Christ's presence, drawing others to Him. Understanding that we are like Jesus empowers us to live boldly and confidently. We can face each day knowing His love is at work in us, shaping us to be more like Him.

Reflect on how you can show Jesus' love today. Choose one way to demonstrate His love and compassion to someone around you.

Today I…

MARCH 25

UNTIL IT IS COMPLETED

I am sure of this: that the One who began a good work among you will keep it growing until it is completed on the Day of the Messiah Yeshua.

PHILIPPIANS 1:6 CJB

God's Word, which is Jesus, does not return void. Isaiah 55:11 says, *"So is my word that goes out from my mouth: It will not return to me empty but will accomplish what I desire and achieve the purpose for which I sent it"* (NIV). Jesus, the creator of all things (John 1:3), cannot fail. We can speak boldly because we know that His Word cannot set out to accomplish something and then return without fruit.

This confidence stems from our trust in God's unchanging nature and His unfailing promises. Philippians 1:6 reminds us that the good work God began in us will continue to grow. As we speak God's Word over our lives and situations, we can rest assured that it will bring forth fruit. His promises are true, and His power is unmatched. Knowing this, we can boldly declare His truths, confident that they will accomplish His purposes.

Speak God's promises over your life today. Trust that His Word will not return void but will accomplish His perfect will.

Today I…

WITH GREAT BOLDNESS

"Now, Lord, consider their threats and enable your servants to speak your word with great boldness."

ACTS 4:29 NIV

The early Christians faced significant threats and opposition. Instead of praying for safety or relief, they asked God for boldness to continue proclaiming His word. This prayer reflects a profound trust in God's protection and a deep commitment to their mission. Their example challenges us to consider how we respond to opposition and difficulties in our own lives. Do we retreat in fear, or do we ask God for the boldness to continue sharing His truth?

The early Christians understood that the power of their message came from God, not from their own strength. They knew that *"the word of God is living and active"* (Hebrews 4:12 ESV) and that it carries the power to change hearts and lives. Whether we face opposition at work, in our communities, or even within our families, we can trust that God will give us the courage and the right words to speak.

Ask God to give you the courage to speak and respond according to His will today in your interactions with others.

Today I…

MARCH 27

USING WISDOM

"Behold, I am sending you out as sheep in the midst of wolves, so be wise as serpents and innocent as doves."

MATTHEW 10:16 ESV

In Matthew 10:16, Jesus described His followers as sheep among wolves, highlighting the dangers and opposition we will encounter as we live our lives on mission. However, He doesn't leave us defenseless. He gives us the Holy Spirit and instructs us to be wise as serpents and innocent as doves. Being wise as serpents means being shrewd and discerning, navigating challenges with godly wisdom. Being innocent as doves means maintaining purity, integrity, and a gentle spirit. This balance ensures our actions are driven by love and righteousness.

As a follower of Christ, you're sent into a world that can be hostile to your message. You need both wisdom to navigate complexities and innocence to maintain your witness. Jesus perfectly modeled this balance, engaging with broken people and confronting evil while remaining blameless. This balance helps you to be an effective witness, demonstrating God's love and truth. When you rely on the Holy Spirit, He gives you the discernment you need to represent Christ faithfully.

Ask God for wisdom and purity as you navigate your day. Seek to be shrewd in your decisions and gentle in your interactions, reflecting Jesus in all you do.

Today I…

MARCH 28

ROAR

They shall go after the Lord; he will roar like a lion; when he roars, his children shall come trembling from the west.

HOSEA 11:10 ESV

Hosea 11:10 paints a powerful image of God's call to His people. The roar of the Lord, like that of a lion, signifies His supreme authority and power. When God roars, it commands attention, evoking awe and reverence. His children respond, coming from all directions, drawn by His mighty presence. This verse reminds us of the importance of pursuing the Lord with our whole hearts. God's roar represents His call to repentance and His desire for our return to Him. When we hear His call, our response should be one of reverent obedience as we recognize His majesty and authority in our lives.

In the same way that a lion's roar can be heard from miles away, God's call to us is unmistakable. It penetrates our hearts and compels us to follow Him. His roar is both a call to action and a reassurance of His protection and sovereignty. As children of God, we are invited to pursue Him passionately, knowing that His powerful presence guides and sustains us. Let us not hesitate when we hear His call but instead respond with trembling reverence and wholehearted devotion.

Reflect on how you can pursue the Lord more passionately.

Today I…

MARCH 29

A PERFECT BLEND

The next day he saw Jesus coming toward him, and said, "Behold, the Lamb of God, who takes away the sin of the world!"

JOHN 1:29 ESV

This profound statement captures the essence of Jesus' mission and character. Jesus embodies both boldness and gentleness, a perfect blend of strength and humility. Jesus' boldness was evident in His ministry. He fearlessly confronted the religious leaders, overturned the tables of the money changers, and spoke truth to those in power. Yet His boldness was always tempered by His gentleness. As the Lamb of God, He willingly sacrificed Himself for the sake of humanity, displaying the ultimate act of meekness and love.

We see Jesus' gentle nature in His interactions with the broken and marginalized. He touched lepers, healed the sick, and showed compassion to sinners. His gentleness did not diminish His strength; rather, it revealed the depth of His love and commitment to His Father's will. As followers of Christ, we are called to emulate this balance of boldness and gentleness. We should stand firm in our faith and speak truth with courage but always from a heart of compassion and humility.

Look for an opportunity to show compassion to the broken and marginalized today.

Today I…

MARCH 30

CLOTHED IN BOLDNESS

Clothed with strength and dignity, she can laugh at the days to come. When she opens her mouth, she speaks wisely; on her tongue is loving instruction.

PROVERBS 31:25–26 CJB

Boldness doesn't come from merely being outspoken or confident—it comes from knowing who you are in Christ and being fully clothed in His strength. The Proverbs 31 woman laughs at the days to come because she knows her future is secure in God's hands. She is bold because she fully trusts in God's promises and lives in the freedom of His protection. She isn't worried about tomorrow because she has a deep-rooted faith that God will provide, protect, and guide her through all circumstances.

Verse 26 highlights that true boldness speaks life into others with wisdom and grace. When you operate from a place of bold faith, your words reflect the power and authority of God, yet they're delivered with love and compassion. Jesus Himself exemplified this combination of strength and wisdom. He boldly spoke truth, but He also reached out in love to heal and restore. The boldness we are called to in Proverbs 31 isn't about dominating others but about being empowered by the Holy Spirit to speak truth in love.

Clothe yourself in truth and love so that you can be bold.

Today I...

MARCH 31

A GENTLE APPROACH

He will tend his flock like a shepherd; he will gather the lambs in his arms; he will carry them in his bosom, and gently lead those that are with young.

ISAIAH 40:11 ESV

Like yesterday's verse, Isaiah 40:11 also beautifully captures the balance of boldness and gentleness we see in Jesus. He gathers us in His arms, carries us close to His heart, and gently guides us as we raise and mentor new believers. This image of a loving shepherd reminds us that God's boldness is perfectly paired with His gentleness. Throughout our journey of boldness this month, we've learned that being bold in our faith doesn't mean being harsh or overbearing. True boldness is rooted in love and compassion, reflecting the heart of our gentle Shepherd. Jesus, the Lamb of God, embodies this balance perfectly—bold in His mission yet gentle in His love.

In this same way, we're called to disciple our children or those young in the faith. As we move forward, let's carry this lesson with us. Be bold in your faith, stand firm in truth, and speak with courage. But also, be gentle and compassionate in your approach, tenderly caring for those around you as Jesus does.

Ask God to help you embody both boldness and gentleness as you grow in your faith.

Today I…

APRIL

Spring-Cleaning

APRIL 1

SPRING-CLEANING

Create in me a clean heart, O God,
and renew a right spirit within me.

PSALM 51:10 ESV

Spring is a time for renewal and fresh beginnings, so it's the perfect opportunity for spiritual "spring-cleaning." Just as you clean your home, it's essential to purify your heart and mind on a regular basis. David wrote Psalm 51 right after the prophet Nathan confronted him about his adultery with Bathsheba. David pleaded,

> *Have mercy on me, O God, according to your unfailing love; according to your great compassion blot out my transgressions. Wash away all my iniquity and cleanse me from my sin.* (vv. 1–2 NIV)

His cry reflects a deep desire for inner cleansing and renewal. David understood that true transformation starts from within. Purifying your heart involves examining your thoughts, attitudes, and behaviors. It's about letting go of anything that hinders your relationship with God—bitterness, unforgiveness, negative thoughts, and sinful habits. When you ask God to create in you a clean heart, you are inviting Him to point out and then remove the impurities, which renews your spirit.

Pray Psalm 51:10. Let God's Word wash over you, cleansing your heart and mind. Allow Him to remove the clutter and fill you with His Spirit, renewing your purpose and passion for Him.

Today I…

APRIL 2

POP QUIZ

Examine me, God, and know my heart; test me, and know my thoughts. See if there is in me any hurtful way, and lead me along the eternal way.

PSALM 139:23–24 CJB

Spiritual spring-cleaning requires honest self-reflection and a willingness to confront areas in your life that need God's transformative touch. God knows everything. He exists outside of time, and in fact, He created time for our finite minds to have something to grasp. Because He knows everything past, present, and future, when He tests us, it's not for His sake but for our own. God already knows what choices we'll make. Each time He tests us, it's to help us process our decisions, evaluate our hearts and minds, and grow. It's to ensure we get back onto the narrow road that leads to life.

Just as you wouldn't ignore a dusty room during spring-cleaning, don't ignore the parts of your heart that need attention. Be proactive in seeking God's help to cleanse your thoughts, attitudes, and behaviors. By allowing Him to examine and know your heart, you invite His healing and transformative power into your life. Let this season be a time of deep spiritual renewal.

Ask God to examine your heart and reveal areas that need cleansing and purification.

Today I…

APRIL 3

PRESUMPTUOUS SINS

Also keep your servant from presumptuous sins, so that they won't control me. Then I will be blameless and free of great offense.

PSALM 19:14(13) CJB

I recently experienced a betrayal, and despite bringing it to the Lord, I couldn't stop overanalyzing. My attempts to understand the situation had consumed me, making it hard to command my heart to be still and look to the cross. One night, I prayed for the Holy Spirit to keep me from harboring bitterness and to help me focus on Him. I heard in my heart, *Read Psalm 19*. Unsure if it was God's voice, I read the passage and wept at today's verse, asking forgiveness for my presumptuous sins.

John Bevere warned, "An offended heart is the breeding ground of deception."[17] Beloved, we all face fiery trials, but keep your eyes on Jesus. He knows the how, the why, the who, and the when, and He alone is the judge. It is presumptuous sin to take His seat of judgment.

When you go through a trial, don't pray for the Lord to remove every obstacle. Pray for His will, guidance, protection, and the grace to get through it so you can be refined in the fire.

Today I…

---

[17] "John Bevere: The Deadly Trap of Defense," CBN, cbn.com.

APRIL 4

WORTHLESS RELIGION

If anyone thinks he is religious and does not bridle his tongue but deceives his heart, this person's religion is worthless.

JAMES 1:26 ESV

Controlling our mouths is a vital aspect of true religion. Words have immense power to build up or tear down, and an unbridled tongue can lead to deception and hurt. It's easy to fall into the trap of speaking without thinking, letting our emotions dictate our words. Yet God calls us to higher standards, commanding us to be mindful of what we say. As believers, our speech should reflect our faith, embodying grace, love, and truth. When we fail to control our tongues, we undermine our testimony and can cause significant harm to ourselves and others.

Beloved, let's remember that our words are a reflection of our hearts. In moments of frustration or anger, take a pause and seek God's wisdom before speaking. A bridled tongue demonstrates self-control and a heart aligned with God's will.

Today, practice mindful speaking. Before you respond in any situation, take a moment to pray silently and ask the Holy Spirit to guide your words to ensure they reflect His love and truth.

Today I…

APRIL 5

HUMILITY CREATES UNITY

Do nothing out of rivalry or vanity; but, in humility, regard each other as better than yourselves.

PHILIPPIANS 2:3 CJB

Humility is the foundation of a Christlike character. Embracing humility feels countercultural because the world's perspective promotes self-importance and competition. However, Jesus taught and exemplified humility throughout His life. When we consider others as better than ourselves, we create an environment of respect, love, and unity.

Practicing humility requires intentionality and a heart transformed by God's love. It's about recognizing our own limitations and relying on God's strength. Humility allows us to build genuine relationships and reflect Christ's love more accurately. Beloved, let's strive to live humbly, seeking to honor others above ourselves. Remember, true greatness in God's kingdom is marked by a servant's heart.

Today, make a conscious effort to practice humility. Look for opportunities to serve others, listen more than you speak, and seek to uplift those around you. Ask God to help you develop a humble heart that reflects His love and grace.

Today I…

APRIL 6

CONFIDENT

Trusting is being confident of what we hope for, convinced about things we do not see.

HEBREWS 11:1 CJB

Faith is the cornerstone of our relationship with God. It's the assurance and conviction that God's promises are true even when we cannot see their fulfillment yet. Living by faith means trusting in God's character and His word, regardless of our circumstances. It means believing that He is working all things together for our good (Romans 8:28) even when we face challenges and uncertainties.

The heroes of faith mentioned in Hebrews 11 lived with an unwavering trust in God's promises. They faced trials, yet their faith remained steadfast because they knew who God was. Similarly, our faith grows as we experience God's faithfulness in our lives. Beloved, let your faith be rooted in the confidence that God is who He says He is. Trust that His promises will come to pass in His perfect timing.

Today, take a step of faith. Reflect on a promise from God's Word that you need to hold on to. Write it down, pray over it, and trust that God will bring it to fulfillment. Let your actions reflect your trust in His promises even when you can't see the outcome.

Today I…

APRIL 7

HEAVEN'S PERSPECTIVE

If you were raised along with the Messiah, then seek the things above, where the Messiah is sitting at the right hand of God. Focus your minds on the things above, not on things here on earth.

COLOSSIANS 3:1–2 CJB

One of life's greatest challenges is keeping our gaze and focus on Jesus amid a world full of distractions and temptations. The Lord does value hard work (Proverbs 10:4–5), but if we take our eyes off Jesus, it's easy to let work, money, and provision take precedence over God's kingdom. And the more we focus on something, the bigger it appears. Worldly problems can become insurmountable mountains if our perspective is off.

When we focus on Jesus, we realize He is far above the problems of this world (Ephesians 1:21). There is nothing too big or impossible for Him. Furthermore, we're spiritually seated with Him in heaven (Ephesians 2:6). From our heavenly perspective, our earthly problems shrink into manageable molehills we can simply step over. And not only is He able to handle our struggles, but He is also able to do *"far beyond all that we ask or imagine"* through His power at work in us (Ephesians 3:20 TLV).

Today, intentionally shift your focus from earthly concerns to heavenly truths.

Today I…

APRIL 8

YOU MUST FORGIVE

Bear with one another; if anyone has a complaint against someone else, forgive him. Indeed, just as the Lord has forgiven you, so you must forgive.

COLOSSIANS 3:13 CJB

Forgiveness is a powerful act of grace that frees us from the chains of resentment and bitterness and aligns us with God's heart and plan for our lives. When we forgive, we release the hold that past hurts have on us. As we choose forgiveness, we open ourselves to God's redemptive work, trusting that He can bring good even out of painful situations.

Consider Joseph, who forgave his brothers despite their betrayal. He forgave because he trusted that God had a greater plan. In Genesis 50:20, Joseph said, *"You intended to harm me, but God intended it for good to accomplish what is now being done, the saving of many lives"* (NIV). His willingness to forgive not only restored his family but also positioned him to fulfill God's greater plan. Sometimes in His wisdom, God allows what He can easily prevent in His power because it will shape us into the person we need to be and carry out a greater plan for our lives that benefits others.

Pray that God blesses your enemy and ask Him to use the experience to make you more like Jesus.

Today I…

APRIL 9

OPEN REBUKE

Now I appeal to Euodia and Syntyche. Please…settle your disagreement. And I ask you…to help these two women, for they worked hard with me in telling others the Good News.

PHILIPPIANS 4:2–3 NLT

Despite the awkwardness in today's passage, Paul's open rebuke was both scriptural and rooted in love. He recognized that Euodia and Syntyche's division threatened both their well-being and the entire church's unity. There should not be dissension in the body of Christ. We are called to a standard of love.

When you experience church hurt, bring it to Jesus. Then follow Jesus' advice:

> *If your brother sins against you, go and tell him his fault, between you and him alone. If he listens to you, you have gained your brother. But if he does not listen, take one or two others along with you.…If he refuses to listen to them, tell it to the church. And if he refuses to listen even to the church, let him be to you as a Gentile and a tax collector.* (Matthew 18:15–17 ESV)

The devil's goal is to divide and destroy (John 10:10; Luke 22:31; 1 Peter 5:8), but Jesus' love can cover every offense.

If you are struggling with this, fast for one to three days, surrender your heartache to Jesus, and pray Psalm 19.

Today I…

APRIL 10

PUT SIN ASIDE

Since we are surrounded by such a great cloud of witnesses, let us, too, put aside every impediment—that is, the sin which easily hampers our forward movement—and keep running with endurance in the contest set before us.

HEBREWS 12:1 CJB

The author of Hebrews encouraged us to run with endurance, shedding anything that hinders our progress. Hindrances could be habitual sins, unhealthy relationships, or negative thought patterns. Life's race is filled with obstacles, but you are not alone; the Bible is full of examples of faithful believers who have gone before you and whose lives testify to God's faithfulness.

The Lord deeply desires for you to surrender every weight and sin so you can endure every trial you encounter. This process requires intentionality, discipline, and a focus on removing anything that hinders your relationship with God. When you encounter difficulties, don't become weary or discouraged. Fix your eyes on Jesus, the author and perfecter of your faith, and He will empower you to keep going (Hebrews 12:2).

Today, identify one area in your life you need to lay down so you can persevere. Pray for grace and wisdom to overcome any hindrance.

Today I…

APRIL 11

UNANSWERED PRAYERS

You do not have because you do not ask God. When you ask, you do not receive, because you ask with wrong motives, that you may spend what you get on your pleasures.

JAMES 4:2–3 NIV

James warns that when we pray for things that are self-serving rather than kingdom-focused, we shouldn't expect God to answer. But when we surrender our desires and trust in His plan, we align with His perfect timing and find our yes through Jesus (2 Corinthians 1:20).

Still, some prayers seem unanswered even when our hearts are pure. But God is *always* faithful. Hebrews 11 recounts the faith of those who trusted God despite not seeing the fulfillment of His promises in their lifetimes: *"God had something better in store for us. And he did not want them to reach the goal of their faith without us"* (Hebrews 11:40 CEV). The promise wasn't abandoned—God fulfilled it by weaving us into their story. His plan was always bigger than one generation; He designed it so we would be part of the fulfillment. God's faithfulness isn't limited by time. Even when we don't see answers right away, we can trust that He's always working for our good.

Ask the Holy Spirit to teach you how to pray according to His will.

Today I…

APRIL 12

LOVE WITHOUT FRIENDSHIP

You unfaithful wives! Don't you know that loving the world is hating God? Whoever chooses to be the world's friend makes himself God's enemy!

JAMES 4:4 CJB

Here, *"wives"* is a metaphor for the church being the bride of Christ (2 Corinthians 11:2). As part of the bride of Christ, we're commanded to love everyone, including our enemies. This verse doesn't nullify that commandment. However, you can love someone without being their friend. Loving someone out of compassion is different than building a deep friendship with them, in which advice and influence are exchanged.

The first person that God called His friend was Abraham. What made Abraham God's friend? God was willing to share His plans with Abraham and even consider his input. This level of closeness with the creator of the universe is almost unfathomable. Imagine being so close to God that He invites you into His plans, allowing you to intercede before He acts. We are to love those in the world, but we shouldn't seek their advice over God's or let their opinions influence us more than God's Word does. Our guidance shouldn't come from worldly influences but from the Holy Spirit and those who also submit to Jesus.

Evaluate where you're getting your information or anything that influences your opinions and actions. Are those sources of God or the world? Commit to renewing your mind.

Today I…

APRIL 13

GOD LONGS FOR YOUR SPIRIT

Do you think Scripture says without reason that he jealously longs for the spirit he has caused to dwell in us?…Submit yourselves, then, to God. Resist the devil, and he will flee from you.

JAMES 4:5, 7 NIV

This verse breaks my heart. I think of the constant war in the spirit world, just behind the veil where we cannot physically see. God jealously longs for our spirits to revive so we can walk in freedom and in service to Him. It seems ironic that freedom includes servanthood. The Bible is full of paradoxes. Remember, Jesus said we will always serve something (Matthew 6:24). There is freedom in serving Christ, for the Holy Spirit is the Spirit of liberty (2 Corinthians 3:17).

Satan knows Scripture better than we ever will. He is a legalist, using God's Word against us. He does everything he can to keep our spirits from yielding to God because he knows how the Lord jealously longs for our spirits. We must continually submit our whole selves and spirits to the Lord to overcome the devil's schemes.

Pray and submit your body, mind, and spirit to the Lord. If this idea gives you pause, explore why and ask the Holy Spirit to help increase your faith.

Today I…

APRIL 14

DAILY SURRENDER

Come near to God and he will come near to you. Wash your hands, you sinners, and purify your hearts, you double-minded.

JAMES 4:8 NIV

There is no one kinder than God. His kindness leads us to repentance (Romans 2:4). God deeply longs to be near to us, closer than the very air we breathe, but sin cannot be in His presence. This is why Jesus' blood covering is so important, profound, and humbling. The minute we forget the great sacrifice the Savior endured on the cross—eternally cleansing us of our sin so we can boldly approach God's throne—is the very moment when sin can easily take hold of our hearts, minds, bodies, and spirits.

It's hard to read *"you sinners"* and think of ourselves, but we must be diligent to keep pride or offense from taking root and to check in with ourselves for anything in us that would set itself against God. Stay vigilant to keep your heart tender. Take up your cross daily and acknowledge that your life is not your own. You have been bought with a price. Then God's Holy Spirit will work in wondrous ways, and you will encounter Jesus and God's kingdom.

Is there anything you're double-minded about? Ask the Holy Spirit to help you identify and conquer it.

Today I…

APRIL 15

ONE JUDGE

Anyone who speaks against a brother or sister or judges them speaks against the law and judges it. When you judge the law, you are not keeping it, but sitting in judgment on it. There is only one Lawgiver and Judge, the one who is able to save and destroy. But you—who are you to judge your neighbor?

JAMES 4:11–12 NIV

The Bible repeatedly warns us not to judge others, but it also calls us to wisdom. God desires that all people come to know Him, so we're called to love without casting aside our discernment and following people on their path to destruction. Love sets boundaries because it discerns the destruction ahead if people don't reroute. We're called to bear each other's burdens, but when someone is hardhearted, we should stop preaching and keep praying.

The Holy Spirit is the only one who can soften a heart and make ears to hear and eyes to see. We cannot force it. We have to trust the Holy Spirit and keep ourselves off the seat of judgment. Only God can discern a person's motives and understand the intricate reasons for someone's behaviors. He can provide the healing salve they need to live in freedom.

Ask the Holy Spirit when to preach versus when to pray.

Today I…

APRIL 16

DISCERNING FRUIT

"Beware of the false prophets! They come to you wearing sheep's clothing, but underneath they are hungry wolves! You will recognize them by their fruit."

MATTHEW 7:15–16 CJB

In Matthew 7, Jesus called us to observe a prophet's fruit to discern if their word is from God. This instruction applies specifically to prophets, and it's crucial to distinguish between discernment and judgment. Discernment protects, but judgment condemns. Discernment says, "I should not partner with this person," while judgment casts them off as beyond hope. Keep God alone on the judgment seat so you can show the love of Jesus to all, hoping to lead them to salvation.

A true prophet's word aligns with Scripture and is fulfilled in God's timing, not ours. Isaiah prophesied the Messiah over seven hundred years before Christ, and Daniel's visions spanned centuries, with some still yet to come. A delayed prophecy doesn't mean it isn't from God— prophecy follows God's appointed time. This is why we must weigh prophets by their fruit. Conduct a Galatians 5 test: Does this prophet's life and message bear fruit of the Spirit, like love, joy, peace, and self-control? If their words promote strife, self-interest, or fear that leads people away from God, they are not speaking for Him.

Ask the Holy Spirit for wisdom as you navigate voices in the church.

Today I…

APRIL 17

NO FAVORITISM

"'Do not pervert justice; do not show partiality to the poor or favoritism to the great, but judge your neighbor fairly.'"

LEVITICUS 19:15 NIV

Some people use Leviticus 19:15 as an excuse to judge others. That's not what this verse means. This verse deals with showing favoritism to the rich while casting down the poor. James 2:1–4 echoes this:

Practice the faith…without showing favoritism. Suppose a man comes into your synagogue wearing gold rings and fancy clothes, and also a poor man comes in dressed in rags. If you show more respect to the man wearing the fancy clothes and say to him, "Have this good seat here," while to the poor man you say, "You, stand over there,"… then aren't you creating distinctions among yourselves, and haven't you made yourselves into judges with evil motives? (CJB)

God desires that all people turn to Jesus and repent, and they won't do that if you judge them. *"God plays no favorites! It makes no difference who you are or where you're from—if you want God and are ready to do as he says, the door is open"* (Acts 10:34–36 MSG).

Ask the Holy Spirit to guide your heart and mind and help you in offering love over judgment.

Today I…

APRIL 18

SPIRITUAL MURDER

> "'Do not go around spreading slander among your people, but also don't stand idly by when your neighbor's life is at stake; I am ADONAI. Do not hate your brother in your heart, but rebuke your neighbor frankly, so that you won't carry sin because of him.'"
>
> LEVITICUS 19:16–17 CJB

No matter what translation of this verse you look at, it's clear that all gossip should end with us. We are called to rebuke the person sharing the information instead of allowing hatred to take root in our hearts. Jesus said,

> *You have heard that it was said to our ancestors, Do not murder, and whoever murders will be subject to judgment. But I tell you, everyone who is angry with his brother or sister will be subject to judgment.* (Matthew 5:21–22 CSB)

Likewise, 1 John 3:15 says, "Everyone who hates his brother is a murderer, and you know that no murderer has eternal life abiding in him" (ESV).

Have you ever heard someone say, "They're dead to me," after learning something unsettling about a person? When we act as if people are "dead to us," it's like committing murder because we're setting aside God's love for that person and writing them off as if they're without hope. If someone has breath in their lungs, there is still hope for their soul.

Ask God to bless someone who wounded you.

Today I…

APRIL 19

PUT ON KINDNESS

Put on then, as God's chosen ones, holy and beloved, compassionate hearts, kindness, humility, meekness, and patience.

COLOSSIANS 3:12 ESV

Kindness, humility, and compassion are powerful expressions of God's love. It's not just about being polite or nice but about genuinely caring for others and showing them honor. God's love means being sensitive to the needs and hurts of others and responding with empathy and compassion. Consider that our acts of kindness shine even brighter because they contrast the harshness and unkindness that people are so accustomed to.

Forgiveness is a vital aspect of kindness. Holding on to grudges or bitterness only harms us and our relationships. Forgiving others as Christ forgave us frees us to live in peace and harmony. Letting go of offenses keeps our hearts tender and helps us see others through Christ's eyes. Beloved, let kindness be a hallmark of your character. Remember that even small acts of kindness can make a big difference in someone's life and open doors to receive healing and hope.

Today, look for opportunities to show kindness. It could be a kind word, a helping hand, or an act of forgiveness. Ask God to help you be tenderhearted and forgiving, reflecting His love through your actions.

Today I…

APRIL 20

PEACE GIVER

"Peace I leave with you; my peace I give to you. Not as the world gives do I give to you. Let not your hearts be troubled, neither let them be afraid."

JOHN 14:27 ESV

In Christ, you are a new creation (2 Corinthians 5:17), a righteous tree bearing the fruit of the Spirit, which includes peace. When you keep your focus on Jesus, the fruit of the Spirit naturally occurs in your life. The world offers temporary peace that is often based on circumstances. But the peace Jesus gives is steadfast, rooted in His unchanging nature and promises. In the midst of chaos and uncertainty, you can have peace because you know Jesus loves you and promises to care for you (Luke 12:25–31).

Jesus is not pacing in heaven with anxiety. He is the Prince of Peace, seated on the throne with all authority and power (Hebrews 1:3). His peace is always available to you because He is with you and in you (John 14:16–17). His presence calms your fears and steadies your heart, reminding you that He is in control.

Let Christ's peace, as a fruit of the Spirit, fill you and be with you throughout the day, spreading to those around you who need it. Be the calm in others' storms.

Today I…

APRIL 21

OBEDIENCE

Just as through the disobedience of the one man, many were made sinners, so also through the obedience of the other man, many will be made righteous.

ROMANS 5:19 CJB

Never underestimate the power of obedience. Obedience is more important to God than sacrifice (1 Samuel 15:22). Adam's disobedience brought sin and separation from God to all humanity, but Jesus' perfect obedience brought righteousness and reconciliation. Your obedience to God's will can have a profound impact, not only on your own life but on the lives of those around you. Obeying God in the small, daily decisions builds a foundation of faith and trust. It aligns your heart with His purposes and allows His blessings to flow through you to others.

Obedience isn't always easy, but it's driven by love. It often requires sacrifice, humility, and a willingness to go against the grain. But remember, Jesus' obedience led Him to the cross, and through His sacrifice, we are made righteous. Following His example, your obedience can lead to transformation and blessing in ways you may not yet see.

Ask the Holy Spirit to fill you with His love and compassion for others. Ask Him to speak to you and empower you to obey God even when it's uncomfortable.

Today I…

APRIL 22

A NEW HEART

"'I will give you a new heart and put a new spirit inside you; I will take the stony heart out of your flesh and give you a heart of flesh.'"

EZEKIEL 36:26 CJB

A heart of flesh is tender and responsive to God's leading—unlike a stony heart, which resists God's guidance. Allowing God to renew your heart involves a willingness to confront and let go of anything that hardens your spirit. This might include unforgiveness, pride, fear, or even a love of comfort and convenience.

Today, actively seek to align your life with God's will. Purpose to open your eyes and ears to those around you and ask the Holy Spirit to help you easily perceive who needs the love of Jesus around you. Your daily encounters with strangers are not a mistake. You might be the only representation of Jesus they'll ever encounter. Remember, God is capable of replacing hearts of stones with hearts of flesh.

Go out of your way to tangibly demonstrate God's love for someone today. Whether it's bringing a coworker coffee or flowers, writing someone an encouraging note, or buying a meal for a person experiencing homelessness, practice love in a practical way and pray for God to transform hearts.

Today I…

APRIL 23

HOLY

On the contrary, following the Holy One who called you, become holy yourselves in your entire way of life; since the Tanakh says, "You are to be holy because I am holy."

1 PETER 1:15–16 CJB

Holiness isn't just about outward behavior or something we do on Sundays. It's about a transformation of the heart and a lifestyle. True holiness stems from a deep relationship with God and a desire to reflect His character in every aspect of our lives. God calls us to be holy because He is holy, and this calling is both a privilege and a responsibility.

We don't strive for holiness to earn salvation; rather, holiness is the fruit of a life surrendered to Christ. Jesus Himself said, *"I am the vine; you are the branches. The one who remains in me and I in him produces much fruit"* (John 15:5 CSB). Just as a branch draws life from the vine, our ability to live a holy life comes from abiding in Him. Let go of anything hindering your spiritual growth and pursue righteousness wholeheartedly. It's not about perfection but about a sincere commitment to live a life that honors God and reflects His love so you can effectively build His kingdom.

Commit to making choices that honor God and allow the Holy Spirit to disciple you.

Today I…

APRIL 24

TRANSFORMED MINDS

Do not let yourselves be conformed to the standards of the 'olam hazeh [the world]. Instead, keep letting yourselves be transformed by the renewing of your minds; so that you will know what God wants and will agree that what he wants is good, satisfying and able to succeed.

ROMANS 12:2 CJB

Transformation begins in the mind. Renewing your mind involves immersing yourself in God's Word, meditating on His truths, and allowing His Spirit to reshape your thoughts and attitudes. It's about seeing through heaven's perspective. Dave Roberson taught that "the prison is in the mind," and it is there that the Enemy wages war against us, attempting to plant seeds of doubt, fear, and unbelief.[18]

In today's digital age, a social media presence is a worldly standard. But studies have shown a significant link between social media use and increased levels of anxiety and depression. The constant exposure to the filtered and curated lives of others can lead to unhealthy comparisons and feelings of inadequacy. In his book *The Digital Fast*, Darren Whitehead said that when you disconnect from digital chaos, you rediscover the art of listening to God's voice.[19]

Consider fasting from social media and news and observe how the change affects you.

Today I…

---

18 Dave Roberson, "The Prison Is in the Mind," Dave Roberson Ministries, daveroberson.org.
19 Darren Whitehead, *The Digital Fast: 40 Ways to Detox Your Mind and Reclaim What Matters Most* (pub. by author, 2024).

APRIL 25

BE SALTY

"You are salt for the Land. But if salt becomes tasteless, how can it be made salty again? It is no longer good for anything except being thrown out for people to trample on."

MATTHEW 5:13 CJB

Salt is used to enhance flavors and make bland food taste delicious. It's also a natural preservative, preventing bacterial growth and extending food's shelf life. Additionally, salt has medicinal benefits, can remove stains, softens hardened water, melts ice, and cleanses wounds. Likewise, Christians are called to be like salt: We are to enhance people's lives by pointing them to Jesus, their Creator and source of meaning and purpose. We're also called to bring out people's God-given gifts and talents so they can live out their divine purpose. We're called to preserve others' values, protect against moral decay, and hopefully extend people's lives eternally.

We lovingly point them to Jesus, who promises, *"Though your sins are like scarlet, they shall be as white as snow"* (Isaiah 1:18 NIV). We direct them to the one who can soften hardened hearts and heal every wound. If we allow ourselves to blend in with worldly standards or become consumed by our own needs, wants, and desires, we lose our divine purpose, influence, and authority.

Go be the salt of the earth today.

Today I…

APRIL 26

TRUE REPENTANCE

"Yet even now," says Adonai, "turn to me with all your heart, with fasting, weeping and lamenting. Tear your heart, not your garments; and turn to Adonai your God. For he is merciful and compassionate, slow to anger, rich in grace, and willing to change his mind about disaster."

JOEL 2:12–13 CJB

In the book of Joel, God called His people to return to Him with all their hearts, emphasizing sincere repentance. The phrase *"Tear your heart, not your garments"* highlights the need for genuine, internal transformation rather than outward displays of sorrow. True repentance involves a heartfelt turning back to God, a recognition of our shortcomings, and a quest for His mercy. As we continue in our spiritual spring-cleaning, we should examine our hearts and remove anything separating us from God. This might involve confessing sins, forgiving others, or realigning our priorities with God's will.

God's promise in Joel is clear: God is merciful, compassionate, slow to anger, and rich in grace. He is always ready to welcome us back and restore our relationship with Him. Let's return to God wholeheartedly, knowing He is eager to renew our spirits and guide us.

Ask God to reveal any areas needing repentance and renewal. Turn to Him with all your heart, trusting in His mercy, compassion, and grace.

Today I…

APRIL 27

WE CARRY A DEEP TREASURE

As God's fellow-workers we also urge you not to receive his grace and then do nothing with it.

2 Corinthians 6:1 cjb

This verse makes me cry for everyone who doesn't know Jesus because they've never heard the good news. They've heard His name, but the idea of hearing His voice or experiencing His presence is a strange concept to them. As an actress, I meet people all over the world from many different cultures, backgrounds, and stages of life. I sit with them, talk to them, observe them, and love them.

It amazes me how those whose grass seems the greenest at a distance are usually applying lawn paint (a Hollywood trick for green grass on screen in the winter) to fool onlookers. These people use drugs, go on meditation retreats, or seek out psychics because they're searching for Jesus without knowing it. They want peace, true joy, unconditional love, and answers to life's questions. As Christians, we carry a deep treasure: Jesus, the answer to every question, the fulfillment of every void. We are His coworkers. It's our job to listen for His voice and share the good news.

Start your day by asking the Holy Spirit to show you whom you need to speak to today. Trust that He'll give you the words in the moment.

Today I…

APRIL 28

HEAVEN'S WHISPERS

> Adonai is my shepherd; I lack nothing. He has me lie down in grassy pastures, he leads me by quiet water, he restores my inner person. He guides me in right paths for the sake of his own name.
>
> PSALM 23:1–3 CJB

God doesn't usually shout over the noise of the world—He whispers in stillness (1 Kings 19:11–12). When you pause and silence distractions, the Holy Spirit speaks. His voice isn't always dramatic. Sometimes, it's a gentle nudge, an impression, a knowing. He invites you to trust Him, to take one step at a time as He orders your steps for His glory. Use wisdom and do whatever He asks. He will stay beside you as you follow the path He lays out.

Too often, we rush ahead, filling our schedules, pursuing dreams, and solving problems without stopping to ask, *Lord, what are You saying?* But everything in life is about listening to God's will through the Spirit and building His kingdom. If we don't quiet our hearts, we risk missing the very guidance that restores us. Open your ears. Yield everything—your dreams, fears, wants, and needs. Surrender. Rest in His presence, breathe in His peace, and respond to His whispers with obedience.

What is God whispering to you today?

Today I…

APRIL 29

WITHOUT LOVE

"Not everyone who says to me, 'Lord, Lord!' will enter the Kingdom of Heaven, only those who do what my Father in heaven wants. On that Day, many will say to me, 'Lord, Lord! Didn't we prophesy in your name? Didn't we expel demons in your name? Didn't we perform many miracles in your name?' Then I will tell them to their faces, 'I never knew you! Get away from me, you workers of lawlessness!'"

MATTHEW 7:21–23 CJB

We must keep this passage at the forefront of our minds to successfully live out God's calling. Proverbs 3:3 reminds us, *"Let love and faithfulness never leave you; bind them around your neck, write them on the tablet of your heart"* (NIV). It's sobering to realize that we can operate in miracles and wonders without truly knowing Jesus. Without love as our motive, we're like *"blaring brass or a clanging cymbal"* (1 Corinthians 13:1 CJB). Have you ever heard someone learning how to play the horn or drums? It's painful!

In the same way, without love, our evangelism deters people from Jesus. Jesus calls those who call on His name but do not know Him *"workers of lawlessness."* This means that without love, we cannot fulfill the law of God. Love is the foundation and essence of God's law. Without it, even our most righteous acts are disgusting to God (Isaiah 64:6).

Lead with love.

Today I…

APRIL 30

GOD'S TAPESTRY

We know that God causes everything to work together for the good of those who love God and are called in accordance with his purpose.

ROMANS 8:28 CJB

Life often presents us with circumstances that are difficult to understand, so I find today's verse so comforting. When we yield our desires and will to God and pray about everything, no matter which way we turn in uncharted waters, we will eventually get to the place God intends.

God's perspective is far greater than ours. What may seem like a setback or a hardship can actually be a part of His greater plan. He has the ability to weave together every experience, whether joyous or painful, into a beautiful tapestry that reveals His glory and fulfills His purpose in our lives. Reflecting on the life of Joseph, we see this truth in action. Despite being sold into slavery and unjustly imprisoned, Joseph's faith in God never wavered. Ultimately, God used Joseph's circumstances to save many lives during a famine. What seemed like misfortune was part of God's divine plan. Nothing is wasted with God.

Thank God for where you are right now and thank Him that He has a plan to get you where you need to go.

Today I…

MAY

Move in the Opposite Spirit

MAY 1

MOVE IN THE OPPOSITE SPIRIT

Repay no one evil for evil, but try to do what everyone regards as good. If possible, and to the extent that it depends on you, live in peace with all people.

ROMANS 12:17–18 CJB

Choosing to take the high road, especially when someone has wronged us, reflects the character of Christ. The world glorifies revenge and retaliation, but God calls us to reflect the character of Christ. Repaying evil with good and striving to live peaceably with everyone are marks of true discipleship. Graham Cooke often speaks of "moving in the opposite spirit," meaning that we should respond to negativity and hostility with their opposites: love, joy, kindness, and peace.[20] It's an act of faith that says, "I trust You, Lord, to handle this situation."

Living honorably in the sight of all means being mindful of your actions and their impact on others, always striving to reflect God's love and grace. By choosing to act "in the opposite spirit," contrary to the world's reactions, you bring heaven's perspective into your circumstances and allow God's love to shine through you.

Today, if you face a situation where you are tempted to repay evil with evil, pause and move in the opposite spirit.

Today I…

---

20 Graham Cooke, "Nothing Works Against the Fruit of the Spirit," *What Is God Really Like?* (podcast), Brilliant Perspectives, September 10, 2018, brilliantperspectives.com.

MAY 2

HE CAME TO SERVE

"Even the Son of Man came not to be served but to serve, and to give his life as a ransom for many."

MARK 10:45 ESV

The world is driven by selfish ambition and pride, but God calls us to live differently. Using your freedom to serve others in love is a profound way to reflect Christ's love. I love that this translation of today's verse says *"even"* Jesus did not come to be served but to serve. He's the ultimate example of humility and generosity. His life was marked by selflessness and compassion, teaching that true greatness lies in serving others. When you humble yourself and prioritize others, you create an atmosphere of love and respect, where God's presence is evident.

Humility allows you to see others through God's eyes so you can foster genuine relationships and meaningful connections. By choosing humility, you invite God's grace into your life and the lives of those around you. Let your actions reflect the love of Christ, who humbled Himself for your sake. In serving others, you honor God and fulfill His command to love one another.

Create a list of ways you could serve someone this week, whether through small acts of kindness or significant gestures of help. Follow through on these acts of service.

Today I…

MAY 3

WEAKNESS

He said to me, "My grace is sufficient for you, for my power is made perfect in weakness." Therefore I will boast all the more gladly of my weaknesses, so that the power of Christ may rest upon me.

2 Corinthians 12:9 ESV

Admitting weakness is not easy in a world that celebrates strength and self-sufficiency. Yet God's perspective is different. Your weaknesses are your testimony. They're opportunities for God's strength to shine through and reveal what He's delivered you from. Acknowledging your limitations opens the door for God's incredible power to work in your life. Vulnerability before God invites His transformative power. By recognizing your dependence on Him, you allow His grace to empower you in ways you could never achieve on your own.

This divine exchange—your weakness for His strength—leads to a deeper experience of His presence and purpose. Don't be discouraged by your weaknesses. Instead, see them as opportunities for God to display His power and grace in your life.

Identify an area of weakness in your life and invite God's strength into it. Pray for His grace to sustain you and His power to be perfected in that area. Embrace your dependence on Him and watch how His strength transforms your weakness into a testimony of His faithfulness.

Today I…

MAY 4

FOCUS

Finally, brothers and sisters, whatever is true, whatever is noble, whatever is right, whatever is pure, whatever is lovely, whatever is admirable—if anything is excellent or praiseworthy—think about such things.

PHILIPPIANS 4:8 NIV

In honor of May the fourth (be with you!), let's recall what a wise Jedi once said: "Always remember, your focus determines your reality."[21] That echoes the profound truth in Philippians. Whatever you choose to fill your mind with ultimately shapes your attitude, behavior, and even your character. Philippians 4:8 urges us to focus on the positive and uplifting aspects of life.

When you dwell on thoughts that are true, noble, right, pure, lovely, admirable, excellent, and praiseworthy, you invite God's peace and joy into your life. These thoughts align your heart with God's will and His perspective, leading to a more joyful and hopeful outlook on life.

Today, intentionally fill your mind with positive and uplifting thoughts. Start your day by reflecting on the goodness of God and the blessings in your life. Throughout the day, whenever negative thoughts arise, consciously replace them with thoughts of gratitude and praise. Write down three things you're thankful for and meditate on them throughout the day.

Today I…

---

21 *Star Wars: Episode I—The Phantom Menace*, directed by George Lucas (20th Century Fox, 1999), DVD.

MAY 5

WITNESSING IS A LIFESTYLE

Rejoice in the Lord always. I will say it again: Rejoice! Let your gentleness be evident to all. The Lord is near. Do not be anxious about anything, but in every situation, by prayer and petition, with thanksgiving, present your requests to God. And the peace of God, which transcends all understanding, will guard your hearts and your minds in Christ Jesus.

PHILIPPIANS 4:4–7 NIV

Witnessing is more than words; it's a lifestyle. Heaven has a language and perspective of its own that's foreign and contrary to the world's, but we can learn it. One of the easiest ways to practice it is by moving in the opposite spirit of our natural flesh. If you're in a crummy situation, instead of grumbling, do the opposite and thank God for something. The more you practice verbal gratitude and praise, the more it will flow out of you naturally.

Another way to live out the heavenly perspective is by being gentle. This is challenging. When we hear people mock Jesus, it's hard not to fight back. While there is a time to speak and not be silent, God doesn't need us to defend Him with words because our actions and reactions speak far louder than clever responses.

Reflect on your lifestyle. Watch your actions today and ask yourself if your behavior naturally witnesses to those around you.

Today I…

MAY 6

A GRATITUDE ATTITUDE

In everything give thanks, for this is what God wants from you who are united with the Messiah Yeshua.

1 Thessalonians 5:18 CJB

Complaining is often our natural inclination when facing challenges. Yet God's way calls us to respond with gratitude. Gratitude is a powerful practice that transforms our perspective and aligns us with God's viewpoint. Paul instructed us to give thanks in all circumstances, not just when things are going well. This isn't about denying our struggles but instead recognizing that God is present and at work in every situation. When we cultivate a heart of gratitude, we shift our focus from what we lack to what we have been blessed with. This practice not only uplifts our spirit but also strengthens our faith and deepens our relationship with God.

A grateful heart is a reflection of trusting God's sovereign plan. It acknowledges His hand in every situation and expresses faith that He is working all things together for our good. Let's make it a daily habit to thank God for His blessings, big and small, and watch how it transforms our lives.

Write down five things you are grateful for and thank God for each one. Let this practice of gratitude become a daily habit, helping you to see God's goodness in every situation.

Today I…

MAY 7

LOVE YOUR ENEMIES

"I tell you, love your enemies!
Pray for those who persecute you!"

MATTHEW 5:44 CJB

The world teaches us to retaliate when someone hurts us, but Jesus calls us to love our enemies and pray for those who persecute us. This radical love reflects the heart of God and demonstrates His transformative power in our lives. Loving our enemies isn't about condoning their actions; it's about choosing to see them through God's eyes—as valuable and worthy of love. When we respond with love instead of retaliation, we break the cycle of hatred and open the door for reconciliation and healing.

Praying for those who persecute us shifts our perspective. It's hard to hold on to anger and bitterness when we're lifting someone up in prayer. Through prayer, we ask God to work in their lives and ours, bringing healing, reconciliation, and peace. Jesus exemplified this on the cross when He prayed for those who crucified Him. His love transcended their actions and offered forgiveness and grace. As we follow His example, we become vessels of God's love, impacting those around us in profound ways.

Think of someone who has wronged you. Pray for them today, asking God to bless them and help you love them as He does.

Today I…

MAY 8

LET GO OF CONTROL

Trust in Adonai with all your heart; do not rely on your own understanding. In all your ways acknowledge him, and he will make your paths straight.

PROVERBS 3:5–6 CJB

Worry is a natural response to uncertainty, but we need to move in the opposite spirit and have faith. Our understanding is limited, but God's wisdom is perfect. Trusting God means letting go of our need for control and believing that He is able to intervene. It's an act of faith that acknowledges His sovereignty and goodness even in the midst of chaos. Jesus taught that when we prioritize seeking God's kingdom, He will meet all our needs.

One profound way to encounter Jesus is by serving others even when we feel lacking. By stepping out in faith and meeting the needs of those around us, we trust that God will supply all our needs. It's a beautiful exchange: As we pour out, God fills us up. Consider the widow of Zarephath who, despite her own scarcity, provided for Elijah. Her act of faith and service resulted in God's miraculous provision. When we serve others, we open ourselves to experiencing God's abundant provision and blessings.

Serve someone in need, trusting that God will meet your needs as you meet the needs of others.

Today I…

MAY 9

CHEERFUL GENEROSITY

Each should give according to what he has decided in his heart, not grudgingly or under compulsion, for God loves a cheerful giver.

2 Corinthians 9:7 CJB

Sometimes generosity can feel like an obligation instead of a joyful act of worship. When this happens, we must remember this verse and check our heart posture. Second Corinthians 9:7 encourages us to give cheerfully, recognizing that everything we have is a gift from God. Every gift we give mirrors God's love while serving as a powerful affirmation of our trust in His provision. God calls us to radical generosity. When we're scared to give up our money, time, emotions, or resources, we need to once again take the Romans 14:23 test—*"anything not based on trust is a sin"*—and ask ourselves what we're trusting in that moment more than God's provision.

On rare occasions, our hesitation to give can be due to discernment, but most of the time, it's because we're scared that if we give, we won't have enough for ourselves. Jesus commended the widow who gave out of her poverty, highlighting that true generosity is measured by the heart, not the amount. Embracing cheerful generosity allows us to break free from self-centeredness and fear and experience faith's joy and freedom.

In faith, do something radically generous today.

Today I…

MAY 10

BE HUMBLED

Humble yourselves before the Lord, and he will lift you up.
JAMES 4:10 CJB

The world celebrates self-promotion and pride, but God calls us to humility. James 4:10 reminds us that when we humble ourselves before the Lord and recognize our dependence on Him, He will lift us up. Humility isn't self-deprecation; it's acknowledging that every gift, strength, and success comes from God. The Bible is full of paradoxes that challenge our natural inclinations. One of these is the idea that true greatness comes from humility. Jesus, the Son of God, exemplified this by washing His disciples' feet, demonstrating that serving others is the path to true greatness.

When we choose humility, we align ourselves with God's heart and open the door for Him to exalt us in His perfect timing. By embracing humility, we can build stronger relationships and create an environment where God's love can flourish. Let's choose to put others first and serve with a humble heart.

Look for an opportunity to serve someone today. Perform an act of kindness that puts their needs above your own.

Today I…

MAY 11

PEACEMAKERS

"How blessed are those who make peace! for they will be called sons of God."

MATTHEW 5:9 CJB

Jesus calls us to be peacemakers. When we pursue peace, we reflect our heavenly Father's character. He is the Prince of Peace (Isaiah 9:6). There's a difference between being peace*keepers* and peace*makers*. Peacekeepers avoid conflict, which sometimes allows unresolved issues to fester, leading to deep resentment and anger. Peacemakers actively seek reconciliation and understanding. They listen more than they speak and value relationships over being right.

Consider the story of Abigail in 1 Samuel 25. When her husband Nabal insulted David, conflict was imminent. Abigail's wise and humble approach prevented bloodshed and brought peace. She acted swiftly, bringing gifts to David and speaking words of wisdom and humility, which diffused the tension. Her actions saved many lives and demonstrated the power of peacemaking. When we strive to be peacemakers, we become agents of God's love and grace in a fractured world.

Seek to resolve any conflict you may have with someone. Remain calm. Hold fast to love. Don't prepare your arguments but instead listen and trust for a godly response. Approach the situation with a heart of understanding and a desire for reconciliation.

Today I…

MAY 12

JOY ISN'T HAPPENSTANCE

"Don't be sad, because the joy of ADONAI is your strength."
NEHEMIAH 8:10 CJB

Life holds seasons of sadness and despair, but Nehemiah 8:10 reminds us that the joy of the Lord is our strength. The word *happiness* comes from the same root word as *happenstance*, meaning happiness depends on our circumstances. Joy, however, comes from our relationship with God and our assurance of His love and faithfulness. Joy is a fruit of the Spirit, cultivated through time spent in God's presence and meditation on His promises. Even in difficult times, we can find joy in knowing that God is with us and that He works all things for our good.

Jesus endured the cross for the joy set before Him, knowing the redemption it would bring. When we focus on the eternal, our current struggles diminish in comparison. The apostle Paul, despite facing numerous hardships, wrote about joy repeatedly in his letters. In Philippians 4:4, he exhorted us to *"rejoice in the Lord always; again I will say, rejoice"* (NIV). Paul's joy was rooted in his relationship with Christ, not in his circumstances. Choosing joy also impacts those around us. A joyful heart is contagious and can uplift others who may be struggling.

Spend time today reflecting on God's goodness and promises. Share this joy with someone who may need encouragement.

Today I…

MAY 13

THE PARADOX OF GIVING

"Give, and you will receive gifts—the full measure, compacted, shaken together and overflowing, will be put right in your lap. For the measure with which you measure out will be used to measure back to you!"

LUKE 6:38 CJB

Society values accumulation, but Jesus teaches a profound paradox: By giving, we receive. Luke 6:38 promises that when we give generously, God blesses us abundantly in return. This principle goes against the world's logic but aligns perfectly with God's kingdom. Consider the second part of this verse. What is your generosity measured with? If you're giving using a teaspoon, God will use a teaspoon to give back to you.

Generosity reflects the heart of God. When we give freely—whether it's our time, resources, talent, support, or love—we trust God to replenish and multiply what we have given. This act of faith not only blesses others but also opens us to receive God's overflowing blessings so we can keep blessing others. The early church exemplified this spirit of giving. They shared all their possessions and cared for one another, resulting in a community marked by unity and joy. The church should be a place where broken people find healing and help in times of need.

Ask your pastor what needs your church has and find a way to help meet them.

Today I…

MAY 14

FINDING LIFE

"For whoever wants to save his own life will destroy it, but whoever destroys his life for my sake will find it."

MATTHEW 16:25 CJB

The world tells us to cling to our lives and pursue our desires, but Jesus presents a paradox: True life is found in surrender. In Matthew 16:25, Jesus taught that by giving up our lives for His sake, we actually find true life and freedom. Surrendering to God means letting go of our own plans and trusting His perfect will for our lives. It's a daily act of faith, believing that God's ways are higher and better than ours. When we surrender, we discover a freedom that comes from aligning ourselves with God's purpose and experiencing His abundant life.

Serving Jesus becomes an adventure. Making room for God to replace our own schedules with His plans for the day makes every day exciting and full of possibilities. Instead of the mundane, life becomes a journey where we witness God's amazing plans and miracles unfold in unexpected ways. Surrendering our daily plans to God transforms our ordinary days into extraordinary adventures.

Give the Holy Spirit room to wreck your schedule. Trust that He can accomplish more in a moment than you can in a day. Embrace the adventure that comes with following Jesus.

Today I…

MAY 15

LOSING IS GAIN

"Whoever wants to save his own life will destroy it, but whoever destroys his life for my sake and for the sake of the Good News will save it."

MARK 8:35 CJB

If the Holy Spirit felt it necessary to repeat this statement in every single gospel, we can review it again, too, and up the ante. Modern culture prioritizes self-preservation, but Jesus offers a profound paradox: We gain by losing. Mark 8:35 tells us that by losing our lives for Jesus, we actually save our lives. This challenges us to move in the opposite spirit by rejecting self-centeredness and embracing selflessness.

Losing our lives for Jesus means prioritizing His mission and values over our own desires. It involves sacrificing our comfort and ambitions to follow Him wholeheartedly. When we do this, we discover a deeper sense of purpose and fulfillment that the world cannot offer. The lives of the apostles demonstrated this truth. They left everything to follow Jesus and spread the gospel, despite facing persecution and death. Yet their sacrifices led to a legacy of faith that continues to impact the world. By losing their lives for Jesus, they gained eternal significance.

Reflect on areas where you can lose your life for Jesus' sake. Prioritize His mission and values in your daily decisions and actions.

Today I…

MAY 16

HUMILITY LEADS TO WISDOM

*Fools suppose their way is straight,
but the wise pay attention to advice.*

PROVERBS 12:15 CJB

The world often tells us to trust our instincts and rely on our own understanding. However, Proverbs 12:15 reveals a paradox: True wisdom comes from acknowledging our own foolishness and seeking advice from others. Recognizing our limitations and seeking godly counsel are acts of humility that lead to greater wisdom.

When we admit that we don't have all the answers and listen to the advice of wise mentors, we open ourselves to growth and learning. This humility aligns us with God's ways, where dependence on His guidance and on the insights of others enriches our lives. King Solomon, known for his great wisdom, sought God's guidance above all. He understood that true wisdom comes from God and not from human intellect alone. By embracing this paradox, we position ourselves to receive the wisdom that God generously offers.

Identify an area in your life where you need guidance. Pray for God's wisdom to lead you and then seek advice from a trusted mentor or spiritual advisor.

Today I…

MAY 17

REAL ABUNDANCE

"In everything I have given you an example of how, by working hard like this, you must help the weak, remembering the words of the Lord Yeshua himself, 'There is more happiness in giving than in receiving.'"

ACTS 20:35 CJB

This verse encourages us to work hard not only to provide for ourselves and our families but also to bless others out of our abundance. When we embrace a lifestyle of generosity, we reflect God's heart. Jesus' entire ministry was marked by giving—healing the sick, feeding the hungry, and ultimately giving His life for our salvation. We are called to follow His example, using our resources and talents to support and uplift those in need.

Working hard has its rewards, but the true joy comes from using our blessings to help others. Whether it's giving financial support, sharing our time, bearing each other's emotional burdens, or offering our skills, every act of generosity contributes to building God's kingdom and demonstrates His love to the world. Let's commit to being conduits of God's blessings, working diligently and giving joyfully, knowing that in doing so, we fulfill our divine purpose and bring glory to Him.

Ask God to show you someone in need and joyfully step into their story.

Today I…

MAY 18

STOP KVETCHING

Do everything without kvetching or arguing, so that you may be blameless and pure children of God, without defect in the midst of a twisted and perverted generation, among whom you shine like stars in the sky.

PHILIPPIANS 2:14–15 CJB

In a world where complaints and disputes are common, we set ourselves apart as followers of Christ when we move in the opposite spirit. By not complaining or arguing, we reflect the purity and blamelessness that God desires in His children. Our reactions should stand in stark contrast to the world's, showcasing the transformative power of God in our lives. Living without grumbling or disputing allows us to shine like stars, illuminating the darkness around us.

Of course, this doesn't mean we ignore injustices or remain silent when things go wrong. It means we handle situations with grace, patience, and a positive attitude. Our responses should be rooted in love and in a desire to bring peace instead of adding to the chaos and negativity. By cultivating a spirit of gratitude and seeking peaceful resolutions, we honor God and provide a powerful witness to those around us. Our lives can inspire others to seek the same joy and contentment that comes from a relationship with Jesus.

Today, make a conscious effort to avoid complaining or arguing.

Today I…

MAY 19

GODLY REPAYMENT

Do not repay evil with evil or insult with insult. On the contrary, repay evil with blessing, because to this you were called so that you may inherit a blessing.

1 Peter 3:9 NIV

In 1 Peter 3:9, we're called to respond to evil and insults with blessing. This teaching is radically different from the world's response, which often involves retaliation and harboring grudges. As followers of Christ, we are called to embody Christ. When someone wrongs us, our natural inclination might be to seek revenge or respond with harsh words. However, Peter reminded us that we are called to a different path. By responding with blessing, we break the cycle of negativity and reflect the love and grace of Jesus.

This doesn't mean we ignore wrongdoing or allow others to harm us. It means we choose to respond in a way that honors God and promotes peace. Blessing those who hurt us can take many forms: praying for them, speaking kindly, or offering help when needed. Jesus modeled this behavior perfectly. Even when He was insulted and persecuted, He responded with love, forgiveness, and wisdom. We're called to do the same.

Look for an opportunity to bless someone, demonstrating the love and grace of Jesus.

Today I…

ANGER DOESN'T ACCOMPLISH

My dear brothers, let every person be quick to listen but slow to speak, slow to get angry; for a person's anger does not accomplish God's righteousness!

JAMES 1:19–20 CJB

Listening actively and attentively demonstrates respect and humility. It shows that we value the thoughts and feelings of others. When we're quick to listen, we gain understanding and prevent misunderstandings that often lead to conflict. Being slow to speak encourages us to choose our words carefully. Remember, words have the power to build up or tear down. By pausing before we speak, we can ensure our words are kind, truthful, and edifying. This practice helps us to communicate with grace and wisdom.

When we allow anger to control us, we may act or say things that we will regret. By being slow to anger, we exercise self-control (a fruit of the Holy Spirit) and demonstrate a heart transformed by God's love. Our reactions in challenging situations should be contrary to the world's. By embodying patience, understanding, and self-control, we reflect Christ's character and advance God's kingdom.

Today, practice being quick to listen, slow to speak, and slow to get angry.

Today I…

MAY 21

BREAK THE CYCLE

See that no one repays evil for evil; on the contrary, always try to do good to each other, indeed, to everyone.

1 Thessalonians 5:15 CJB

It astounds me how much the Bible repeats itself even though it has many authors. That's proof of the Holy Spirit. For example, just like 1 Peter 3:9 from a couple days ago, today's verse also encourages us to break the cycle of retaliation. It takes strength and grace to choose to do good in the face of evil. This response not only reflects Christ's character but also has the potential to soften hearts and open doors for reconciliation.

Doing good to everyone means showing kindness and compassion to all, regardless of how they treat us. It means going out of our way to help, encourage, and uplift others, even those who may not deserve it by the world's standards. By doing this, we embody the love and mercy of Jesus, who taught us to love our neighbors as ourselves. This proactive approach to doing good can have a ripple effect, influencing others to act similarly and creating a more loving and compassionate community.

Today, make a conscious effort to do good to someone who has wronged you or to someone in need.

Today I…

MAY 22

A GENTLE RESPONSE

A gentle response deflects fury,
but a harsh word makes tempers rise.

PROVERBS 15:1 CJB

A gentle response shows restraint, wisdom, and a desire for peace. It demonstrates that we value the relationship and the person more than winning an argument or proving a point. This kind of response can de-escalate tense situations and open the door for constructive dialogue. On the other hand, harsh words fuel anger and can quickly turn a disagreement into a full-blown conflict. They can damage relationships, hurt feelings, and lead to long-lasting resentment. By choosing our words carefully and responding with gentleness, we reflect the character of Christ, who was described as *"gentle and humble in heart"* (Matthew 11:29 NIV).

Practicing gentle responses requires self-control and a heart aligned with God's will. It involves listening actively, understanding the other person's perspective, and responding with kindness and respect. This approach not only helps to maintain peace but also serves as a powerful witness to others of God's love and wisdom.

When faced with a difficult conversation or conflict, choose to respond gently. Reflect on how your words can bring peace and demonstrate the love of Christ.

Today I…

MAY 23

OVERCOME WITH LOVE

Do not be conquered by evil, but conquer evil with good.
ROMANS 12:21 CJB

The only way we can overcome evil is by making sure the hurting world knows there's a better way—demonstrated by love in action. Evil tempts us to turn a blind eye to suffering and embrace what's comfortable. But the Bible challenges us to act in love even when it's difficult.

Consider the over three hundred fifty thousand children in foster care in the United States.[22] With an estimated three hundred fifty thousand churches across the country,[23] imagine the possible impact of showing these children and their families that they are valued and loved by God and His people! We'd break the cycle of abuse and introduce a cycle of love and healing. It would be a powerful witness of Christ's light and love to the world. Our communities can be places of hope and transformation, where the love of Jesus is not just spoken about but visibly demonstrated.

Rise to the challenge and be the hands and feet of Jesus. Do not allow the comfort of your routines to numb you to the needs around you.

Today I…

---

22 "Data and Statistics: AFCARS," Children's Bureau: An Office of the Administration for Children and Families, March 20, 2024, acf.hhs.gov.
23 "Are There Too Many Churches in the United States?" *The Burge Report*, Church Answers, May 17, 2024, churchanswers.com.

MAY 24

MARKED BY EXCELLENCE

Whatever you do, work at it with all your heart, as working for the Lord, not for human masters, since you know that you will receive an inheritance from the Lord as a reward. It is the Lord Christ you are serving.

COLOSSIANS 3:23–24 NIV

We are to do everything with excellence as an act of worship to the Most High God. It doesn't matter if you don't like your boss, your workplace environment, or your circumstances—do *all* things to the best of your ability because you're actually serving Christ. We are created in the image of the ultimate source of all creativity. God is the wisest, most compassionate, most hilarious, most adventurous, and most colorful being. We are created in His image, and when we're in tune with the source, who is Jesus, we should be the most creative and inspiring people on the planet.

Consider Daniel and his three godly friends: *"In every matter of wisdom and understanding about which the king questioned them, he found them ten times better than all the magicians and enchanters in his whole kingdom"* (Daniel 1:20). They were ten times better than the world's best. It's time for the Daniels of the world to rise up!

Purpose in your heart to do all things with excellence as if it were for Jesus.

Today I…

MAY 25

IT'S NOT IN VAIN

> Let us not grow weary of doing what is good; for if we don't give up, we will in due time reap the harvest. Therefore, as the opportunity arises, let us do what is good to everyone, and especially to the family of those who are trustingly faithful.
>
> GALATIANS 6:9–10 CJB

Doing good can sometimes feel overwhelming, especially when we face challenges and opposition. However, God sees our efforts and promises a reward in due time. Our labor is not in vain. We are called to do good to everyone, seizing every opportunity to make a positive impact. This includes acts of kindness, generosity, and support. It means being a light in dark places and offering hope to those in despair.

Our actions should reflect the love and grace of Jesus, making a tangible difference in the lives of others. In his letter to the Galatians, Paul also emphasized the importance of supporting our fellow believers. The family of faith is a source of strength and encouragement, and by doing good to one another, we build a strong, supportive community that can withstand trials and challenges.

Look for opportunities to do good today to those around you and especially to your fellow believers. Trust that your efforts will bear fruit in due time.

Today I…

MAY 26

PROMOTE PEACE

Make every effort to live in peace with everyone and to be holy; without holiness no one will see the Lord.

HEBREWS 12:14 NIV

Pursuing peace involves actively seeking harmony in our relationships. It means resolving conflicts, forgiving offenses, and extending grace to others. Peace is not merely the absence of conflict but the presence of reconciliation and unity. By promoting peace, we reflect the heart of Jesus, the Prince of Peace, and create an environment where love and understanding can flourish. Striving for holiness is about living a life set apart for God. It involves making choices that honor Him and align with His will. Holiness is not about perfection but about dedication to God's standards and allowing His Spirit to transform us. Without holiness, we cannot fully experience or reflect the presence of the Lord.

The call to pursue peace and holiness is a call to live contrary to the world's ways. It requires intentionality and effort, but the reward is profound. By embodying peace and holiness, we become living testimonies of God's transformative power and draw others to Him.

Reflect on areas in your life where you can pursue peace and live in a way that honors God.

Today I…

MAY 27

CAUSING AN EMOTIONAL RESPONSE

If someone who hates you is hungry, give him food to eat; and if he is thirsty, give him water to drink. For you will heap fiery coals [of shame] on his head, and ADONAI will reward you.

PROVERBS 25:21–22 CJB

Proverbs 25:21–22 challenges us to respond to our enemies with kindness, a concept that is both counterintuitive and profoundly transformative. When we choose to feed the hungry and give drink to the thirsty even if they are our enemies, we reflect God's unconditional love and mercy. This act of kindness can break down barriers of hostility and resentment, creating opportunities for reconciliation and peace. Remember, *"God's kindness is intended to lead you to repentance"* (Romans 2:4 NIV).

The phrase *"heap fiery coals [of shame] on his head"* can be understood as an ancient metaphor. It signifies causing an emotional response in the one who has wronged us. This response can lead to a change of heart, a sense of shame, and potentially repentance. By showing unexpected kindness, we may prompt our adversaries to reflect on their actions and consider a different path.

Reflect on someone who has wronged you or holds animosity toward you. Find a way to show them kindness through a word, gesture, or act of generosity.

Today I…

MAY 28

HEAVENLY WISDOM

The wisdom from above is, first of all, pure, then peaceful, kind, open to reason, full of mercy and good fruits, without partiality and without hypocrisy. And peacemakers who sow seed in peace raise a harvest of righteousness.

JAMES 3:17–18 CJB

Heavenly wisdom is first and foremost pure, indicating that it is free from any moral defilement or selfish motives. Purity in wisdom means seeking God's truth and applying it with a heart that is clean and devoted to Him. This purity sets the foundation for all other qualities, ensuring our actions and decisions are aligned with God's will.

Wisdom from above is peaceful and kind, promoting harmony rather than strife. This wisdom is also open to reason, which means being willing to listen and consider others' perspectives, fostering an environment of mutual respect and learning. This openness reflects humility and a readiness to grow. Mercy, another crucial aspect of divine wisdom, means showing compassion and forgiveness, echoing God's merciful nature. Mercy tempers justice with grace, ensuring that our actions are not only fair but also compassionate.

Reflect on how you can embody the qualities of heavenly wisdom in your daily interactions.

Today I…

MAY 29

BEAR AND BUILD

> We who are strong have a duty to bear the weaknesses of those who are not strong, rather than please ourselves. Each of us should please his neighbor and act for his good, thus building him up.
>
> ROMANS 15:1–2 CJB

The world teaches us to climb the ladder and do whatever it takes to reach our goals. But Jesus calls us to bear each other's burdens and build each other up. This verse is not merely about physical strength, though helping your neighbor move something heavy is appreciated. It's also about bearing emotional, mental, and even financial burdens. By doing so, we fulfill the law of Christ and reflect His love and compassion.

Bearing each other's burdens means stepping into someone's struggles and offering support. Building others up involves encouraging and strengthening others to keep going. Living out this principle requires sensitivity to the needs around us and a willingness to act. We must see beyond our own circumstances and recognize opportunities to serve. Consider the story of the Good Samaritan, who went out of his way to help a stranger in need. His actions exemplified true neighborly love, putting the injured man's needs above his own convenience and safety.

Offer someone in need your support and encouragement.

Today I…

MAY 30

BUILD BRIDGES, NOT BARRIERS

Let's stop passing judgment on each other! Instead, make this one judgment—not to put a stumbling block or a snare in a brother's way.

ROMANS 14:13 CJB

Social Media PSA: People do not go to social media to have their minds changed. Don't post or look at upsetting things. It only drives a deeper wedge into the great divide facing our nation. Paul urged us to stop passing judgment on each other. In the context of social media, this means resisting the urge to criticize or condemn others based on their posts or opinions. Instead of engaging in arguments or making harsh comments, we are called to approach others with grace and understanding.

Our words and actions should build bridges, not barriers. When we post or share content, we should consider whether it will help or hinder someone's faith journey. Controversial or inflammatory posts can create stumbling blocks, deepening divides rather than fostering understanding and unity. Living out this principle requires discernment and self-control. It means thinking carefully before we post or comment, considering whether our words will lift others up or tear them down.

Before posting or commenting on social media, ask yourself if your comments will build up or create a stumbling block for others. Choose to share content that promotes peace, positivity, and unity.

Today I...

MAY 31

INSTEAD

He has sent me…to bestow on them a crown of beauty instead of ashes, the oil of joy instead of mourning, and a garment of praise instead of a spirit of despair. They will be called oaks of righteousness, a planting of the Lord for the display of his splendor.

ISAIAH 61:1, 3 NIV

The word *instead* signifies God's divine exchange. He's so kind! God offers us a crown of beauty instead of ashes. Ashes represent mourning, loss, and destruction. In ancient times, people would sit in ashes to signify their grief. But God promises to replace our ashes with a crown of beauty, signifying restoration, honor, and new beginnings. The oil of joy instead of mourning signifies a profound change in our emotional state. Mourning is a natural response to loss and hardship, but God promises to anoint us with the oil of joy: healing, comfort, and restoration.

God also offers a garment of praise instead of a spirit of despair. Despair makes us feel hopeless and disconnected. But when we praise, we experience breakthroughs. Those who receive this divine exchange are *"oaks of righteousness, a planting of the Lord for the display of his splendor."* Oaks are strong, enduring trees with deep roots. Likewise, the more you depend on Jesus, the deeper your roots will grow.

Listen to the song "Beauty for Ashes" by UpperRoom.

Today I…

JUNE

The Promises of God

JUNE 1

CHRIST, OUR GUARANTEE

However many promises God has made, they all find their "Yes" in connection with him; that is why it is through him that we say the "Amen" when we give glory to God.

2 CORINTHIANS 1:20 CJB

God's promises are a testament to His faithfulness and love, and they're guaranteed in Jesus. This means that whatever God has promised in Scripture—whether it's provision, protection, guidance, or eternal life—is all fulfilled and affirmed in Christ. Jesus is the embodiment of God's faithfulness, the ultimate yes to all His promises.

Understanding that God's promises are yes in Jesus gives us a firm foundation. It means we can live with confidence and assurance, knowing that God will always be true to His word. This should transform how we live, think, and respond to life's challenges. When we say amen, we are expressing our agreement and trust in God's promises. It's a declaration of faith, an acknowledgment that we believe God will do what He has said. This amen is not just a passive agreement but an active participation in God's promises. It releases divine power to accomplish the impossible for us. You do your part in the natural, and God will do the supernatural.

Reflect on a specific promise of God that you need to hold on to today. Declare it!

Today I…

JUNE 2

HE'S IN OUR FUTURE

"Adonai—it is he who will go ahead of you. He will be with you. He will neither fail you nor abandon you, so don't be afraid or downhearted."

Deuteronomy 31:8 CJB

Fear and discouragement can paralyze us, but knowing that God is with us empowers us to move forward with confidence. One of the most comforting aspects of God's promise is that He goes ahead of us. This means that He is already in our future, preparing the way for us. Whatever challenges or unknowns we face, we can trust that God is already there, making a path for us. His foreknowledge and sovereignty ensure that nothing takes Him by surprise.

God's promise to be with us provides immense comfort and strength. In moments of fear, uncertainty, or loneliness, we can rest in the assurance that God is right there with us. His presence is a constant source of peace, guiding us through every situation. Human relationships can fail, and people may abandon us, but God's commitment to us is unchanging. His reliability means we can depend on Him completely. He is our Rock and Fortress, steadfast and true.

Pray for the courage to move forward without fear, knowing that God will never fail or abandon you.

Today I…

JUNE 3

HE'S WATCHING YOU

*"I will instruct and teach you in this way that you are to go;
I will give you counsel; my eyes will be watching you."*

PSALM 32:8 CJB

This verse encapsulates the intimate relationship God desires to have with us, in which He actively participates in our journey and directs our paths. The phrase *"teach you in this way that you are to go"* highlights the personalized nature of God's guidance. He knows our unique circumstances, strengths, and weaknesses, and He tailors His teaching to fit our individual needs. This personalized attention ensures that we are equipped to fulfill the specific purposes He has for us.

The promise that God's eyes will be watching us underscores His constant vigilance and care. We are never out of His sight or beyond His reach. This assurance means that He is always aware of our needs and ready to intervene on our behalf. His watchful presence provides comfort and security. We can know that we are under His protective gaze. As we live in the promise of God's protection, we must actively seek His instruction and counsel. This involves praying daily, reading Scripture, and being sensitive to the Holy Spirit's leading.

Reflect on an area in your life where you need God's guidance. Seek His instruction and counsel through listening prayer and Scripture.

Today I…

JUNE 4

EVERY NEED

Moreover, my God will fill every need of yours according to his glorious wealth, in union with the Messiah Yeshua.

PHILIPPIANS 4:19 CJB

God's promise to fill every need underscores His role as our provider. He is aware of our physical, emotional, and spiritual needs and is committed to meeting them. This provision is not limited or scarce but comes from His glorious wealth, indicating its abundance and richness. God's resources are limitless, and He generously supplies us according to His riches in glory.

The key to accessing God's provision is our union with Messiah Yeshua. Through our relationship with Jesus, we are connected to the source of all blessings. This union ensures that we are not only recipients of God's provision but also partakers in His divine nature. Understanding that God will fill every need allows us to live with confidence and peace. We can approach each day without fear, knowing that our heavenly Father is attentive to our circumstances and is working on our behalf. This confidence frees us to focus on our relationship with Him and our service to others rather than being consumed by our own needs.

Trust God's promise to meet your needs today.

Today I…

JUNE 5

SEEK WISDOM

If any of you lacks wisdom, let him ask God, who gives to all generously and without reproach; and it will be given to him.

JAMES 1:5 CJB

God gives wisdom without reproach, meaning He doesn't criticize us for asking. Sometimes we might hesitate to ask for help because we fear God's judgment. But God invites us to come to Him freely, for He already knows our limitations and needs. His response is always one of grace and generosity. Aren't you grateful you don't have to know all the answers because you know Jesus? I sure am! Still, there are some practical steps for seeking wisdom:

- **Pray regularly:** Make it a habit to ask God for wisdom in all areas of your life. Bring your decisions, challenges, and uncertainties to Him in prayer.
- **Read Scripture:** God's Word is a rich source of wisdom. Spend time in the Bible, allowing God's teachings to guide your thoughts and actions.
- **Listen to the Holy Spirit:** Be sensitive to the leading of the Holy Spirit, who speaks to us and provides guidance in our hearts.
- **Seek godly counsel:** Surround yourself with wise, godly people who can offer advice and perspective based on biblical principles.
- **Trust:** Remember that God promises to lead us even when we don't know where we're headed.

Follow the steps to seek wisdom.

Today I…

JUNE 6

CONFESSION'S PROMISE

If we acknowledge our sins, then, since he is trustworthy and just, he will forgive them and purify us from all wrongdoing.

1 JOHN 1:9 CJB

Today's verse offers a profound promise of forgiveness and purification. This verse underscores the importance of regular confession and the transformative power of God's grace. When we acknowledge our sins and struggles, we open the door to God's forgiveness and cleansing, which renews our hearts and restores our relationship with Him. Confession is the first step in experiencing God's forgiveness. It involves recognizing our wrongdoings and admitting them both to ourselves and to God. This act of humility allows us to confront our faults honestly and seek God's mercy.

Acknowledging our sins is not about dwelling in guilt but about taking responsibility and seeking restoration. God's promise to forgive is rooted in His trustworthy and just nature. He is faithful to His word and righteous in His actions. When we confess and repent, we can be confident that God will forgive us—not because of anything we have done but because of His character. His justice ensures that He deals with sin appropriately and credits Jesus' righteousness to our accounts through the blood of Christ.

Ask the Holy Spirit to quickly convict you of anything you need to repent of.

Today I…

JUNE 7

ROD AND STAFF

> Even if I pass through death-dark ravines, I will fear no disaster; for you are with me; your rod and staff reassure me.
>
> PSALM 23:4 CJB

In Hebrew, the rod (שֵׁבֶט, *shebet*) and staff (מִשְׁעֶנֶת, *mishʿenah*) are tools used by shepherds. The rod is a symbol of protection and authority while the staff represents support and guidance. Together, they provide a comprehensive picture of God's care for us. The rod is used by the shepherd to defend the flock from predators and to exert authority. It is a powerful symbol of God's protection over us. Just as a shepherd uses the rod to protect his sheep from harm, God uses His authority to safeguard us from spiritual and physical dangers. His power and sovereignty ensure that we are secure under His watchful eye.

The staff, often depicted with a crook, is used to guide and support the sheep. It helps the shepherd lead the flock and rescue them from difficult situations. This symbolizes God's guidance and support in our lives. He directs our paths and provides the necessary support to navigate life's challenges. His guidance keeps us on the right track and helps us find our way when we are lost.

Reflect on Psalm 23:4 and ask God to reassure you with His presence today.

Today I…

JUNE 8

NEW EVERY MORNING

The grace of ADONAI is not exhausted, his compassion has not ended. [On the contrary,] they are new every morning! How great your faithfulness!

LAMENTATIONS 3:22–23 CJB

The promise that God's mercies are new every morning provides a profound sense of hope and renewal. No matter what happened yesterday, today is a new day filled with God's grace and compassion. The grace of Adonai is never exhausted. No matter how many times we fail or fall short, God's grace remains abundant and sufficient.

This grace is His unmerited favor toward us and does not depend on our actions but solely on His character. We are always welcome to come back to Him, no matter our circumstances. God's compassion is never-ending. His mercies are new every morning, meaning that each day brings a fresh outpouring of His love and kindness. This continual renewal of mercy speaks to God's deep care for us, His understanding of our struggles, and His desire to uplift and sustain us.

Thank God for this new day and commit to intentionally showing the love of Jesus to one person today.

Today I…

JUNE 9

YOUR HEART'S DESIRE

You will delight yourself in Adonai,
and he will give you your heart's desire.

PSALM 37:4 CJB

This verse isn't a promise that God will fulfill every fleeting wish—it's an invitation to align our hearts with His. When we delight in Him, our desires change, and we begin longing for what He longs for. And in His goodness, He doesn't just transform our hearts. He also provides in ways we never imagined.

Jesus echoed this truth in Matthew 6:33: *"Seek first the kingdom of God and his righteousness, and all these things will be added to you"* (ESV). When we prioritize God's will even at the cost of our own comforts and conveniences, He takes care of everything else. Have you ever sacrificed your own plans to follow a prompting from God? Maybe you stopped to help someone even though you had a tight deadline—only to find that somehow, your work still got done. God multiplies time. He opens doors we were striving to open. He honors those who honor Him. What if your heart's desire is on the other side of surrender?

Take time today to seek God's kingdom first, trusting that He will give you everything you truly need—at just the right time.

Today I…

JUNE 10

THROW THEM

*Throw all your anxieties upon him,
because he cares about you.*

1 Peter 5:7 cjb

The act of throwing or casting our anxieties upon God signifies a deliberate and decisive action. It means taking the worries, fears, and concerns that weigh us down and placing them into the hands of God. This requires trust and a willingness to let go of our need to control every situation. The reason we can confidently cast our anxieties on God is rooted in His profound care for us. God is not distant or indifferent to our struggles. Instead, He is intimately aware of our needs and deeply concerned about our well-being. His care is personal and constant, offering us reassurance and comfort.

When we cast our anxieties on God, we experience freedom from the weight of worry. This freedom allows us to live more fully in the present, trusting that God is in control and working for our good. It shifts our focus from our problems to His promises, from our fears to His faithfulness.

Identify specific anxieties or worries that you are holding on to. Take a moment to pray and consciously cast these anxieties upon God, trusting in His deep care for you.

Today I…

JUNE 11

PACKED WITH PROMISES

"Don't be afraid, for I am with you; don't be distressed, for I am your God. I give you strength, I give you help, I support you with my victorious right hand."

Isaiah 41:10 CJB

Today's verse is packed with promises. *"Don't be afraid, for I am with you."* Knowing that the creator of the universe is with us in every situation dispels fear. We're never alone, no matter what challenges we face. God is always by our side. *"Don't be distressed, for I am your God."* This statement emphasizes God's identity and His relationship with us. He's not a distant deity; He is our God. This personal relationship means that He knows us intimately and cares deeply for us. He has the power and authority to handle anything we encounter.

"I give you strength, I give you help." God promises to provide us with the strength we need to face our challenges. This strength is not merely physical but also emotional and spiritual. *"I support you with my victorious right hand."* The right hand symbolizes power and victory. God's support is not passive; it is powerful and active. We can overcome any obstacle with His help.

Reflect on a challenge you face today and pray for God's strength and support. Then move forward with confidence in His promises.

Today I…

JUNE 12

REVIVAL STARTS WITH US

"If my people, who bear my name, will humble themselves, pray, seek my face and turn from their evil ways, I will hear from heaven, forgive their sin and heal their land."

2 CHRONICLES 7:14 CJB

Revival and healing begin with the people of God returning to Him with sincere hearts. We must recognize the ways we've prioritized comfort and convenience over our commitment to build God's kingdom. Experiencing revival and healing involves humility, prayer, and repentance. Humility is the first step. It means acknowledging our sins, shortcomings, and the ways we've strayed from God's commands. Humility involves a posture of submission, a recognition that we depend on God for everything. This recognition opens up new possibilities for blessings.

Prayer is the pathway to restoration. Prayer is a powerful weapon because it disrupts the war going on in the unseen realm and asks God to intervene. Finally, we must embrace repentance, which requires action. It's not enough to feel remorse for our sins; we must also turn away from them and choose God's path. This means making changes in our behavior, priorities, and attitudes. True repentance is marked by a transformed life.

God promises that if we follow these steps, He will hear from heaven, forgive our sins, and heal our land. Today, let us begin a collective repentance and trust that it will lead to national restoration and blessing.

Today I…

JUNE 13

LORD, HEAR OUR PRAYERS

"We know that God doesn't listen to sinners, but he is ready to hear those who worship him and do his will."

JOHN 9:31 NLT

John 9 recounts the healing of a man born blind. This man that Jesus healed made a statement about God's responsiveness to people's prayers. This verse can be unsettling at first glance, because it seems to suggest that God only listens to those who worship Him and do His will. Does God only listen to those who have been made righteous through Jesus?

When we accept Jesus, we're clothed in His righteousness, meaning we are acceptable before God (Romans 3:22). Because of Jesus' sacrifice and His role as our High Priest, we have direct access to God. This means that when we worship Him and strive to do His will, God hears our prayers. However, God is not deaf to the cries of sinners who have not accepted Christ's gift. Throughout the Bible, we see instances where God hears the cries of those who are seeking Him even if they have not yet given their lives to Him. God answers prayers according to His will. He always reveals Himself and saves those who cry out to Him.

Approach God in prayer with confidence.

Today I…

JUNE 14

NO WEAPON WILL PREVAIL

"No weapon made will prevail against you. In court you will refute every accusation. The servants of Adonai inherit all this; the reward for their righteousness is from me," says Adonai.

Isaiah 54:17 CJB

Isaiah 54:17 promises that no weapon formed against us will prevail. The Enemy cannot prevail or prove more powerful than God and His purposes and promises. Isaiah 54:17 also promises victory over false accusations. *"In court you will refute every accusation,"* God said, reminding us that He equips us with the truth and wisdom we need to destroy false accusations. This is a promise we can stand on.

Understanding this allows us to live in confidence. We can move forward without fear, trusting that God's promises are true and that He is always in control. Even when we face opposition, we can rest in the knowledge that God's purpose will prevail and that no weapon or lies formed against us will succeed. Consider David. Though King Saul relentlessly pursued him, falsely accused him, and sought to destroy him, God's hand remained on David's life. Despite years of exile and injustice, David trusted God's plan, refusing to retaliate against Saul. In the end, God's promise prevailed: Saul's schemes failed, and David became king.

When faced with challenges, move forward with confidence and in love, knowing God has you covered.

Today I…

JUNE 15

UNITED

"If you remain united with me, and my words with you, then ask whatever you want, and it will happen for you."

JOHN 15:7 CJB

Jesus promised that we can ask whatever we want and it will happen. This promise is rooted in our union with Jesus and His words dwelling in us. When we are closely connected to Jesus, our desires begin to reflect His. Our prayers align with His will, and therefore, He will answer them. This promise isn't a blank check for selfish requests but an assurance that when we pray according to God's will, He responds powerfully.

Remaining united with Jesus implies an intentional relationship in which we continually seek His guidance, follow His example, and live in obedience to His commands. When we meditate on Christ's teachings, they shape our character, align our desires with His will, and increase our faith. Consider the example of Jesus Himself, who lived in perfect union with the Father. His prayers were always in alignment with God's will, and as a result, they were powerful and effective. Jesus taught us that this same union and effectiveness in prayer is available to us when we abide in Him.

Ask Jesus to help you see what He sees and hear what He hears about others and the circumstances around you. Respond to this new perspective accordingly.

Today I…

JUNE 16

SUN AND SHIELD

Adonai, God, is a sun and a shield; Adonai bestows favor and honor; and he will not withhold anything good from those whose lives are pure.

Psalm 84:12(11) cjb

Scripture describes God as both a sun and a shield. As a sun, He is the source of light, life, and sustenance. Just as the sun gives energy to sustain life on earth, so God provides everything we need to thrive. His light illuminates our path, guiding us through life's challenges. As a shield, God is our protector, standing between us and harm. A shield is a defensive weapon, designed to block attacks and provide safety. God's favor is His grace and empowerment to accomplish His will. His honor reflects the dignity and value He places on us as His children.

God promises that He will not withhold anything good from those whose lives are pure. Purity is living in alignment with God's will with a heart devoted to Him. When we walk in purity, God's blessings flow freely into our lives. This doesn't mean we will get what we want but rather that God, in His wisdom, will provide what is truly good for us and what will help us fulfill His plans.

Thank God aloud for this promise.

Today I…

JUNE 17

LIVING WATER

> Yeshua answered, "I am the bread which is life! Whoever comes to me will never go hungry, and whoever trusts in me will never be thirsty."
>
> JOHN 6:35 CJB

Pastor D. T. Niles defined evangelism as "one beggar telling another beggar where to get food."[24] Our first encounter with Jesus transforms our lives, filling our voids and providing us with hope and purpose. This realization should humble us, removing any sense of superiority. We're merely recipients of God's grace, sharing the good news with others who have the same desperate need for salvation. Evangelism isn't about boasting of our spiritual status but about compassionately pointing others to Jesus.

Evangelism often involves listening to people's struggles, offering hope, and demonstrating Christ's love through our actions. After encountering Jesus at the well, the Samaritan woman eagerly went back to her village to tell others about Him (John 4:1–42). She was so undone by His kindness that she left her water jar and her shame at the well and ran to tell her village about Jesus and the transformative experience she had in His love.

Watch *The Chosen* season 1, episode 8.

Today I…

---

24 D. T. Niles, *That They May Have Life* (Harper & Brothers, 1951), 96.

JUNE 18

PERFECT PEACE

"You keep him in perfect peace whose mind is stayed on you, because he trusts in you."

ISAIAH 26:3 ESV

The phrase *"perfect peace"* in Hebrew is *shalom shalom*, which emphasizes a peace that's complete, whole, and unshakable. It's more than the absence of conflict; it's a deep, abiding sense of well-being and tranquility that comes from being in harmony with God. Peace is all about where we put our focus. Fear is misfocused faith. When we're afraid, it's because we've shifted our focus away from God and onto our circumstances, believing more in the power of our problems than in the power of our God.

    To experience perfect peace, we must trust that God is who He says He is. Getting to know His promises and character allows us to relinquish our need for control and to trust in His plans. We're called to act out of the atmosphere of heaven, not the atmosphere of the world or our emotions. When chaos comes, keeping our hearts and minds focused on God enables us to shift the atmosphere of the rooms we're in and point people to Jesus. Think about when Jesus calmed the storm. While His disciples panicked, Jesus remained completely at peace because His focus and trust was in His Father, not the storm.

Move in the atmosphere of heaven today.

Today I…

JUNE 19

COMPLETE DEPENDENCE

*"Blessed are the poor in spirit,
for theirs is the kingdom of heaven."*

MATTHEW 5:3 NIV

Being poor in spirit means recognizing our complete dependence on God. We acknowledge our spiritual poverty—that we have nothing of true worth to offer on our own and that we desperately need God's grace. This humility is the foundation of a right relationship with God, where we understand that every good thing comes from Him, not from our own efforts.

Cultivating a spirit of humility transforms how we interact with God and others. It keeps us grounded in the truth that we are deeply loved and valued by God not because of what we do but because of who He is. This humility also opens us to receive all that God has for us—His guidance, His blessings, and His peace. When we allow the Holy Spirit to lead us daily, our perspective shifts. We begin to see the people around us through Jesus' eyes and respond with love and understanding rather than judgment. This Spirit-led living is a powerful witness of God's kingdom at work within us.

Ask the Holy Spirit to guide you. Trust that you will see God's kingdom at work as you walk in humility and dependence on Him.

Today I…

JUNE 20

MOTIVATED DELAYS

The Lord is not slow in keeping his promise, as some people think of slowness; on the contrary, he is patient with you; for it is not his purpose that anyone should be destroyed, but that everyone should turn from his sins.

2 Peter 3:9 CJB

It's easy to become impatient or doubtful when we feel like God is taking too long to fulfill His promises. But He is not slow in the way we understand slowness. Instead, God is patient, giving us time to turn from our sins and draw closer to Him. His delays are not denials but opportunities for more people to experience His grace and salvation. Second Peter 3:9 is a powerful reminder of God's patience and His deep desire for all people to repent. His delays are motivated by His love and mercy.

God's patience has a purpose: He doesn't want anyone to be destroyed but desires that everyone would turn from their sins and embrace His love. This reveals God's heart for humanity—His desire for redemption rather than judgment. Every moment of God's patience is an invitation to repent, realign our lives with His will, and experience His mercy.

Ask God to give you His heart and patience for others. Then carry His love to the hurting.

Today I…

JUNE 21

TOTAL RESTORATION

"I will restore to you the years that the locusts ate, the grasshoppers, shearer-worms and cutter-worms, my great army that I sent against you."

JOEL 2:25 CJB

The thought of locusts devouring the land conjures images of total destruction. A locust plague can wipe out an entire harvest, leaving nothing. This devastation symbolizes the times in our lives when it feels like everything we've worked for or hoped for has been stripped away. But God's promise is to restore even those years—He can bring new life, new opportunities, and new hope out of what seems like total loss.

What's striking about today's verse is that God acknowledges that He allowed the locusts—He sent them as part of His divine plan. Yet in His mercy, He promises to restore. This highlights God's sovereignty: He has the power not only to allow difficult seasons for a purpose but also to redeem and restore those seasons for our good and His glory. No matter what we have lost, God is fully capable of restoring it in ways that are beyond our imagination. Our past does not define our future when we are in God's hands.

Reflect on areas of loss in your life and trust God to restore them. Pray for His renewal and believe in His promise of restoration.

Today I…

JUNE 22

UNWAVERING STANDARDS

If you fully obey the LORD your God and carefully follow all his commands I give you today, the LORD your God will set you high above all the nations on earth. All these blessings will come on you and accompany you if you obey the LORD your God.

DEUTERONOMY 28:1–2 NIV

Deuteronomy 28 continues to list incredible promises, but all of them are contingent upon our obedience to the Father and making Him the supreme ruler of our lives. If you need a healthy dose of the fear of the Lord, I encourage you to read all of Deuteronomy 28. We do not serve a weak God but one who is able to bless us or bring about our demise.

    The Bible explicitly states that God never changes (Malachi 3:6; Hebrews 13:8). So God's standards and demands have not changed. What changed was Jesus' own sacrifice, which covered us in His perfect blood as the required payment for our sins (Leviticus 17:11). It is because of the Father's indescribable generosity and Jesus' obedience even unto death in our place that we are considered righteous. We are in grave danger if we trample or mock the blood of Jesus by continuing in sin and expecting God's grace (Hebrews 10:28–30).

Read Deuteronomy 28.

Today I…

JUNE 23

COMING AND GOING

You will be blessed when you come in and blessed when you go out.

DEUTERONOMY 28:6 NIV

When we yield our lives to the Lord and obey Him, He promises that He will bless us in our coming and going. This assurance is powerful, especially when we face challenging situations, like the complexities of workplace politics. Every profession has its own set of challenges, and as Christians, it sometimes feels like we're caught between a rock and a hard place, with no room to move or even breathe.

In these moments, it's crucial to remember and declare God's promises over our lives. Deuteronomy 28:6 promises God's encompassing blessing in every aspect of our lives, whether we're entering into new opportunities or exiting difficult situations. As we carry God's favor with us, we become a source of blessing to others in ways we may not even realize. Our presence can bring peace, encouragement, and light to those who interact with us. Whether we are stepping into new endeavors or simply enduring the daily grind, His presence goes with us, and His favor surrounds us—allowing us to be a blessing to others as well.

In your daily routine, especially in moments of frustration or uncertainty, take a moment to pause and speak God's promises over your life.

Today I…

JUNE 24

UNFAILING LOVE

Love never fails.

1 Corinthians 13:8 niv

"Love never fails" because God is love (1 John 4:8). Yet we often misunderstand this promise. We assume that if love never fails, then our relationships will be free of challenges. But the promise here is not that love will protect us from pain or difficulty. Rather, love will sustain us through them. Even when relationships are tested, love provides the strength to persevere. Consider how Jesus embodied this unfailing love. He loved His disciples, knowing they would abandon Him. He loved the crowds even as they shouted for His crucifixion. On the cross, He demonstrated the ultimate act of love by forgiving those who nailed Him there and offering redemption to all who believe.

Love does not depend on the worthiness of its object but on the character of the one who loves. Jesus' love never fails because it flows from His perfect nature. We are called to reflect this unfailing love. There will be moments when our patience is tested, when kindness feels like a burden, and when forgiveness seems impossible. But in those moments, our love must be rooted in God's love—a love that empowers us to rise above our limitations.

Choose love in the moments that test your limits today.

Today I…

JUNE 25

RELIABLE

*"I will not violate my covenant
or alter what my lips have uttered."*

PSALM 89:34 NIV

Trust is the foundation of any meaningful relationship. To violate a covenant is to break a sacred bond, to undermine the very trust that binds the agreement. But God declares that He will never break His word or alter what He has spoken because doing so would deny His own nature. *"God is not a man, that he should lie, nor a human being, that he should change his mind"* (Numbers 23:19 NET).

This truth is both comforting and challenging. It's comforting because it means we can trust God. Every promise He has made—whether in the Old Testament covenants or in the New Covenant through Jesus Christ—is reliable. It also challenges us to reflect on our own faithfulness. How often do we make commitments to God in moments of passion or desperation, only to forget them when the situation changes? How frequently do we alter our promises when they become inconvenient? God's unwavering commitment to His word calls us to a higher standard of integrity and faithfulness in our own lives. If we are to reflect His character, we must strive to be people of our word—reliable, trustworthy, and true.

Declare a promise of God that you need right now.

Today I…

JUNE 26

PERSEVERE

Blessed is the one who perseveres under trial because, having stood the test, that person will receive the crown of life that the Lord has promised to those who love him.

JAMES 1:12 NIV

The book of James begins with a paradox: *"Blessed is the one who perseveres under trial."* The word *"blessed"* here carries the connotation of deep, abiding happiness or of being in a state of divine favor. It may be difficult to feel abiding happiness or favor during trials. But trials are not meaningless; they serve a divine purpose. They are the crucibles in which our faith is refined, our character is shaped, and our love for God is tested and deepened. Trials refine our faith, just as fire refines gold. The heat may be intense, but it is through this process that impurities are burned away, leaving behind a purer, stronger faith.

The crown James spoke of is not a physical one but the spiritual reward of eternal life and glory. The crown signifies victory over sin, death, and every force that seeks to separate us from God. Therefore, we must view our trials with an eternal perspective. Our struggles, when we face them with faith, are never in vain and are part of a larger narrative.

Consider the trials you're currently facing. Instead of focusing on the difficulty, ask God for the strength to endure and trust that He is refining your faith.

Today I…

JUNE 27

OUR ADVOCATE

"I will ask the Father, and he will give you another advocate to help you and be with you forever."

JOHN 14:16 NIV

As Jesus prepared His disciples for His departure, He promised them the Advocate—the Holy Spirit—whom the Father would send to be with us eternally. The term *advocate*, from the Greek *parakletos*, means "counselor," "helper," or "one who comes alongside." The Holy Spirit embodies all these roles, providing wisdom for decisions, strength in weakness, and unwavering companionship along our journey of faith, ensuring we are never alone.

Jesus knew that His followers would need this divine help. Following Christ is not easy. It requires us to live in a world that often opposes God's kingdom, to endure trials, and to resist temptations. But the Holy Spirit empowers us to live out our faith boldly. He equips us with spiritual gifts, enables us to understand and apply God's Word, and empowers us to witness to others. He transforms our hearts, molding us into the image of Christ. The presence of the Holy Spirit in our lives is a testament to God's unending love and His commitment to our spiritual growth.

Acknowledge the Holy Spirit and invite Him to guide your decisions, strengthen you in your challenges, and deepen your understanding of God.

Today I…

JUNE 28

TEMPTATION

No temptation has seized you beyond what people normally experience, and God can be trusted not to allow you to be tempted beyond what you can bear. On the contrary, along with the temptation he will also provide the way out, so that you will be able to endure.

1 CORINTHIANS 10:13 CJB

Temptation is a reality we all face, but it's important to remember that temptation itself is not sin—it's an invitation to sin. In 1 Corinthians 10:13, Paul reminded us that no temptation is unique or beyond what others have experienced, and God is faithful in every situation. When we keep our eyes on Jesus, we gain the clarity to recognize the snares set before us.

Temptation often thrives in the shadows. But when we're actively seeking God—through prayer, His Word, and worship—our awareness of His presence is heightened, and the allure of sin loses its grip. God promises a way out. This *"way out"* might be a verse that comes to mind, sudden clarity about the consequences of a decision, or even physical removal from a bad situation. The key is to be attentive to these divine escapes and to act on them.

When you face temptation, pause and focus your eyes on Jesus. Pray for the strength to resist and the discernment to see the way out.

Today I…

JUNE 29

WHOSE WATERS NEVER FAIL

"The LORD will guide you always; he will satisfy your needs in a sun-scorched land and will strengthen your frame. You will be like a well-watered garden, like a spring whose waters never fail."

Isaiah 58:11 NIV

Today's verse begins with a simple but powerful truth: *"The LORD will guide you always."* The Holy Spirit is not a distant observer; He's an involved, caring guide who leads us with wisdom and love. What does it mean to be guided by God? It means allowing His will to shape our decisions and trusting in His direction even when the path seems unclear. It means not leaning on our own understanding but acknowledging Him in all our ways (Proverbs 3:5–6).

God's guidance is not just about making the right choices; it's also about walking in step with His Spirit, staying attuned to His voice, and following where He leads even when it's into the unknown. In seasons of desolation, God promises to satisfy your needs. In weakness, God will *"strengthen your frame."* This promise applies to physical, mental, and emotional strength. God desires for us to be like *"a well-watered garden"* flourishing in His presence and like *"a spring that never fails,"* drawing from His endless supply of grace, love, and provision.

Speak these promises over yourself.

Today I…

JUNE 30

OPEN DOORS

"Ask and it will be given to you; seek and you will find; knock and the door will be opened to you."

MATTHEW 7:7 NIV

"Ask, and it will be given to you." Asking implies humility. It forces us to acknowledge our dependence on God for needs we can't fulfill ourselves. The Creator delights in giving good gifts to His children (Matthew 7:11). *"Seek, and you will find."* Seeking involves pursuit. It's actively searching for God's presence, wisdom, and guidance. Our efforts to draw closer to God and understand His will are not in vain. God isn't hiding from us; He desires to be found, and He rewards those who earnestly seek Him (Hebrews 11:6).

"Knock, and the door will be opened to you." Knocking is an act of faith and determination. It's what we do when we stand before a closed door, believing that there is something worth encountering on the other side. Knocking requires effort and the willingness to wait for the door to open. But the promise is clear: When we knock, the door will be opened. No door remains permanently closed to those who knock with faith.

Don't lose hope. Keep asking, seeking, and knocking.

Today I…

JULY

Freedom and Authority in the Kingdom of Heaven

JULY 1

POWERED BY THE HOLY SPIRIT

The Spirit of *Adonai* E<small>LOHIM</small> is upon me, because A<small>DONAI</small> has anointed me to announce good news to the poor. He has sent me to heal the brokenhearted; to proclaim freedom to the captives, to let out into light those bound in the dark.

I<small>SAIAH</small> 61:1 <small>CJB</small>

"The Spirit of Adonai E<small>LOHIM</small> *is upon me"* highlights that this mission is powered by the Holy Spirit. As Christians, we're vessels of God's Spirit, called to proclaim good news, heal the brokenhearted, and bring liberty and light to everyone. *"To proclaim freedom to the captives"* refers to those who are imprisoned, not just physically but also spiritually and emotionally. Sin, shame, guilt, addiction, fear—these are the chains that bind people. Jesus came to break these chains, and He empowers us to do the same by His Spirit.

Darkness in the Bible often symbolizes ignorance, sin, and separation from God. To be bound in darkness is to be trapped in a state of hopelessness, cut off from the light of God's truth and love. But the anointing of the Holy Spirit brings light—truth, hope, and revelation—to those lost in darkness. This light exposes the lies that keep people bound and illuminates the path to freedom.

Think about how you can be an instrument of God's freedom to others.

Today I…

JULY 2

BE INTENTIONAL

"Learn to do good! Seek justice, relieve the oppressed, defend orphans, plead for the widow."

ISAIAH 1:17 CJB

In context, today's verse from Isaiah rebukes those practicing religious rituals without true righteousness or compassion. God is not interested in empty worship; He desires lives that reflect His justice, mercy, and love, especially to the marginalized. The command *"Learn to do good!"* suggests that doing good is something we must be intentional about. It's not our natural inclination to seek the welfare of others, especially when it requires sacrifice. But God calls us to cultivate goodness as a defining characteristic of who we are.

"Seek justice," Isaiah's prophecy directed. Justice in the biblical sense goes beyond legal fairness. It involves restoring right relationships, ensuring equity, and upholding the dignity of every person as an image-bearer of God. The oppressed, the orphaned, the widow, and in modern day, the single parent all represent individuals who have no one to stand up for them, to protect or provide for them. God's heart is especially tender toward these groups, and He calls His people to reflect that same compassion. To *"plead"* is to intercede, to stand in the gap for someone else, to make their cause our own.

Ask God to show you specific ways you can take action for the vulnerable and commit to being a vessel of His compassion.

Today I…

JULY 3

A 2D WORLD

Now we see obscurely in a mirror, but then it will be face to face. Now I know partly; then I will know fully, just as God has fully known me.

1 CORINTHIANS 13:12 CJB

In *Imagine Heaven*, John Burke offered an analogy to grasp the concept in today's verse. He compared our current life to living in a colorless, two-dimensional painting. You can only perceive what's within this two-dimensional world of lines and shapes. But after death, you're lifted out of the painting into a vibrant, three-dimensional reality, full of color and depth beyond anything you could've imagined.[25]

Our current understanding is limited by the confines of our earthly existence. We see God's work, but it's like seeing through a foggy mirror. We grasp spiritual truths, but they are only a shadow of the fullness we will one day experience. There's freedom in partial knowledge—we're relieved from the pressure of knowing every answer or detail. We can walk *"by faith, not by sight"* (2 Corinthians 5:7 NIV), knowing that one day God will fulfill our longing for fullness of vision.

How can you embrace the freedom of trusting God with the unknown?

Today I…

---

[25] John Burke, *Imagine Heaven: Near-Death Experiences, God's Promises, and the Exhilarating Future That Awaits You* (Baker Books, 2015), 122–23.

JULY 4

TRUE FREEDOM

"If the Son sets you free, you will be free indeed."
JOHN 8:36 NIV

True freedom begins with recognizing our need for it. In John 8, Jesus spoke to people who believed they were already free because of their heritage and religious practices. But He challenged them, pointing out that anyone who sins is a slave to sin. This sobering truth applies to us all: Without Christ, we are bound by something, whether it's addiction, pride, fear, or the expectations of others. Our freedom in Christ doesn't erase the natural consequences that come with our choices, but it does empower us to live differently moving forward. This is why it's crucial to take every thought captive and align our actions with God's will.

Freedom in Christ isn't a license to live as we please; it's an invitation to live in a way that honors God and reflects our new identity in Him. Staying free requires vigilance and a commitment to walking in the Spirit. Remember, true freedom in Christ is not just about being set free—it's about staying free and living in the fullness of His love each day.

Let go of what binds you and walk confidently in His grace, knowing He empowers you to live fully and freely in His love.

Today I…

JULY 5

DON'T BE BURDENED AGAIN

It is for freedom that Christ has set us free. Stand firm, then, and do not let yourselves be burdened again by a yoke of slavery.

GALATIANS 5:1 NIV

Freedom is the very purpose of Christ's sacrifice. Yet how often do we return to the familiar chains that once bound us? Paul urged us to *"stand firm"* and resist the temptation to slip back into old patterns, habits, and mindsets that once enslaved us. The *"yoke of slavery"* he spoke of can take many forms—legalism, addiction, fear, shame, or the relentless pursuit of approval from others. Each of these can quietly creep back into our lives, attempting to reclaim the power over us that Christ has already broken.

Imagine being set free from a prison cell only to voluntarily walk back inside and close the door. It seems absurd, yet spiritually, we do this when we allow ourselves to be burdened again by what Christ has already overcome. There is a comfort in familiarity even when that familiarity means bondage. But Christ calls us to stand firm and to refuse to be shackled by anything that diminishes the full life He offers.

Identify any yokes you've been tempted to take back. Bring them to God and stand firm, refusing to be burdened again by what Christ has already overcome.

Today I…

JULY 6

MULTIFACETED FREEDOM

Where the Spirit of the Lord is, there is freedom.
2 Corinthians 3:17 NIV

Freedom in Christ is not just a theological concept; it is a lived reality that comes from the presence of the Holy Spirit in our lives. The freedom the Spirit brings is multifaceted. It's freedom from sin's power, from fear, from the need to perform, and from the pressures of the world. The Holy Spirit liberates us to be who God created us to be, without the constraints of worldly expectations or the bondage of our past.

The Spirit continually works within us to break chains, renew our minds, and lead us into deeper intimacy with God. As we yield to the Spirit's leading, we experience greater levels of freedom in our thoughts, actions, and relationships. As you reflect on today's verse, consider how the Holy Spirit is bringing freedom into your life. Where do you feel liberated, and where might you still need to invite the Spirit's transforming power? The more we allow the Spirit to fill and guide us, the more we will experience the fullness of the freedom Christ has provided.

Invite the Holy Spirit to reveal areas where you need His freedom.

Today I…

JULY 7

LAW OF THE SPIRIT

There is therefore now no condemnation for those who are in Christ Jesus. For the law of the Spirit of life has set you free in Christ Jesus from the law of sin and death.

ROMANS 8:1–2 ESV

Before Christ, we were bound by a law that, while good and just, revealed our sin and left us powerless to conquer it. The law of sin and death held us captive, demanding death as the payment for our sins, constantly reminding us of our failures and separating us from God. Condemnation wasn't a feeling; it was a reality. The law declared us guilty and deserving of judgment.

But then, Christ came. Through Jesus' life, death, and resurrection, He did what we could not, fulfilling the law's demands and breaking the power of sin and death. Now in Christ, our sin no longer defines us or determines our fate; our guilt has been replaced by righteousness and our death penalty by life. The *"law of the Spirit who gives life"* (v. 2 NIV) is now our reality—centered on the Holy Spirit's presence, empowering us to live in the freedom Christ won for us. Let this freedom shape your identity, decisions, and walk with God.

Leave the past and embrace the liberating truth that you are fully loved, accepted, and free in Christ.

Today I…

JULY 8

NO CONDEMNATION

There is therefore now no condemnation for those who are in Christ Jesus. For the law of the Spirit of life has set you free in Christ Jesus from the law of sin and death.

ROMANS 8:1–2 ESV

Continuing with the verses from Romans we discussed yesterday, we see that the *"law of the Spirit"* isn't about rules and regulations. It's about the indwelling presence of the Holy Spirit, who empowers us to live in the freedom Christ provided. The Holy Spirit reminds us we aren't bound by our past. We're new creations, no longer subject to the old order of sin and death. This freedom means that the accusations of the Enemy—the voices that tell you you're not good enough, that you've failed too many times, that you're beyond redemption—are lies.

In Christ, you're free from condemnation. You're loved, accepted, and secure in your relationship with God. Paul's declaration of *"no condemnation"* is followed by a call to live according to the Spirit, not the flesh. Freedom in Christ isn't a license to sin; it's the power to overcome sin. We're called to live in this newness of life and walk in step with the Holy Spirit.

Embrace the freedom Christ has given you and extend His grace to others.

Today I…

JULY 9

FREEDOM TO SERVE

You, my brothers and sisters, were called to be free. But do not use your freedom to indulge the flesh; rather, serve one another humbly in love.

GALATIANS 5:13 NIV

The world equates freedom with doing whatever we want, but Christian freedom is different. It liberates us from self-centeredness and invites us into love, humility, and service. The paradox of Christian freedom is that by laying down our rights and serving others, we find fullness in Christ. When Paul said, *"Do not use your freedom to indulge the flesh,"* he was warning against prioritizing self. The *"flesh"* is our fallen nature, the part of us that's inclined to sin and self-centeredness. As believers, we're called to use our freedom to serve others in love.

Serving others in love is the very heart of Christ's ministry and the gospel. Jesus, who had all the freedom and authority in the universe, chose to humble Himself and serve humanity even to the point of death on a cross (Philippians 2:5–8). As His followers, we are called to imitate His example: to consider others before ourselves, to seek the good of those around us, and to express God's love in tangible ways.

Today, use your freedom in Christ to serve others. Seek opportunities to show love and kindness.

Today I…

JULY 10

FREEDOM-GIVING LAWS

Whoever looks intently into the perfect law that gives freedom, and continues in it—not forgetting what they have heard, but doing it—they will be blessed in what they do.

JAMES 1:25 NIV

In James 1:25, we encounter a powerful and perhaps unexpected connection between law and freedom. The phrase *"perfect law that gives freedom"* may seem contradictory at first. How can law, often associated with restrictions and limitations, offer freedom? But James was speaking of a different kind of law, one that is not about legalism or rigid rules but about the law of Christ, which is rooted in love and grace.

This *"perfect law"* is the law of liberty, found in the teachings of Jesus. It's a law that doesn't constrain but rather liberates us to live the way God intended. When we continue to follow this law, we are not bound by fear, guilt, or the weight of legalistic obligations. Instead, we are free to love, serve, and walk in the fullness of life that Christ offers. James emphasized that it's not enough to merely hear this law; we must *"look intently"* into it, allowing it to shape our thoughts, attitudes, and actions.

Actively seek ways to apply Jesus' teachings by serving someone in need or encouraging someone who needs it.

Today I…

JULY 11

FREEDOM'S PARADOX

Live as free people, but do not use your freedom as a cover-up for evil; live as God's slaves.

1 PETER 2:16 NIV

This verse highlights the tension between freedom and accountability. Peter's call to live as *"God's slaves"* represents a paradoxical freedom. How can we be both free and slaves? The answer lies in understanding the concept of being a bondservant of Christ. In biblical times, a bondservant was someone who willingly chose to serve their master for life, acting out of love and loyalty. Similarly, as followers of Christ, we are called to willingly submit to God's authority, not out of obligation but out of love for the one who has set us free. This kind of freedom is deeply fulfilling because it aligns us with the very purpose for which we were created.

When we misuse our freedom, using it as a *"cover-up for evil,"* we distort the gift that Christ has given us. As bondservants of Christ, our freedom is not marked by a constant excusing of behavior that contradicts His will. Instead, our freedom manifests in a commitment to His lordship and a desire to glorify Him in all we do.

Embrace your role as a bondservant of Christ by using your freedom to serve God and others in a tangible way.

Today I…

JULY 12

FREEDOM IN KNOWING HIM

"If you hold to my teaching, you are really my disciples. Then you will know the truth, and the truth will set you free."

JOHN 8:31–32 NIV

It's important to consider the context in which Jesus spoke these words. He was speaking to Jewish believers, but during the conversation, a debate arose. The religious leaders were confident in their freedom because of their heritage as descendants of Abraham. They believed that their lineage guaranteed their spiritual freedom. However, Jesus clarified that true freedom doesn't come from heritage or religious practices but from knowing and following Him. While the Jews claimed Abraham as their father, their actions and hearts revealed a different allegiance. They weren't following Abraham's example of faith but were instead under the influence of the Father of Lies—the devil (John 8:44).

This was a startling revelation, highlighting that even church leaders can be deceived if they don't fully embrace Christ. Christ is the truth (14:6). His freedom provides discernment even when falsehoods are cloaked in religious or cultural traditions. It sharpens our ability to recognize when teachings, traditions, or even our own thoughts aren't aligned with God's Word.

Be mindful of theology you've been taught. Make sure it actually aligns with the full Word of God, not just verses out of context.

Today I...

JULY 13

ETERNAL LIFE STARTS NOW

Now that you have been set free from sin and have become slaves of God, the benefit you reap leads to holiness, and the result is eternal life.

ROMANS 6:22 NIV

Before Christ transformed us through salvation, we were enslaved to our own desires, unable to break free from the patterns and behaviors that separated us from God. Sin, in its deceptive allure, promised fulfillment but always led to emptiness and death. But through Christ, we have been set free from sin's power. This freedom, however, should not prompt a return to living for ourselves; rather, it is a call to a new kind of servanthood—a willing submission to God as our Master.

Paul emphasized that the *"benefit"* of this new life is holiness. Holiness is not just a moral standard; it is the very character of God being formed in us. As we walk in obedience to God, allowing His Spirit to lead us, we are transformed into the image of Christ. This transformation is a process—often slow and challenging—but it is the pathway to true fulfillment. Eternal life starts now as we encounter the Holy Spirit and experience the abundant life Jesus promised.

Identify one area where you can make a change that aligns your life more closely with God's will.

Today I…

JULY 14

MESSIAH LIVES IN ME

When the Messiah was executed on the stake as a criminal, I was too; so that my proud ego no longer lives. But the Messiah lives in me, and the life I now live in my body I live by the same trusting faithfulness that the Son of God had, who loved me and gave himself up for me.

GALATIANS 2:20 CJB

This statement in today's verse captures the heart of what it means to follow Jesus—our old self, driven by pride and ego, has been put to death, and in its place, the Messiah Himself now dwells within us. The imagery of being executed alongside the Messiah is not just symbolic; it speaks to the reality that our old nature, with its selfish desires and sinful tendencies, has been crucified with Him. The life we now live *"in the body"* is radically different from our former life.

Each day, we are invited to wake up to the truth that the Messiah lives in us, guiding our actions, shaping our thoughts, and empowering us to live according to God's will. We are vessels through whom God's love and power flow.

The Messiah lives in you. Seek to embody His character in your daily encounters, knowing that you are called to be a living expression of His grace.

Today I…

JULY 15

KINGDOM PRINCIPLES

It is he who has rescued us from the domain of darkness and transferred us into the Kingdom of his dear Son. It is through his Son that we have redemption—that is, our sins have been forgiven.

COLOSSIANS 1:13–14 CJB

The kingdom of heaven isn't just a place but also a present reality we're transferred into when we accept Jesus. Heaven operates under principles vastly different from the world's. In the world, we gain power through dominance, wealth through accumulation, and freedom through the exercise of personal rights. But in God's kingdom, power is found in servitude, wealth in generosity, and freedom in surrendering our will to the Father.

We were once held captive by the kingdom of darkness. But through Jesus, we're forgiven, released from Satan's grip, and transferred into God's kingdom, where grace reigns, where our value is found in Christ, and where our purpose aligns with God's eternal plan. The kingdom of heaven calls us to live by its principles here and now. We are to reflect the light of Christ in a world still shrouded in darkness, to live with hope in a world plagued by despair, and to operate in love where hatred abounds.

How can you reflect the principles of the kingdom of heaven in your daily life?

Today I…

FREEDOM TO BREATHE

*When hard pressed, I cried to the LORD;
he brought me into a spacious place.*

PSALM 118:5 NIV

Freedom in the kingdom of heaven often comes in ways we don't expect. Psalm 118:5 speaks to a moment of intense pressure, when the psalmist felt confined and restricted by circumstances. Yet he called out to God, who responded by bringing him into a spacious place of freedom and relief.

Many times, we feel *"hard pressed"* by various challenges—whether they're personal struggles, societal pressures, or spiritual battles. These moments can make us feel trapped, with no clear way out. But in the kingdom of heaven, confinement is never the final word. When we call on God, He answers, often in ways that enlarge our territory both physically and spiritually. God's response to our cries for help is not always to remove the challenge but to give us the strength, wisdom, and grace to overcome it.

Today, if you find yourself feeling restricted or overwhelmed, take a moment to call out to God. Trust that He will answer, not necessarily by removing the obstacles but perhaps by providing you with more room to maneuver—more spiritual, emotional, and even physical freedom. Look for ways in which God might be expanding your boundaries and walk boldly in the freedom He has provided.

Today I…

JULY 17

FREEDOM IS OUR IDENTITY

The Spirit you received does not make you slaves, so that you live in fear again; rather, the Spirit you received brought about your adoption to sonship. And by him we cry, "Abba, Father."

ROMANS 8:15 NIV

In the kingdom of heaven, freedom isn't just a concept—it's our identity. We are no longer slaves to fear; we are children of God. This shift from slavery to adoption is at the core of the freedom we have in Christ.

Our identity as God's heirs and children empowers us to live boldly, to take risks in faith, and to love others without fear of rejection because we know that our identity is anchored in God's unchanging love. As children of God, we're invited to participate in the family business, spreading the love, grace, and truth of the kingdom to a world still enslaved by fear and anxiety.

Reflect deeply on your identity as a child of God. Are there areas in your life where fear or anxiety still grips you? Bring these before your Abba Father and ask Him to replace that fear with His perfect love. Then walk in the confidence that you are fully loved and free. Look for opportunities to extend that freedom to others, inviting them into the same liberating relationship you enjoy with God.

Today I…

JULY 18

OVERCOMER

Since the children have flesh and blood, he too shared in their humanity so that by his death he might break the power of him who holds the power of death—that is, the devil—and free those who all their lives were held in slavery by their fear of death.

HEBREWS 2:14–15 NIV

The fear of death is one of the most pervasive and paralyzing fears in human existence. It drives people to cling to life at all costs and to live in constant anxiety. Before Christ, this fear dictated our decisions and overshadowed our lives with a sense of impending doom. But Jesus' death and resurrection have liberated us to live with boldness and peace. By sharing in our humanity, Jesus not only empathized with our struggles but overcame them. He faced death head-on and emerged victorious, breaking its power once and for all.

In the kingdom of heaven, we're overcomers. The freedom we have in Christ means that death is no longer the end but a transition into eternal life with God. This truth empowers us to live fully, love deeply, and serve others fearlessly, knowing that nothing—not even death—can separate us from God's love.

Live boldly, knowing you're no longer a slave to fear but a child of God, secure in His promise of eternal life.

Today I…

JULY 19

IN CASE YOU MISSED IT

In the same way, count yourselves dead to sin but alive to God in Christ Jesus.

ROMANS 6:11 NIV

In case you need the reminder: You are no longer defined by your past, your failures, or the labels the world places on you. Instead, you are made completely and utterly new through Jesus. When you understand that you're no longer a slave to sin but are alive to God, it changes everything. Your old nature no longer has control over you. You're free to live out the righteousness that has been given to you through Christ.

This freedom is practical and powerful. It means sin no longer has a hold on you. It no longer defines you, no longer controls you, and no longer dictates your actions. You are alive to God—your life is now defined by His love, His righteousness, and His power at work within you. Many believers continue to live in bondage because they haven't fully grasped that they are no longer who they used to be. You don't have to struggle and strive in your own strength to overcome wrongdoing. Instead, you can rest in the truth that you are dead to sin.

Declare aloud that you are dead to sin and alive to God. Proclaim that sin doesn't define you.

Today I…

JULY 20

PUT OFF, PUT ON

You were taught, with regard to your former way of life, to put off your old self, which is being corrupted by its deceitful desires; to be made new in the attitude of your minds; and to put on the new self, created to be like God in true righteousness and holiness.

EPHESIANS 4:22–24 NIV

Many believers remain entangled in old patterns of thinking because they haven't fully embraced the principle in today's passage. To walk in the freedom Christ offers, you must shed your old self, which is driven by deceitful desires and worldly values. When it seeks to regain control, you must take up your cross and die to yourself again. As we've discussed, Jesus commands us to die to ourselves daily because He knows the depths of Satan's desire to sift us like wheat.

This continuous process of daily renewal and aligning your thoughts with God's truth reshapes your thinking and perspective. It opens your heart, enabling you to see, hear, and love people the way Jesus does. You have the Holy Spirit and this biblical command. Claim it so you can live authentically and powerfully as God's child and coworker.

Ask God to open your heart to those around you today. Then move when He prompts you.

Today I…

JULY 21

FREE TO FORGIVE

If you forgive others their offenses, your heavenly Father will also forgive you.

MATTHEW 6:14 CJB

Freedom in Christ means being free to love as God loves. His love isn't conditional or self-seeking; it's sacrificial, patient, and kind. It doesn't keep a record of wrongs, nor does it rejoice in evil. Instead, it rejoices in the truth, always protecting, trusting, hoping, and persevering (1 Corinthians 13:4–7). When you walk in love, you're set free from the prisons of your own making. Bitterness and unforgiveness can no longer hold you captive because you understand that you've been forgiven much, and therefore, you forgive others (Matthew 6:14–15).

Self-centeredness loses its grip on your heart because you're no longer concerned with your own gain but with the well-being of others. This is the love that compels you to go the extra mile, to turn the other cheek, and to love your enemies (Matthew 5:38–48). Walking in love isn't always easy. It requires a daily surrender to God's Spirit, allowing Him to work in you and through you. Real love means choosing to love when it's inconvenient, when it's costly, and when it hurts. Yet in these moments, you'll experience the depth of true freedom—the freedom to love without fear, without reservation, and without end.

Choose forgiveness.

Today I…

JULY 22

CONTENT

I know what it is to be in need, and I know what it is to have plenty. I have learned the secret of being content in any and every situation, whether well fed or hungry, whether living in plenty or in want. I can do all this through him who gives me strength.

PHILIPPIANS 4:12–13 NIV

Paul's strength was anchored in his unchanging relationship with Jesus. Your freedom is rooted in your relationship with Christ. His Holy Spirit empowers you to live above your circumstances rather than being defined or controlled by them. You are a righteous tree. You bear the good fruit of the Spirit. You have peace and joy unshakeable! You're called to live with a peace that transcends your circumstances, a joy that isn't dictated by external factors, and a freedom that remains intact no matter what.

Jesus Himself modeled this freedom. In the midst of a storm, Jesus slept peacefully (Mark 4:37–39). He wasn't oblivious to the storm; He simply wasn't controlled by it. His peace came from His intimate connection with the Father and His authority over the situation. By God's power, you, too, have the authority to speak peace into your storms.

Are there areas where you've allowed your peace or joy to be dictated by your circumstances? Give them to Jesus.

Today I…

JULY 23

FREEDOM TO RISE ABOVE

Everything which has God as its Father overcomes the world. And this is what victoriously overcomes the world: our trust.

1 JOHN 5:4 CJB

Your faith connects you to the victory that Jesus has already secured. Faith doesn't deny the reality of your challenges; rather, it enables you to rise above them. It's the assurance that God is with you even in the midst of the storm and that He is working all things together for your good (Romans 8:28). When you live in this freedom, your life becomes a testimony of God's power and grace, showing the world that true victory is found in Christ alone.

Faith transforms how you approach life's difficulties. Instead of being overwhelmed by fear, you stand firm in God's promises. Instead of succumbing to despair, you hold on to the hope that Christ has given you. Instead of allowing bitterness to take root, you choose to walk in love, knowing that God's love has already conquered the power of sin and death. Your faith in the one who is greater than any circumstance you will ever face is the victory that overcomes everything.

Remember, you are more than a conqueror through Him who loves you.

Today I...

JULY 24

SPIRITUAL SEASONS

For everything there is a season, a right time for every intention under heaven.

ECCLESIASTES 3:1 CJB

Understanding the times and seasons is not just about recognizing the changing circumstances around you. It's also about discerning what God is doing in the spiritual realm and aligning yourself with His purposes. Discernment is crucial for living effectively in the kingdom of God. Just as the natural world has seasons—spring, summer, fall, and winter—your spiritual life also goes through seasons of growth, harvest, rest, and preparation. Each season has its own unique purpose and opportunities, and recognizing the season you are in is key to experiencing the fullness of what God has for you.

Discernment allows you to understand whether you are in a time to plant or a time to reap, a time to wait patiently or a time to move forward in faith. When you're in sync with God's timing, you're able to avoid the frustration and exhaustion that come from trying to force things to happen outside of their appointed time. In seasons of waiting, you can rest, knowing that God is preparing you for what's to come. In seasons of action, you can move boldly, knowing that God has gone before you.

Take time to seek God's guidance on the season you are currently in.

Today I…

JULY 25

KINGDOM AUTHORITY

"Remember, I have given you authority; so you can trample down snakes and scorpions, indeed, all the Enemy's forces; and you will remain completely unharmed."

LUKE 10:19 CJB

Jesus gave you His authority. The *"snakes and scorpions"* mentioned in today's verse may represent spiritual threats the Enemy uses to attack and discourage you, but you have authority over them. Christ's authority also has a physical dimension. In Acts 28:3–6, Paul was bitten by a venomous snake while gathering firewood. The people watching expected him to die, but Paul simply shook the snake off into the fire and moved on. This event illustrates the reality of the protection and authority you have in Christ—even in times of physical danger.

Christ's authority in you is essential for you to live free from fear and oppression. The one who is in you is greater than all hell (1 John 4:4). The Enemy may try to intimidate, deceive, or discourage you, but when you stand in the authority Christ gave you, you can confidently resist the Enemy, knowing that he has no power over you that you do not permit.

Don't permit Satan any authority over you. You are empowered by Christ to live victoriously. Use that authority to bring freedom to those around you.

Today I…

JULY 26

KINGDOM AMBASSADORS

We are therefore Christ's ambassadors, as though God were making his appeal through us. We implore you on Christ's behalf: Be reconciled to God.

2 Corinthians 5:20 NIV

You're not just a citizen of God's kingdom. You're also an ambassador of His kingdom, carrying the authority of the King wherever you go. As an ambassador, you represent Christ in every interaction, every decision, and every challenge you face. Whether you're dealing with personal trials, spiritual battles, or challenges in your family or workplace, you have been given authority over them by Christ Himself. This authority empowers you to stand firm, speak truth, and act with the wisdom and love that reflect your King.

As a representative of Christ, you are called to use your authority to help set others free from fear, oppression, and the lies of the Enemy. You have the authority to speak life, bring healing, declare truth, and release God's power into every situation. But this authority is not to be wielded carelessly or arrogantly. We must exercise it with humility, knowing that it comes from Christ and is for the purpose of advancing His kingdom, not our own agendas.

How can you use the authority God has given you to impact the lives of those around you?

Today I…

JULY 27

KINGDOM FAVOR

> [God] mocks proud mockers
> but shows favor to the humble and oppressed.
>
> PROVERBS 3:34 NIV

A life marked by humility and integrity is a life unbound by the snares of pride and sin. Humility is not just a virtue; it's also a key that unlocks the door to God's grace and favor. Character and humility are closely intertwined. A person of character is someone who lives with integrity, whose actions align with their values, and who seeks to do what is right even when no one is watching. Humility, on the other hand, is the recognition that everything you have and everything you are is a gift from God. It's the understanding that you are utterly dependent on Him for every good thing in your life.

This combination of character and humility frees you from the need to prove yourself, strive for recognition, or compete with others. Pride, on the other hand, binds you. It leads to a life of striving, comparison, and ultimately, disappointment. When you embrace humility, you are free to be who God created you to be, and you open yourself up to the fullness of His grace and favor.

Examine your heart for pride today. Ask God for humility and look for ways to serve others.

Today I…

JULY 28

HE SECURED YOUR FREEDOM

You, children, are from God and have overcome the false prophets, because he who is in you is greater than he who is in the world.

1 John 4:4 cjb

Satan has prophets who speak lies, death, and destruction. After all, one of the Enemy's primary tactics is deception—convincing you that you are powerless, unworthy, or still bound by your past. But the truth is that Jesus has already defeated the powers of darkness on the cross, and through His resurrection, He has secured your freedom. This victory is not just a future hope; it's also a present reality that you are called to live in today. When you stand firm in your identity in Christ, you are enforcing the victory that Jesus has already won.

This awareness of the spiritual battle empowers you to live unshaken by opposition. When challenges arise, you can recognize them for what they are—attempts by the Enemy to steal your peace, joy, and confidence in Christ. But rather than being overwhelmed, you can stand firm, knowing that the power of Christ within you is greater than any force that comes against you.

Renew your mind with God's truth, speak His Word over your life, and take authority over the spiritual forces that seek to hinder you.

Today I…

JULY 29

I RECOGNIZE THEM

"My sheep listen to my voice, I recognize them, they follow me."

JOHN 10:27 CJB

When you're sensitive to God's voice, you're freed from the confusion and uncertainty that clouds decision-making and direction. Knowing God's voice enables you to navigate life's challenges with the confidence that you are aligned with God's perfect will. Notice in today's verse that Jesus said He recognizes His sheep. He recognizes you because you spend time with Him in the heavenly realm, engaging with Him through worship, His Word, prayer, and fasting. And this recognition is reciprocal. As He knows you, you also come to know His voice more clearly, distinguishing it from the many other voices vying for your attention.

It's in this intimate exchange that you find the freedom to live with purpose and direction, unshaken by the uncertainties of life. This includes being open to God's unexpected leading. His guidance may take you in unanticipated directions, often leading to the most profound growth and freedom. Trust His leading even when it defies your natural understanding, knowing that His ways are higher than yours (Isaiah 55:9) and always for your good (Jeremiah 29:11).

Spend time in worship, immerse yourself in God's Word, and engage in regular prayer. Consider fasting to sharpen your spiritual sensitivity and ask God to make you more attuned to His voice.

Today I…

JULY 30

UNOFFENDABLE

Good sense makes a person slow to anger, and it is to his credit when he overlooks an offense.

PROVERBS 19:11 EHV

Throughout his book *The Bait of Satan*, John Bevere emphasized that taking offense is one of the most dangerous traps set by the Enemy.[26] Offense has the power to ensnare you and prevent you from walking in love, unity, and the freedom that Christ offers. Offense is a subtle but powerful tool the Enemy uses to create division, bitterness, and isolation. When you hold on to offense, it festers, leading to resentment and a hardened heart. It disrupts your relationship with God and others, blocking His flow of love and grace in your life.

By choosing to forgive and release offenses, you can avoid this trap and experience the true freedom that comes from living in Christ. You are called to be unoffendable—living in a way that offenses roll off you, unable to take root in your heart. It's not about excusing wrong behavior but about releasing yourself from the chains of bitterness and anger. It's about choosing to respond with love to make room for God to encounter the other person. When you forgive, you're trusting God with the situation.

Choose to live unoffendable, knowing that this is the path to true freedom in Christ.

Today I…

---

[26] John Bevere, *The Bait of Satan: Living Free from the Deadly Trap of Offense* (Charisma House, 2014).

JULY 31

THE KEY TO WISDOM

The fear of the Lord is the beginning of wisdom, and knowledge of the Holy One is understanding.

PROVERBS 9:10 NIV

As we've discussed, the fear of the Lord isn't about being afraid of God. Rather, it's about cultivating a deep reverence and awe for Him, and it's foundational for walking in freedom. In his book *The Awe of God*, John Bevere taught that the fear of the Lord brings freedom because it protects us from the traps of sin and deception.[27] When we have a deep respect for God's holiness, we naturally avoid anything that would grieve His Spirit or lead us away from His truth. This fear acts as a safeguard, keeping us on the path of righteousness and away from the pitfalls that entangle and enslave us.

This reverence for God also brings clarity and discernment. It allows you to see through the lies of the Enemy and the world's empty promises. The fear of the Lord is like a compass, always pointing you toward what is true, pure, and right. As you grow in this fear, you also grow in wisdom, understanding more of God's character and His ways.

Ask God to increase your awe of and respect for Him. Let that reverence guide your thoughts, words, and actions as you witness to others.

Today I…

---

[27] John Bevere, *The Awe of God: The Astounding Way a Healthy Fear of God Transforms Your Life* (Thomas Nelson, 2023), 245.

AUGUST

Acts of God's Kindness

AUGUST 1

ARE YOU AWAKE YET?

In the same way, faith by itself, if it is not accompanied by action, is dead.

JAMES 2:17 NIV

Faith isn't meant to be a passive belief system that stays hidden in your heart. True, living faith is an active force that compels you to move, reach out, and make a tangible difference in the world around you. It's more than just believing in God's promises; it's engaging in the work He is doing and expressing your beliefs through love, service, and obedience. In today's verse, James wasn't suggesting that works earn your salvation; instead, he was emphasizing that genuine faith naturally produces good works. If your faith is real, it will manifest in how you live.

We're over halfway through the year. Check in on the vitality of your faith. Is it awake and visible? Can others see the evidence of your faith through your actions—through acts of kindness, compassion, and generosity that reflect the love of Christ? Or has your faith become stagnant, reduced to words and intentions that never fully materialize into deeds? Living faith is dynamic, continually growing, and doesn't wait for things to happen. It actively engages with the world, bringing God's kingdom through every action, word, and choice.

Faith check: How are you doing?

Today I…

AUGUST 2

YOU DID IT FOR ME

> "'I was hungry and you gave me something to eat, I was thirsty and you gave me something to drink, I was a stranger and you invited me in, I needed clothes and you clothed me, I was sick and you looked after me, I was in prison and you came to visit me.'…'Truly I tell you, whatever you did for one of the least of these brothers and sisters of mine, you did for me.'"
>
> MATTHEW 25:35–36, 40 NIV

Jesus' words in today's passage should be a foundational belief for every church. As the body of Christ, we often excel in providing clothing, food, and care for the needy and sick. But what about inviting strangers into our community or visiting prisoners? These are the words of Jesus, reflecting God's profound love for the marginalized.

As a teenager, I participated in detention-home ministry, and it remains my most cherished outreach experience. I believe that no one is more receptive to the love of Jesus than a prisoner. Alone with their thoughts, many have little hope for the future. But God works powerfully in prisons and jails, and within those walls, there are people searching for the deeper purpose that only the Savior can provide.

Consider how you can extend Christ's love to those whom others overlook.

Today I…

AUGUST 3

ENTERTAINING ANGELS

Do not forget to show hospitality to strangers, for by so doing some people have shown hospitality to angels without knowing it.

HEBREWS 13:2 NIV

This verse makes me a little weepy when I think about the reason angels would be the strangers around us. My guess is it's a test, and it's one I'm sure I've failed before. Testing is an interesting biblical concept. Testing isn't for God to discover our choices—He already knows them. The Almighty exists outside of time, seeing our past, present, and future all at once. The best analogy I've heard to describe God's perspective is of someone watching a parade. We observers can see the performers right in front of us, those who just passed by, and those coming up next.

But God sees the whole parade at once, so He doesn't need to test us for His own sake. Testing is for us. How often have we been so driven by our to-do list that we've failed to notice the needs of those around us? Have we passed by angels disguised as strangers in need?

Today, pause and look beyond your own plans. Be open to the possibility that God has placed someone in your path for a reason.

Today I…

AUGUST 4

HIS MERCY

When the kindness and love of God our Savior appeared, he saved us, not because of righteous things we had done, but because of his mercy. He saved us through the washing of rebirth and renewal by the Holy Spirit.

Titus 3:4–5 NIV

God's kindness came when we were least deserving. It's from His mercy, not our merit. Consider this: God's kindness appeared in a world that rejected Him. It's as if light burst into the darkest place not because the darkness had lessened but because God, in His infinite love, chose to pierce through it. His kindness aims to fundamentally transform us from the inside out. His kindness led to our rebirth and renewal by the Holy Spirit—a complete overhaul of who we were, moving us from death to life, from darkness to light.

True kindness that reflects God's heart isn't about good deeds. Instead, it's about engaging with others in a way that brings life, hope, and renewal. It's about seeing people as God sees them—valuable, loved, and worth the ultimate sacrifice. It's about choosing to act in love, even when it's inconvenient or we think the other person doesn't deserve it, simply because that's what God did for us.

Today, see and treat others as valuable and worthy. Reflect God's kindness in a tangible way.

Today I…

AUGUST 5

RESPONDING TO GRACE

This is a trustworthy saying. And I want you to stress these things, so that those who have trusted in God may be careful to devote themselves to doing what is good. These things are excellent and profitable for everyone.

TITUS 3:8 NIV

Building on yesterday's reminder of God's kindness and mercy in Titus 3:4–5, Paul, in verse 8, emphasized the need for intentional living in response to God's grace. Consider the impact of your actions on others. Are you living in a way that visibly reflects the kindness and love that God has shown you? It's not enough to simply believe; we must express our faith through good works that benefit others. Otherwise, our faith is dead (James 2:17). Again, this isn't about earning God's favor. It's about responding to His grace.

Good works are a natural and necessary response or outflow of our faith. When we truly understand the depth of God's love and mercy, it should compel us to be intentional about doing good, seeking out opportunities to serve, and making a positive impact on those around us. This kind of devotion to good works wakes up our faith.

Be intentional about seeking out opportunities to serve that are *"excellent and profitable for everyone."*

Today I…

AUGUST 6

A HIGHER STANDARD

"Love your enemies, do good to them, and lend to them without expecting to get anything back. Then your reward will be great, and you will be children of the Most High, because he is kind to the ungrateful and wicked."

LUKE 6:35 NIV

The people of the world often exchange kindness like currency. That is, they give something with the expectation of receiving something in return. But God calls us to a higher standard. His kindness—a transformative act that brought us from death to life—is a call to radical, unconditional love. It's a call to see beyond the surface, to extend grace where it's least expected, and to offer a hand of compassion without calculating the cost.

This is the kind of kindness that changes lives, the kind that can soften even the hardest hearts, the kind that mirrors the heart of God. Let us be beacons of His love in a world that desperately needs it.

Ask God to open your eyes to those around you who need to experience His kindness through you. Challenge yourself to offer life-giving kindness even to the undeserving.

Today I…

AUGUST 7

THE IMPACT OF KINDNESS

Those who are kind benefit themselves, but the cruel bring ruin on themselves.

PROVERBS 11:17 NIV

There's a profound truth about the impact of kindness: It affects not only others but yourself as well. When you choose to act with kindness, you are sowing seeds that ultimately benefit your own life. Kindness has a ripple effect, touching the lives of those around you and reflecting God's love in a tangible way. Kindness softens hearts, builds bridges, and opens doors for deeper relationships and understanding.

Today's verse also serves as a warning. The opposite of kindness—cruelty—leads to ruin. It destroys trust, damages relationships, and isolates you from others. Cruelty may provide a momentary sense of power or control, but it leaves behind a trail of brokenness that ultimately harms the one who practices it. God's design is that kindness should be the foundation of your interactions with others. It's not just a nice thing to do; it's also a reflection of God's nature within you. When you choose kindness, you align yourself with God's heart and His purposes, bringing blessings not only to others but to your own life as well.

Challenge yourself to let kindness be your default response and watch how it transforms your relationships and brings peace and joy into your life.

Today I…

AUGUST 8

GO FOR THE GOLD

"Treat other people as you would like them to treat you."
LUKE 6:31 CJB

Today's verse, referred to as the Golden Rule, is one of the most universally recognized principles of kindness and fairness. It's a simple yet profound directive to consider the impact of our actions and to live with empathy, treating others with the same respect, kindness, and love that we desire. At its core, this principle is about seeing others as God sees them: valued, loved, and worthy of compassion.

It's easy to treat others well when they are kind to us, but this command pushes us to go further: to extend the same kindness to *everyone*, regardless of how they treat us, mirroring the unconditional love that God shows us. Living out this verse requires intentionality. It means pausing before we act or speak, asking ourselves, *How would I want to be treated in this situation?* It's about shifting our perspective from self-centeredness to others-centeredness, allowing the love of God to guide our interactions.

Make it a point to treat others as you would want to be treated. Whether in your family, at work, or with strangers, let empathy guide you. Challenge yourself to go beyond mere politeness and truly consider how your words and deeds can reflect God's love.

Today I…

AUGUST 9

BE UNSHAKEABLE

"Though the mountains be shaken and the hills be removed, yet my unfailing love for you will not be shaken nor my covenant of peace be removed," says the Lord, who has compassion on you.

Isaiah 54:10 niv

Consider the depth of this promise. The mountains and hills represent the most stable and enduring parts of the earth, yet even if they crumbled, God's love and His covenant of peace would remain. This is the essence of divine kindness: It's not an emotional response but a steadfast commitment rooted in God's very character. His compassion isn't dependent on your circumstances or your behavior. It is a reflection of His unchanging nature.

But this promise isn't just for your comfort; it's also a call to action. Just as God's kindness and love are unwavering, you are called to be a reflection of Jesus in the lives of others. While so many people are shaken by uncertainty and fear, your acts of kindness can serve as a tangible expression of God's unshakeable love. When you show compassion, offer a listening ear, or lend a helping hand, you are embodying the covenant of peace that God has extended to you.

Be a stabilizing presence in the lives of others.

Today I…

AUGUST 10

TRUE KINDNESS

The Lord's servant must not be quarrelsome but must be kind to everyone, able to teach, not resentful.

2 TIMOTHY 2:24 NIV

As God's bondservant, you are called to rise above the temptation to engage in quarrels or to let resentment take root in your heart. You must embody kindness even in situations where it's difficult. This doesn't mean avoiding all confrontation but approaching conflicts with a spirit of gentleness and a desire to teach rather than to win. Kindness, in this context, is not about being passive or avoiding difficult conversations. It's about maintaining a posture of grace and humility even when standing firm on the truth. Living out this form of kindness requires intentionality and reliance on the Holy Spirit.

It's easy to become frustrated or defensive when others challenge your beliefs or values, but 2 Timothy 2:24 calls us to respond differently. A true servant of the Lord is marked by a kindness that transcends personal offense, one that seeks to build bridges rather than walls. In a culture that often celebrates the loudest voices and the sharpest arguments, choosing kindness can be a radical act. It's a declaration that your identity isn't rooted in being right but in God's righteousness.

Let your words and actions reflect God's heart.

Today I…

AUGUST 11

A HEALING WORD

Gracious words are a honeycomb, sweet to the soul and healing to the bones.

PROVERBS 16:24 NIV

This verse paints a vivid picture of the power of words by comparing words filled with kindness, compassion, and love to honeycomb, a natural source of sweetness and nourishment. But the impact of these words goes beyond just being pleasant; they bring healing and restoration to those who hear them. The world uses words to wound, tear down, or divide, but this verse reminds us that our words have the potential to bring life and healing.

Think about the last time someone spoke a kind word to you. Chances are, it lifted your spirits, gave you hope, or encouraged you to keep going. This is the power of gracious words. They can reach deep into the soul, offering sweetness that revives and strengthens. But more than just making someone feel good, gracious words have a healing quality. They can soothe emotional wounds, mend broken relationships, and restore hope where it has been lost. Your words hold incredible power to either bring healing or harm. Let today's verse challenge you to be intentional with your speech, recognizing that every word you speak has the potential to affect someone's soul deeply.

Today, focus on the power of your words.

Today I…

AUGUST 12

FAITH EXPRESSED THROUGH LOVE

In Christ Jesus neither circumcision nor uncircumcision has any value. The only thing that counts is faith expressing itself through love.

GALATIANS 5:6 NIV

In today's verse, Paul cut to the heart of what truly matters in the life of a believer: faith that is expressed through love. The world is consumed with outward appearances, rituals, and rules, but external markers hold no real value in Christ. What counts is the authenticity of your faith and how it manifests in love. Here, Paul was addressing a significant debate in the early church: whether Gentile believers needed to follow Jewish customs, such as circumcision, to be truly saved. But Paul made it clear that these outward signs are irrelevant in Christ because God is interested in the condition of your heart.

Faith naturally flows into love. Love is the visible evidence of your faith in Christ. Remember that it's not about following a set of rules to prove your righteousness. It's about allowing your faith to transform you from the inside out, leading you to love others as Christ loves you.

Do the people around you see the love of Christ in the way you interact with them? If not, His mercies are new every morning, so repent and start again.

Today I…

AUGUST 13

WHAT A GIFT

As each one has received some spiritual gift, he should use it to serve others, like good managers of God's many-sided grace—if someone speaks, let him speak God's words; if someone serves, let him do so out of strength that God supplies; so that in everything God may be glorified through Yeshua the Messiah—to him be glory and power forever and ever. Amen.

1 Peter 4:10–11 CJB

Each of us has unique spiritual gifts that reflect God's diverse grace. These gifts are not meant to be hidden or used solely for personal gain but are intended to serve others and glorify God's name. Our ultimate purpose in this life is to love God wholeheartedly and to love others in such a profound way that we lead them to Jesus, thus building His kingdom on earth.

When we serve others using the gifts God has given us, we engage in the divine work of His kingdom. Whether we speak or serve, our actions and words should consistently point others to Jesus, bringing honor to His name. By using our gifts in this way, we become conduits of God's grace, showcasing His love and power in every aspect of our lives.

Consider how you can use your gifts or talents to serve others today.

Today I…

AUGUST 14

A LIVING SACRIFICE

Do not forget to do good and to share with others, for with such sacrifices God is pleased.

HEBREWS 13:16 NIV

It's easy to overlook the small opportunities to show kindness and generosity. Yet these very acts of goodness and sharing are what please God. They are sacrifices—not always in the grand or dramatic sense but in the everyday sense in which you put others' needs before your own even when it is inconvenient.

These acts of kindness don't have to be elaborate. They can be as simple as offering a listening ear, sharing a meal, or giving your time to help someone in need. The key is the intention behind the action—doing good and sharing because it aligns with God's heart, not for recognition or reward. Small acts of kindness ripple outwards, impacting lives in ways you may never fully see or understand.

Look for opportunities to bless someone, whether it's through a kind word, a helping hand, or a generous gift. Remember that these acts, no matter how small, are sacrifices that please God.

Today I…

AUGUST 15

OUR DESTINY

We are God's handiwork, created in Christ Jesus to do good works, which God prepared in advance for us to do.

EPHESIANS 2:10 NIV

This is your identity: You are God's handiwork, intricately designed and uniquely crafted with a specific purpose in mind. And this is your destiny: the good works God has prepared in advance for you to do. Your life is not random or without meaning; it is part of a divine plan that was set in motion long before you were born. Being God's handiwork means that you are a masterpiece, intentionally created with care and precision. Every detail of who you are—your gifts, talents, and passions—was crafted by God for a purpose. Your purpose is not just about fulfilling personal goals or ambitions. It's about building God's kingdom.

This understanding of destiny challenges you to view your life through the lens of God's plan. It calls you to seek His guidance and to be attentive to the opportunities He places before you. Whether it's in your career, relationships, or daily interactions, God has prepared specific good works for you to do.

Look for tangible opportunities to show God's love today and remember, you were destined to read this passage and act on it.

Today I…

AUGUST 16

I STAND IN AWE

Look out for each other's interests and not just for your own.

PHILIPPIANS 2:4 CJB

In today's verse, Paul called us to a life marked by genuine concern for others. We do not have to neglect our own needs but rather balance them with a sincere effort to care for those around us. It's a mindset that reflects the heart of Christ, who, as Paul later described in this chapter, humbled Himself and put the needs of humanity above His own even to the point of death on a cross (Philippians 2:5–8). Let's just pause here a moment and be struck with wonder at who God is: all-powerful yet always humble, loving, and sacrificial. Can we recognize the depth of His love and the lengths He went to redeem us?

When you truly grasp what Jesus did for you, it becomes the driving force behind your willingness to put others first, to serve, and to live a life marked by humility. When you shift your focus from yourself to others, you begin to see the world through God's eyes. You become more attuned to the needs of those around you, more compassionate in your responses, and more willing to lend a hand, no matter the cost.

See the world through God's eyes.

Today I…

AUGUST 17

TRUE RELIGION

Religion that God our Father accepts as pure and faultless is this: to look after orphans and widows in their distress and to keep oneself from being polluted by the world.

JAMES 1:27 NIV

James 1:27 cuts to the core of how God views true faith. It's not about rituals or appearances but about showing tangible love to those who are hurting and marginalized. This verse speaks to the depth of God's heart for orphans. To open your home, life, and heart to a child in need reflects God's heart. After all, God describes Himself as a *"father to the fatherless"* (Psalm 68:5 NIV).

I recognize that becoming a foster or adoptive parent isn't everyone's calling, but as believers, we are *all called* to care for these modern-day orphans. There are countless ways to support children who are navigating the foster care system. You might be able to mentor them or simply offer your God-given talents. For example, someone who is a hairdresser can offer free haircuts to kids in foster care. Think outside the box. Each act of care reflects God's love for the fatherless and demonstrates true religion.

Write down a practical way you can help a family or kids in foster care.

Today I…

AUGUST 18

MODERN-DAY WIDOWS

Religion that God our Father accepts as pure and faultless is this: to look after orphans and widows in their distress and to keep oneself from being polluted by the world.

JAMES 1:27 NIV

Since there's a lot to unpack in James 1:27, we're looking at it again today. Yesterday we focused on children, but today we'll consider single moms, who face similar struggles to those that widows faced in biblical times. Like some widows, single mothers shoulder the heavy burden of raising children, often with little support and few resources. We're called to stand in the gap for these women, offering community and practical help. Remember, true religion isn't a passive set of rules but rather an active expression of love and care for the most vulnerable. God's heart beats for those who are struggling. He calls His people to step in, stand with, and lift up those who cannot carry their burdens alone.

James highlighted another key aspect of pure faith: keeping yourself *"from being polluted by the world."* While the world encourages self-interest and convenience, God calls us to reject these temptations. Instead of looking away from that struggling mom who has no support system, we're called to run toward her brokenness with open arms. Embracing compassion, selflessness, and holiness demonstrates a heart that's unstained by the world.

Encourage or assist a single mom today.

Today I…

AUGUST 19

GENEROUS HEARTS, OPEN HOMES

*Share with the Lord's people who are in need.
Practice hospitality.*

ROMANS 12:13 NIV

Romans 12:13 commands us to share what we have with fellow believers in need and to open our hearts and homes in hospitality. This instruction speaks to the interconnectedness of the Christian community, where each person's well-being is a shared responsibility. Whether it's through financial help, time, or simply offering a meal, sharing what we have isn't just about meeting material needs. It's also about mirroring the love and generosity of Christ in practical ways.

Hospitality, too, is a key expression of God's love. Hospitality goes beyond entertaining or hosting parties to the simple act of creating a space where others feel seen, cared for, and welcome. Hospitality is more than opening our homes—it's opening our lives to others, offering them a place of belonging, warmth, and connection just as God welcomes us into His presence. Sharing and practicing hospitality requires us to step outside our comfort zones, to sacrifice time, resources, and even convenience. Yet in doing so, we build deeper relationships, strengthen the community, and reflect God's kingdom values of love, generosity, and unity.

Today, look for a way to share what you have or make someone feel welcome, wanted, and seen.

Today I…

AUGUST 20

THE LAW OF LOVE

Carry each other's burdens, and in this way you will fulfill the law of Christ.

GALATIANS 6:2 NIV

In today's verse, Paul called us to something deeper than sympathy. He invited us to actively engage in the struggles of others. To *"carry each other's burdens"* is to shoulder the weight of someone else's pain, hardship, or difficulty as though it were our own. This is the essence of community in Christ—a bond so strong that our brothers or sisters do not face their challenges alone but in union with the entire body of Christ. This act of bearing one another's burdens fulfills the *"law of Christ,"* which is the law of love (John 13:34).

Jesus Himself demonstrated the ultimate burden-bearing when He took our sins upon Himself on the cross. His selfless love set the standard for how we are to live in community with one another—carrying each other's physical, emotional, and spiritual burdens with compassion and grace. Whether it's listening, offering help, or praying, bearing burdens requires an active response. Though the burdens may remain, their weight becomes more bearable when they are shared.

Today, seek out someone carrying a burden. Reflect Christ's love by offering support through your prayers, help, or presence.

Today I…

AUGUST 21

GOD'S ECONOMY

Whoever is kind to the poor lends to the Lord, and he will reward them for what they have done.

PROVERBS 19:17 NIV

This verse is a beautiful reminder that when we show kindness to the poor, we are not just helping others but also lending to the Lord Himself. What an incredible thought! God, in His infinite love and mercy, sees every act of compassion you show, and He considers it as if you were giving directly to Him.

Matthew Henry, a renowned seventeenth-century preacher and Bible commentator, noted that when we're kind to the poor, we're lending to God, who will repay us with interest. Henry's insight reminds us that when we give to those in need, it is not a loss but an investment in God's economy. God, who owns everything, sees our kindness and repays us in ways that far exceed material gain. So when you show compassion, you're not just helping the needy. You're also partnering with God in His mission, and He promises to bless you for it.

Seek out a way to help someone in need, knowing that God not only sees your generosity, but He will also repay it with interest.

Today I…

AUGUST 22

SPEAK UP

Speak up for those who cannot speak for themselves; ensure justice for those being crushed.

PROVERBS 31:8 NLT

Many—including those crushed by poverty, discrimination, or exploitation—are silenced by systems of injustice. Proverbs 31:8 is a call to courage. Your voice has power, and God has given you the responsibility to use it. Edmund Burke is thought to be the person who said, "The only thing necessary for the triumph of evil is for good men to do nothing." Silence allows injustice to thrive, but speaking up aligns you with God's heart for justice.

Speaking for the voiceless goes beyond surface-level empathy. It's a heart-level commitment to reflect God's justice and mercy. Jesus modeled this when He defended the woman caught in adultery (John 8:1–11). The religious leaders sought to condemn her to death, using her as a pawn to trap Jesus. Instead of joining in their judgment, Jesus defended her when she was crushed under the weight of societal and legalistic condemnation. Standing for justice may bring criticism, but God promises to be with you. He empowers those who defend the vulnerable, and your courage can bring light and hope where it's needed most.

Think of someone you can speak up for. Pray for the right strategy, then act.

Today I…

AUGUST 23

WHEN IT'S IN YOUR POWER

Do not withhold good from those to whom it is due, when it is in your power to act.

PROVERBS 3:27 NIV

The verse is straightforward: When you have the ability to do good, don't hesitate—act. James 4:17 offers a sobering complement to this message: *"So then, anyone who knows the right thing to do and fails to do it is committing a sin"* (CJB). Here, Scripture makes it clear that neglecting to act when you know you should isn't just a missed opportunity—it's a sin. When you turn a blind eye to a need, you're withholding the goodness God has equipped you to offer.

God doesn't call you to wait for the perfect moment or for someone else to act. He calls you to step in when you can. Whether it's helping a neighbor, providing for someone in need, or offering support to a struggling friend, when God puts the opportunity to do good in front of you, He expects you to act.

Don't let the thoughts *I'm too busy* or *Someone else will help* become a stumbling block in your walk of faith. Be aware of opportunities to reflect God's love and act.

Today I…

AUGUST 24

EMPATHY IN ACTION

The wicked don't care about the rights of the poor, but good people do.

PROVERBS 29:7 CEV

God's concern for justice goes beyond sympathy. It's a call to empathy, or sympathy in action. Being good in God's eyes means actively engaging with the needs of the disadvantaged, whether through advocacy, assistance, or speaking up when their voices go unheard. True righteousness is measured by how we respond to the needs and rights of the vulnerable.

The indifference of the wicked speaks volumes. To ignore the struggles of the poor is to deny them the dignity and justice they deserve. It reflects a heart hardened against the compassion and righteousness that God calls His people to embody. Conversely, caring for the rights of the poor is a reflection of God's justice and mercy. Today's verse asks you to evaluate your own heart. Do you care about the rights of the poor, or have you become indifferent to their struggles? Good people—God's people—do more than just notice the injustice around them. They act.

Take time today to research the rights or resources available to the poor in your community. Ask God to show you how you can help.

Today I…

AUGUST 25

GOD'S MIRROR TO THE WORLD

*Adonai is merciful and compassionate,
slow to anger and rich in grace.*

Psalm 103:8 CJB

Psalm 103:8 beautifully captures the very foundation of who God is—merciful, compassionate, patient, and overflowing with grace. His mercy means that He withholds the punishment we deserve while His compassion reflects His deep concern for us even in our brokenness. God is slow to anger. He isn't quick to judge or punish even when we fall short. Instead, He waits with open arms, giving us the opportunity to repent, grow, and turn back to Him.

His grace covers us completely not because we've earned it but because it flows abundantly from His character. He doesn't respond with frustration or impatience but with tender love and mercy. As we receive His grace, we're also called to reflect it. This is how we can embody the love and character of God in our daily interactions.

As you reflect on God's grace, challenge yourself to extend that same grace to others. Be slow to anger, rich in kindness, and merciful in your interactions, reflecting the heart of God.

Today I…

AUGUST 26

DIVINE DELIVERANCE

Blessed is the one who considers the poor! In the day of trouble the Lord delivers him.

PSALM 41:1 ESV

God's desire is for us to deeply engage with the needs of the poor, seeing their inherent dignity with the eyes of Christ and responding with compassion. When you make their struggles a priority, God makes your deliverance His priority. One story that illustrates this well is from the life of George Müller, a Christian evangelist and orphanage director in the nineteenth century. Müller dedicated his life to caring for orphans—all without ever asking for donations.

Time and time again, when there wasn't enough food or resources, Müller would pray, and God would miraculously provide just what was needed. One famous story recalls how the hundreds of children at the orphanage sat down to an empty table, and Müller prayed, trusting that God would provide. Just then, a baker arrived with enough bread to feed all the children, followed by a milkman who offered George free milk because he was worried that it would spoil after his cart had broken down outside the orphanage.[28] The Lord delivered Müller in his time of need because Müller had devoted his life to the poor.

Trust that as you care for others, God will care for you.

Today I…

---

[28] "A Famous Story About Muller's Faith," George Muller, June 29, 2016, georgemuller.org.

AUGUST 27

OPEN HEART, OPEN HANDS

"If there is a poor person among you,…do not be hardhearted or tightfisted toward your poor brother."

DEUTERONOMY 15:7 CSB

When you see someone in need, you are called to soften your heart and loosen your grip on what you have. It's easy to feel protective of your resources, especially in times of uncertainty, but God calls you to take a different approach. When you hold on to your resources too tightly, your heart follows, making you less aware of God's promptings. But when you open your hand in generosity, your heart remains soft, and you make room for God to move in your own life and to use you to meet the needs of others.

Ultimately, generosity isn't just about giving money; it's also about living with an open hand and heart. When you see someone in need, you have a choice: to hold on tightly to your comfort or to respond with compassion. God's Word encourages you to release the tight grip of self-protection and trust that when you give to others, He will supply your needs in return. This openhanded approach reflects God's own nature. He's never hard-hearted or tightfisted toward us but always ready to bless and provide.

Today, open your heart and hands to someone in need.

Today I…

AUGUST 28

A SOBERING THOUGHT

Whoever closes his ear to the cry of the poor will himself call out and not be answered.

PROVERBS 21:13 ESV

Today's verse carries a sobering reminder about the relationship between how we treat others and how God responds to us. It speaks to those who wonder why their prayers seem unanswered. The message is clear: If we close our ears to the poor, our own cries may go unheard. Have you ever felt your prayers were met with silence? While God's timing is often beyond our understanding, this verse challenges us to reflect on whether our unanswered prayers result from our neglect of the needs of the less fortunate.

This might feel like a sharp rebuke, but let it be a loving one. God, in His mercy, invites us to reflect on our actions. He desires not to condemn us but to realign us with His will. If you're caring for the poor and still feel unheard, remember God's delay is not denial. Sometimes He's preparing something so wonderful that He needs your patience to refine you for the breakthrough.

If you feel as if your prayers are unanswered, reflect on how you've cared for the poor. Trust that as you align with God's heart, He'll move in unexpected ways.

Today I…

AUGUST 29

DON'T SHRINK BACK

"My righteous one will live by faith. And I take no pleasure in the one who shrinks back."

HEBREWS 10:38 NIV

Living by faith is not just a concept but should be a daily experience of walking with God. Faith isn't just something you know in your mind—it's something you live out from your spirit. Faith and love are the substance of God, and they shape how you live, act, and engage with the world around you. When you encounter God's love, faith transforms from an abstract idea into a tangible reality that drives your life forward. Faith doesn't originate in your mind. It's born in your spirit because it comes from God.

Your spirit embraces faith not because you've reasoned it out, but because you've encountered the truth of God's love and grace. This isn't head knowledge—it's an encounter with the living God, and that encounter changes you. I once heard Pastor Joe Moniz preach, "Your belief system must match your sound system," meaning what you say and how you live should reflect the faith that has transformed you. True faith doesn't shrink back in fear or doubt but trusts God's promises, speaks them out, and moves forward with confidence.

Today, commit to living by faith, not shrinking back.

Today I…

AUGUST 30

OUTSIDERS

"You must not oppress foreigners. You know what it's like to be a foreigner, for you yourselves were once foreigners in the land of Egypt."

Exodus 23:9 NLT

This verse highlights the biblical principle of remembering where you've come from so that you can show mercy to those who are in similar situations today. God calls us to treat others with dignity and kindness, especially those who may feel like outsiders. Whether they are immigrants, refugees, or individuals who feel displaced in society, God's heart is always for the marginalized. We're called to look beyond differences to offer love and support.

Yet this Scripture passage goes deeper than simply avoiding oppression. It calls us to actively engage with those who are different from us. God's command is rooted in understanding and compassion. We are called to remember our own experiences, our own moments of being in need, and to let that inform how we treat others, show compassion, offer help, and stand up for those who feel out of place. By doing this, we reflect God's love and fulfill His command to care for the foreigner and the marginalized.

Is there someone in your life who feels like an outsider? Extend kindness and compassion, knowing that God has called you to love and welcome them.

Today I…

AUGUST 31

SPIRITUAL WATER

*A generous person will be enriched,
and the one who gives a drink of water will receive water.*

PROVERBS 11:25 CSB

This proverb reminds me of Jesus' encounter with the woman at the well (John 4). He offered her not physical water but living water that satisfies the spirit (vv. 13–14). Similarly, Proverbs 11:25 applies not only to physical water but also to spiritual water—the gospel! When we share the gospel, it's like we're spiritually unplugging a dam and letting fresh living water rush in—bringing with it fresh revelation, empowerment, giftings, and authority.

Consider the Dead Sea: It has only one inlet and no outlet. The water flows in but has nowhere to go, so it becomes stagnant and lifeless. The same thing happens to our spirits when we don't share the gospel. The living water we received when we first encountered Jesus grows stagnant if we keep it to ourselves. Stagnant water breeds disease and death, but fresh, flowing water brings life. When we fail to share the good news with others, our spirits become like the Dead Sea—closed off to the flow of the Holy Spirit. Though we might still encounter the Holy Spirit, it's in small doses because our spirits have less room to receive Him.

Share the gospel.

Today I…

SEPTEMBER

Worship:
Becoming a Person
After God's Own Heart

SEPTEMBER 1

AFTER GOD'S OWN HEART

> One thing I ask from the Lord, this only do I seek: that I may dwell in the house of the Lord all the days of my life, to gaze on the beauty of the Lord and to seek him in his temple.
>
> PSALM 27:4 NIV

I'm amazed and encouraged that David—though he killed thousands and was so full of lust for Bathsheba that he orchestrated her husband's death—was still called the man after God's own heart (Acts 13:22). God didn't excuse David's actions, but we can marvel at God's kindness and mercy: He made David's scarlet sins *"white as snow"* (Isaiah 1:18 NIV).

When we repent and yield our hearts, minds, dreams, and even our finances to the Lord, living entirely in a posture of worship, God softens our hearts and calls us people after His own heart. I love that one of David's greatest prayers was that he would dwell in God's presence and behold His beauty. We have this ability now because of the Holy Spirit. Though we live in this world, we're no longer of it. We should spend more time in the Spirit than in the flesh. Worship is a portal to heaven.

This month, commit to starting each day with a worship song. Sing along! "Nothing Else" by Cody Carnes or "Trust in God" by Elevation Worship is a solid starting place.

Today I…

SEPTEMBER 2

PROPHETIC WORSHIP

The tongue can bring death or life; those who love to talk will reap the consequences.

PROVERBS 18:21 NLT

It's fascinating how Satan distorts biblical principles and twists them to be human-centered. For example, what the world calls "manifesting" is simply a biblical truth: The power of life and death is in the tongue. Scripture repeats this principle often, reminding us that our words influence our reality.

When we worship through song, we're actually prophesying and speaking life over ourselves. However, even in worship, we must be mindful of the lyrics we sing. There are songs I choose not to sing—even if the writer penned them with a sincere heart—because sincerity alone doesn't equal truth. After all, Peter's motive was sincere when he told Jesus not to go to the cross, but Jesus sharply rebuked him (Matthew 16:22–23). Some worship lyrics, though well-intended, can contain biblically inaccurate statements, emphasize struggles over God's power, or reinforce an identity Christ has already redeemed. Starting our days with worship is a powerful way to align our hearts with God's truth. This isn't New Age teaching—it's how God designed us. He *spoke* the world into existence, and as His image-bearers, we have the ability to prophesy and speak life.

Listen to the song "New Thing Coming" by Elevation Worship.

Today I…

SEPTEMBER 3

WORSHIP IN THE WILDERNESS

"Therefore, behold, I will allure her, and bring her into the wilderness, and speak tenderly to her."

HOSEA 2:14 ESV

Wilderness seasons can feel isolating, confusing, and painful, but Hosea 2:14 reminds us that sometimes, God leads us into these quiet places not to abandon us but to draw us closer to Him. In the wilderness, distractions fall away, and God has our full attention. It's here that He speaks tenderly to us, inviting us into deeper intimacy, worship, and surrender. In these seasons, God may be calling you to listen, pause, and refocus. Here, God lovingly rebukes you, gently highlighting areas in your life that need change.

Wilderness seasons are also times of tender care, when God fills you with His love, renews your spirit, and redirects your steps. God doesn't draw you into the wilderness to punish or abandon you—He does it to be with you, to recalibrate your heart, and to lead you into a deeper walk with Him. The wilderness can be a place of worship, where in the quiet, you experience the tenderness and love of the Father, the guidance of the Holy Spirit, and the closeness of Jesus.

Listen to the song "Love Note" by Abbie Gamboa and imagine God singing this over you.

Today I…

SEPTEMBER 4

A NEW SONG

He put a new song in my mouth, a song of praise to our God. Many will look on in awe and put their trust in Adonai.

Psalm 40:4(3) CJB

Psalm 40 begins with David crying out to God for help and God answering by lifting him out of a pit of despair and giving David *"a new song"* of praise. When you go through seasons of difficulty, God can transform your experiences into testimonies that glorify Him. The *"new song"* is your response, a song of worship that flows from deep within, declaring His praise despite the immense pressure you're under.

Worship transforms your outlook. It brings peace, life, and joy into even the darkest circumstances because it shifts your focus back to God's ability to change everything in a moment. Others see the transformation in your life and wonder what changed. Worship, then, leads to testimonies, and testimonies lead to organic opportunities to share the gospel in a way that doesn't feel dogmatic but sincere. Our testimonies often inspire others to trust in the Lord themselves.

Do you need to sing a new song to the Lord? Get alone with Him and spontaneously sing of God's love. Thank Him in song for who He is even if you're tone deaf. The Lord listens to your heart.

Today I…

SEPTEMBER 5

NATURAL RESPONSE

When the waters saw you, O God,…they were afraid; indeed, the deep trembled.…The crash of your thunder was in the whirlwind; your lightnings lighted up the world; the earth trembled and shook. Your way was through the sea, your path through the great waters; yet your footprints were unseen. You led your people like a flock by the hand of Moses and Aaron.

PSALM 77:16, 18–20 ESV

Asaph, a worship leader and prophetic seer in King David's court (1 Chronicles 16:4–7; 2 Chronicles 29:30), penned Psalm 77 as a cry when he felt abandoned by God. Yet in the midst of his sorrow, Asaph reflected on God's faithfulness in parting the Red Sea. The imagery is stunning. All creation responded to the power of God as He made a way through impossible circumstances.

Faith is trusting God when the way forward is unclear, and God often moves when things seem impossible because He loves getting the glory. We see this again at Jericho. Israel's victory didn't come by force but by obedient worship—marching, shouting, and trusting God to fight for them (Joshua 6). Worship is warfare. When we praise God in our darkest moments, we declare His sovereignty over every obstacle.

Trust God's ability to lead you—even when you can't see His footprints.

Today I…

SEPTEMBER 6

MY HIDING PLACE

You are a hiding-place for me, you will keep me from distress; you will surround me with songs of deliverance. (Selah)

PSALM 32:7 CJB

Worship isn't just about singing songs or lifting hands in praise. It's also about finding your refuge in God and allowing Him to be your hiding place. It's about soaking in God's presence. Worship is about more than what we offer to God—it's also about receiving Him. Worship spiritually translates us into heaven, right before the throne of God, where God's presence shelters us as His love and deliverance envelop us in song even if we don't physically hear it.

No matter how distressed we feel, God is working on our behalf. Worship allows us to silence the noise of the world and tune in to the melodies of heaven that declare our freedom. When you feel overwhelmed, turn to God as your hiding place. Let His songs of deliverance surround you, lifting you out of despair and into hope. As you worship, you not only express your love for Him, but you also experience His deliverance in ways that go beyond your understanding.

Listen to a worship song and close your eyes, imagining yourself being translated to God's literal throne room in heaven. What is He saying to you?

Today I…

SEPTEMBER 7

DEEP CALLING TO DEEP

Deep is calling to deep at the thunder of your waterfalls; all your surging rapids and waves are sweeping over me. By day Adonai commands his grace, and at night his song is with me as a prayer to the God of my life.

PSALM 42:8–9(7–8) CJB

Charles Spurgeon said, "I have learned to kiss the waves that throw me up against the Rock of Ages." In today's passage, the psalmist described feeling the presence of God like surging rapids and waves sweeping over him as though to wash away his anxieties and draw him close. The psalmist also spoke of the deep calling to deep—God's Spirit connecting with ours, inviting us into deeper intimacy. The force of God's love and presence washed over him like a waterfall, refreshing his soul and reminding him of God's faithfulness.

When you feel like you're drowning in fear and anxiety, God's presence invites you to stop swimming, stop striving, and sink into the ocean of His love. Let God's grace, love, and peace wash away every trace of fear. By day, God commands His steady current of grace to empower and equip you, and by night, He sings over you with prayer.

Stop swimming. Stop striving. Give it to Jesus.

Today I…

SEPTEMBER 8

TRUE HEARTS

Let us draw near with a true heart in full assurance of faith, with our hearts sprinkled clean from an evil conscience and our bodies washed with pure water.

HEBREWS 10:22 ESV

Worship is about drawing near to God with a true heart, fully assured of His love and grace. Through the sacrifice of Jesus on the cross, we're no longer separated from God by sin, so we don't have to stand far off. We can come into His presence worshiping with a heart that knows it is accepted and loved. We're invited and welcomed into the fullness of His grace and into a relationship with Him.

Drawing near to God is at the heart of true worship. It's not about singing songs or saying prayers—it's about coming close to God with a genuine heart, full of faith that we're cleansed by His Spirit. Worship is where we find that our past is washed away and that our future is held secure in His hands. When we worship, we're responding to the open invitation God gives us through Christ.

Let your worship flow from the assurance that God is with you, welcoming you into His presence.

Today I…

SEPTEMBER 9

WORTHY OF IT ALL

The four living creatures…never cease to say, "Holy, holy, holy, is the Lord God Almighty, who was and is and is to come!"…The twenty-four elders fall down before him.…They cast their crowns before the throne, saying, "Worthy are you, our Lord and God, to receive glory and honor and power."

REVELATION 4:8, 10–11 ESV

Worship is about recognizing God's supremacy and responding with humility. Today's Scripture passage gives us a glimpse into heaven's throne room, where worship is an eternal response to God's glory.

I believe that in every moment, God reveals a new and awe-inspiring facet of Himself, giving fresh reason for our endless worship. The elders, holding positions of honor, lay their crowns—symbols of their authority and accomplishments—before God, acknowledging that their greatest achievements pale before His majesty. They surrender their crowns before Him in recognition that everything they have comes from His will and exists for His glory. In the same way, our worship shifts our focus from ourselves to God's greatness, submitting all we are in response to His majesty.

Listen to the song "Worthy of It All" by Abbie Gamboa and join in with heaven as you cast your entire self, your goals, and your hopes and dreams before the Lord.

Today I…

SEPTEMBER 10

UNDIGNIFIED WORSHIP

David danced and spun around with abandon before Adonai, wearing a linen ritual vest.

2 Samuel 6:14 cjb

In his uninhibited worship, David expressed total devotion to God, unashamed of how he appeared to others. His focus was solely on giving glory to Adonai, reflecting the truth that worship is about Him, not us. David's dance was an outward expression of his joy and reverence for God. But though he was king, he wasn't exempt from judgment—his wife Michal looked on with disgust. Yet David didn't let her disapproval hinder his worship.

Even when others don't understand our worship, when our focus is on God, it elicits a spontaneous and genuine response. It's easy to let fear of judgment hold us back. But true worship isn't about what others see. It's about the posture of our hearts and our response to God's goodness. Worship requires vulnerability and a willingness to surrender our pride. Like David, when we worship with abandon, we encounter God more deeply and experience the freedom of worshiping in spirit and truth.

Today, worship God with complete abandon just as David did. Let go of any concerns about how you look or what others may think. Focus solely on giving God the honor and glory He deserves.

Today I…

SEPTEMBER 11

IN SPIRIT AND TRUTH

"God is Spirit, so those who worship him must worship in spirit and in truth."

JOHN 4:24 NLT

God is Spirit, and for us to truly connect with Him, we must worship Him in spirit and truth. Worship is not just a physical act; it's a spiritual encounter. When we worship, we are translated to the heavenly realm, seated with Christ in the kingdom of heaven, far above the rulers, authorities, and spiritual forces of this world. Though we live in this world, we are not of it (John 17:16). Our citizenship is in heaven.

When we worship, we're not just singing or praying—we're also engaging with the eternal, joining in the chorus of heaven. We're seated with Christ, who has authority over all powers and dominions (Ephesians 2:6). Worship is an act of warfare as much as it is an act of reverence. When we worship in spirit and truth, we rise above the influence of the world and the demonic forces that seek to oppress us. We step into our identity as children of God. We're more than conquerors in Christ, who gave us His authority over darkness.

With a kingdom mindset, worship in spirit and truth.

Today I…

SEPTEMBER 12

BOW DOWN

*Come, let us bow down in worship,
let us kneel before the L<small>ORD</small> our Maker.*

P<small>SALM</small> 95:6 <small>NIV</small>

Bowing and kneeling in worship isn't just a physical act. It's also an outward expression of an inward reality. When we bow down in worship, we are acknowledging God's supreme authority and majesty and recognizing that He is our Creator, the one who formed us with His hands and breathed life into us. To bow before the Lord is to surrender our will, our desires, and our ambitions to Him. It's a recognition that we are not in control—God is. Kneeling before God reminds us of our dependence on Him for every breath, every step, and every provision in life.

When we kneel in worship, we are symbolically lowering ourselves, setting aside our pride and ego, and exalting the Lord in His rightful place above all things. He is the creator, and we are the created. This humbling realization draws us deeper into His presence, where we find peace, strength, and purpose. Worship is about magnifying God, realizing that He is larger than our problems and wants.

Today, bow before God in both body and spirit. Take time to kneel in His presence, surrendering your plans and desires and worshiping Him as the Lord, your Maker.

Today I…

SEPTEMBER 13

OFFERING YOURSELF

I urge you, brothers and sisters, in view of God's mercy, to offer your bodies as a living sacrifice, holy and pleasing to God—this is your true and proper worship.

ROMANS 12:1 NIV

This verse calls us to a radical form of worship: to offer our bodies as living sacrifices to God. Worship, in its truest form, is the complete surrender of our lives to God in response to His mercy. We present every part of ourselves—our thoughts, actions, and desires—as an offering that reflects our gratitude for His grace.

In the Old Testament, people offered sacrifices on altars to atone for sins and express devotion. Jesus' sacrifice calls us to live as sacrifices, holy and pleasing to God. Our lives, in every moment, are acts of worship. We must continually lay our lives and desires on the altar, submitting to God's will and allowing Him to mold us into vessels that are holy and pleasing to Him. It is a sacrifice to choose holiness over worldly pleasures and align our actions with God's standards, but in this surrender, we find freedom and purpose.

Ask God to reveal areas of your life that you need to surrender.

Today I…

SEPTEMBER 14

DIVINE HARMONY IN WORSHIP

Ascribe to the Lord the glory due his name;
worship the Lord in the splendor of holiness.

PSALM 29:2 ESV

The psalmist, having inscribed God's Word on his heart, echoed 1 Chronicles 16:29: *"Ascribe to the Lord the glory due his name; bring an offering and come before him. Worship the Lord in the splendor of his holiness"* (NIV). Like the psalmist, when we memorize God's Word, we're engaging in something far deeper than simply committing verses to memory. We're witnessing the incredible harmony of the Holy Trinity. Jesus is the Word made flesh, and when we internalize His Word, we allow the Holy Spirit to call it to our remembrance. Then the Holy Spirit, in perfect unity with the Son and the Father, uses the Word to magnify Jesus and glorify the Father.

Memorizing Scripture invites us to encounter this divine harmony. This encounter enriches our worship and draws us into deeper reverence and intimacy with God. In both Psalm 29:2 and 1 Chronicles 16:29, God's majesty, power, and splendor are magnified, and 1 Chronicles further reminds us to bring our whole selves as an offering before God. As we do, we step into the fullness of true worship.

Commit to memorizing one verse or passage and allow the Holy Spirit to bring it to life in your worship.

Today I…

SEPTEMBER 15

A CONSUMING FIRE

Since we are receiving a kingdom that cannot be shaken, let us be thankful, and so worship God acceptably with reverence and awe, for our "God is a consuming fire."

HEBREWS 12:28–29 NIV

The unshakable nature of God's kingdom should stir in us a deeper awareness of His sovereignty and our dependence on Him. The phrase *"Our 'God is a consuming fire'"* reminds us not to approach God casually or lightly but with utmost respect. Throughout Scripture, God's consuming fire is not only a display of His power but also a refining force. Malachi 3:3, for example, describes God as a refiner, purifying us like silver. Isaiah 48:10 reminds us that God refines us in the furnace of affliction. His fire isn't meant to destroy but to cleanse and purify our hearts, making us holy as He is holy.

When we come before God in worship, we do so with reverence, acknowledging that we are standing before a holy and all-powerful God whose presence demands awe. This reverence doesn't restrict our worship—it deepens it. When we recognize God's greatness, our awe and wonder for Him elicits an authentic outpouring of worship.

Let God's consuming fire refine your heart as you humbly approach Him in worship.

Today I…

SEPTEMBER 16

HE IS BEING MADE KNOWN

> "Sing to Adonai, for he has triumphed—this is being made known throughout the earth."
>
> ISAIAH 12:5 CJB

I love the Complete Jewish Bible translation of this verse because it feels like a prophetic declaration that God has triumphed, that He will continue to triumph, and that He *"is being made known throughout the earth."* That makes me want to shout. What a mighty God we serve! Who can compare to Him? Who can thwart His plans? Who can stand against Him and succeed? No one!

"With my God, I can scale a wall" (Psalm 18:29 NIV), I can outrun horses (1 Kings 18:46), and I can do all things (Philippians 4:13). Can sickness stand against Him? No, nothing. Still struggling to believe it? Check out Exodus 15:6; 2 Chronicles 20:6; Job 42:2; Proverbs 21:30; Isaiah 14:27; Matthew 19:26; Romans 8:31–39; and 1 John 4:4, to name a few.

Feast on these verses today and prophetically declare these truths over yourself, your circumstances, your family, your work, and your neighborhood.

Today I…

SEPTEMBER 17

BY GOD ALONE

"'You are Adonai, you alone. You made heaven, the heaven of heavens, with all their array, the earth and all the things that are in it, the seas and all that is in them; and you preserve them all. The army of heaven worships you.'"

NEHEMIAH 9:6 CJB

Nehemiah 9:6 declares God's sovereignty as the creator and sustainer of all things. It affirms that He alone is worthy of worship. Everything in heaven and on earth exists by His will and is sustained by His power. When we worship, we recognize God's supremacy and acknowledge our dependence on Him for all things. This verse offers a glimpse into heaven, where the army of heaven worships God without ceasing, constantly in awe of His majesty. Their unending adoration shows us that worship is the natural response to God's greatness.

When we worship, we join this eternal chorus, echoing the heavenly response to His glory. The same God who spoke the universe into existence holds together every breath, heartbeat, and moment of our lives. Think about that: The God who upholds the stars is intimately involved in your life, sustaining you every moment.

Listen to the song "We Crown You King of Glory" by Lindy Cofer.

Today I…

SEPTEMBER 18

WORSHIP FROM VICTORY

Oh, clap your hands, all you peoples!
Shout to God with the voice of triumph!

Psalm 47:1 nkjv

Today's verse is a joyful call to worship, urging all people to respond to God with exuberant praise. Clapping hands and shouting to God with triumph are expressions of victory and celebration. When we worship God with such passion, we declare His sovereignty over every situation in our lives. Worship becomes a powerful and prophetic act of faith as we acknowledge that God has already won the victory. Tony Evans reminded us, "You are not fighting *for* victory—you are fighting *from* victory. This battle has already been won!"[29] This truth transforms our worship, filling it with boldness and joy.

In Christ, we have triumphed over sin, death, and the forces of darkness, and our worship should reflect this victory with joy that knows no bounds. As we worship with a sense of triumph, we are connecting to the heart of God, who desires to see His people filled with the joy of His victory. Every clap, every shout, declares that no matter what we face, God is in control, and He is victorious.

Worship from a place of victory.

Today I…

---

29 Tony Evans, *Victory in Spiritual Warfare* (Harvest House, 2011), 12.

SEPTEMBER 19

I BREATHE YOU IN

Serve the Lord with gladness!
Come into his presence with singing!

PSALM 100:2 ESV

Worship through song is a pathway to encountering God. Singing doesn't just bring us into His presence, but it also reflects the divine exchange that takes place in worship. When we sing, we are mirroring God Himself. God sings over us with joy (Zephaniah 3:17), and in response, we breathe in His love and breathe out our praise. It's a beautiful, cyclical exchange: Our songs of worship rise to God, and His love and presence fill us in return. This divine exchange draws us into a deeper relationship with Him, making our singing more than just melody. It becomes communion with our Creator.

Singing also allows us to express emotions and truths that go beyond words. As we lift our voices in worship, we enter a space of vulnerability where God meets us. In those moments, anxiety can give way to peace, and sorrow can turn to joy as the power of song shifts our perspective and fills us with His strength.

Listen to the song "All of a Sudden" by Elevation Worship and breathe in the Holy Spirit.

Today I…

SEPTEMBER 20

KEYS TO THE KINGDOM

Enter into His gates with thanksgiving, and into His courts with praise. Be thankful to Him, and bless His name.

PSALM 100:4 NKJV

In today's verse, we see a clear order for approaching God: first with thanksgiving, then with praise. Thanksgiving opens the gates, and praise brings us into His courts. This isn't random: Gratitude and worship are key to experiencing God's presence. Thanksgiving sets the foundation, shifting our focus from our circumstances to God's faithfulness. It's the first step through the gates, and it allows us to leave behind distractions. Gratitude opens our hearts to receive from God by recognizing His goodness.

Praise then draws us deeper into His presence, into His courts. While thanksgiving acknowledges what God has done, praise focuses on who He is—His holiness, love, and power. This progression moves us closer to God's heart, drawing us into a deeper encounter with God, filling us with His glory, making room for us to hear from heaven.

Begin your day by thanking God for His blessings, then transition into praising Him for His character. Note how this flow leads you deeper into His presence.

Today I…

SEPTEMBER 21

SPEAK LIFE

All day long my mouth will tell of your righteous deeds and acts of salvation, though their number is past my knowing.

PSALM 71:15 CJB

In heaven, we'll never exhaust reasons to praise God—His greatness is endlessly revealed. But here and now, sometimes worship can feel difficult, usually because we've stopped truly worshiping and allowed our thoughts to drift to our problems instead of God's majesty. When this happens, we should follow David's example—preaching truth to our own souls and shifting our focus from our struggle to the greatness of God. Remember, your words have power (Proverbs 18:21). Likewise, science shows that your brain responds to the words you speak as if they are reality. This is called neuroplasticity—the brain's ability to reorganize itself based on thoughts and experiences.

When we speak the truth of who God is despite our circumstances, we shift our perspective and renew our minds. For example, when we're in financial trouble, we should declare, "God, I praise You because You are my Provider, and You promise to meet all my needs." In doing so, we retrain our thoughts and usher in peace. Speaking life isn't just positive thinking—it's actually transforming our hearts and minds with God's truth.

Thank God for five things about Him. Chances are you'll keep going.

Today I…

SEPTEMBER 22

PRAISE THE LORD

> Praise the LORD, my soul; all my inmost being, praise his holy name. Praise the LORD, my soul, and forget not all his benefits—who forgives all your sins and heals all your diseases, who redeems your life from the pit and crowns you with love and compassion, who satisfies your desires with good things so that your youth is renewed like the eagle's.
>
> PSALM 103:1–5 NIV

Psalm 103 is a beautiful call to worship God with everything in us, especially when we're in difficult seasons. It's easy to become overwhelmed by life's challenges and lose sight of the blessings God has already poured out. Yet as we reflect on His benefits, we're reminded of who God is. He's the one who forgives our sins, heals our diseases, redeems us from despair, and crowns us with His love and compassion. These are promises that God continues to fulfill.

God satisfies our desires with good things and renews our strength like the eagle's (Isaiah 40:31). His love doesn't just meet our needs—it also lifts us up, restores our energy, and gives us hope.

Pause and remember all that God has done. Let this reflection fill your heart with praise. You can know that the God who forgives, heals, redeems, and renews is faithful in every circumstance.

Today I…

SEPTEMBER 23

HIGHER WAYS

Seek Adonai while he is available, call on him while he is still nearby. Let the wicked person abandon his way and the evil person his thoughts; let him return to Adonai, and he will have mercy on him; let him return to our God, for he will freely forgive. "For my thoughts are not your thoughts, and your ways are not my ways," says Adonai. "As high as the sky is above the earth are my ways higher than your ways, and my thoughts than your thoughts."

Isaiah 55:6–9 CJB

Understanding Scripture in context is crucial. Otherwise, we risk adopting incomplete theology that misrepresents God's character. We often hear the statement "God's ways are higher than ours" used as a blanket explanation for things we don't understand. While true, that's not what this passage means.

Isaiah 55:6–9 reveals God's heart of mercy. While our natural inclination might be to punish those who do wrong or seek retribution, God's response is radically different. He offers mercy and forgiveness. This is what makes God's ways higher than ours: His endless compassion even for those we might consider undeserving. When we see how God chooses grace over judgment and forgiveness over punishment, our hearts should be moved to praise Him.

Let your worship flow from a heart that praises God's compassion.

Today I…

SEPTEMBER 24

GOD'S RADICAL NATURE

The LORD is compassionate and gracious, slow to anger, abounding in love. He will not always accuse, nor will he harbor his anger forever; he does not treat us as our sins deserve or repay us according to our iniquities. For as high as the heavens are above the earth, so great is his love for those who fear him; as far as the east is from the west, so far has he removed our transgressions from us.

PSALM 103:8–12 NIV

Today's Scripture passage echoes yesterday's verses from Isaiah 55, revealing more of God's character. He's compassionate, gracious, slow to anger, and overflowing with love. Remember, God's love for us is not bound by human limitations; His ways are higher. Instead of repaying us for our sins, He separates them from us *"as far as the east is from the west,"* removing our guilt and shame. His love is immeasurable, endless, and freely available to those who fear Him.

We're called to reflect God's radical nature, and we are empowered by the Holy Spirit to respond to situations in ways contrary to our flesh. As new creations, we're no longer bound by old ways, and God's love enables us to extend His mercy and grace to others.

Worship God for His infinite love and mercy in paying the wages of our sin in full.

Today I…

SEPTEMBER 25

TO THE KING OF THE AGES

To the King of the ages, immortal, invisible, the only God, be honor and glory forever and ever. Amen.

1 TIMOTHY 1:17 ESV

Today's verse offers a beautiful doxology that lifts our eyes to the majesty of God. He's the *"King of the ages,"* reigning not just over our present circumstances but over all time. He's eternal, immortal, and invisible, standing outside the limitations of time and space. His greatness is unmatched. He's beyond human comprehension yet intimately involved in our lives. No human can fully grasp His essence, yet we're invited to worship Him, giving honor and glory to the one who rules forever.

Again, Paul reminded us that God's ways are higher than ours and His existence is beyond what our finite minds can fully understand. And yet this eternal, all-powerful God, in His boundless love, draws near to us. This verse challenges us to worship Him with awe and reverence. God isn't just a powerful historical figure—He's the eternal King, sovereign over every moment of our lives. When we acknowledge His greatness, we're joining in an eternal chorus that gives honor and glory to the only true God.

Ask the Holy Spirit to reveal another aspect of His limitless nature to you.

Today I…

SEPTEMBER 26

ALL CREATION SINGS

"I tell you," he replied, "if they keep quiet, the stones will cry out."

LUKE 19:40 NIV

Jesus responded to the religious leaders who wanted to silence the people's praise during His triumphal entry, revealing a profound truth: Worship is unstoppable. Creation is designed to worship the Creator. This idea deepens with the knowledge that stones vibrate at frequencies beyond human hearing. Scientists are finding that when these vibrations are translated into a range we can hear, they sound like music.

Even the seemingly silent stones beneath our feet are reverberating with sound. They bear witness to the Creator in their own way, testifying that all of creation is meant to give God glory. The very earth will continue the symphony of worship, whether or not we join in. Yet for us, worship is not an obligation; it's a spiritual necessity. It aligns us with the deepest truths of the universe—that God is worthy of all praise. When we lift our voices, we join a chorus that transcends time and space. As Jesus told us, if we remain silent, even the stones—ever vibrating in imperceptible music—will cry out.

Don't let a rock cry out in your place! Join with creation and praise Him.

Today I…

SEPTEMBER 27

A SACRIFICE OF PRAISE

Through him, therefore, let us offer God a sacrifice of praise continually. For this is the natural product of lips that acknowledge his name.

HEBREWS 13:15 CJB

Sacrifice implies that something costs us dearly. Sacrifice may require physical effort, surrender of our time or possessions, or perseverance through trials. A sacrifice of praise means praising God not only in times of joy but also in moments of pain, loss, or confusion. Offering praise in difficult seasons reminds us that our circumstances don't define our worship; God's unchanging nature does. When we truly consider who Jesus is and what He's done for us, praise becomes an instinctive response, regardless of the season we're in.

By praising God through hardships, we declare both His sovereignty over our lives and our trust in His goodness. Our praise becomes a fragrant offering, rising up to heaven as a testament to our faith in who God is. Worship as a response expedites the refining process of our hearts, matures us, and readies us for whatever God is preparing in our current season. It is an act of faith that transcends our emotions and current struggles as we recognize that God is worthy of praise in every season.

Worship the Lord. Pour yourself out so He can pour Himself in.

Today I…

SEPTEMBER 28

THE HEART OF WORSHIP

You do not delight in sacrifice, or I would bring it; you do not take pleasure in burnt offerings. My sacrifice, O God, is a broken spirit; a broken and contrite heart you, God, will not despise.

PSALM 51:16–17 NIV

God doesn't desire external sacrifices but a heart posture that's humbled, yielded, and teachable. It's easy to fall into the trap of performing religious duties or singing songs out of routine, but God isn't impressed by outward rituals. He wants our hearts. Worship flows from a place of humility, from the recognition that we need God's mercy and grace. When we truly worship, we are real with God, coming before Him with a heart laid bare, not trying to impress but simply offering Him all that we are.

When you approach God with a broken and contrite heart, acknowledging your weaknesses and failures, He draws near. True worship happens when you set aside your pride and allow God to transform your heart. In those moments of vulnerability, your connection with God deepens, and you experience His love and grace in profound ways.

Listen to the song "On the Altar" by UpperRoom. Bring your heart to God exactly as it is. Don't focus on external acts but focus on offering Him your true, authentic self.

Today I…

SEPTEMBER 29

WORSHIP'S HEALING PROMISE

"Worship the LORD your God, and his blessing will be on your food and water. I will take away sickness from among you."

EXODUS 23:25 NIV

Worship not only expresses our love for God but also activates the promise of God's protection and healing. Worship is a powerful spiritual tool that aligns us with God's heart. Through worship, we move beyond the natural realm and enter into God's presence, inviting His transformative power into our lives. Worship not only brings us closer to God but also creates an atmosphere where His healing and provision can manifest.

A powerful testimony from Joseph Prince's ministry recounts a man who, after suffering a heart attack, attended a church service. During worship, he felt a healing power flow through him, leading to a complete and unexplainable recovery.[30] His testimony serves as a powerful reminder that worship invites God's intervention. When we take time to truly worship, we set the stage for physical, emotional, and mental healing as well as spiritual renewal. In moments of genuine worship, God's presence can profoundly impact our daily struggles and needs, bringing peace, restoration, and divine intervention.

Worship God despite your health or circumstances.

Today I…

---

30 Gayle B. Tate, "Praise Report: Damaged Heart Healed During Worship," JosephPrince.com, blog.josephprince.com.

SEPTEMBER 30

A FINAL INVITATION

"The hour is coming, and is now here, when the true worshipers will worship the Father in spirit and truth, for the Father is seeking such people to worship him."

JOHN 4:23 ESV

Jesus repeated this phrase, and so will I to close our month on worship. True worshipers must worship in spirit and truth. This type of worship transcends location, form, or tradition. It's not about performing a ritual or being in a particular place. It's about the posture of our hearts and our connection with the Holy Spirit.

Worship in spirit is led by the Holy Spirit, who draws us into deeper intimacy with God. It's a spiritual encounter that lifts us beyond the natural world into the heavenly realm. Worship in truth is about aligning our worship with the reality of who God is. It's rooted in the truth of His Word, not in our emotions or circumstances. When we worship in truth, we're declaring the unchanging nature of God—His holiness, power, love, and grace. God is seeking worshipers who will approach Him with sincere hearts, worshiping in spirit and truth.

Make it a daily habit to invite the Holy Spirit into your morning. Listen to at least one worship song as you get ready.

Today I…

OCTOBER

Spiritual Warfare:
Satan, We're Gonna Tear
Your Kingdom Down

OCTOBER 1

THIS IS WAR

We are not struggling against human beings, but against the rulers, authorities and cosmic powers governing this darkness, against the spiritual forces of evil in the heavenly realm.

EPHESIANS 6:12 CJB

October is a month of high demonic activity. Witches are real, and they're not cute or innocent. But they're also not more powerful than even a new Christian. Satan is not God's counterpart—that would imply that Satan is equal and opposite to God. Satan is a created being, and all of hell trembles at even the thought of Jesus (James 2:19). To overcome Satan, your focus must remain on Jesus. The Enemy wants to divert your attention to himself and sin, but your victory comes by exalting Jesus, who has already overcome the Enemy.

The more you fix your eyes on Christ, the less room the Enemy has to distract or discourage you. Graham Cooke teaches extensively on the concept of different levels of heaven throughout Scripture and how they relate to spiritual warfare. He emphasizes that as we pray for God's kingdom to come, it crushes the enemies residing in the lower heaven as it descends.[31]

This month, let's remember whom we are at war against, focus on how big God is, and call down His presence and kingdom.

Today I…

---

31 Graham Cooke, *Beholding and Becoming* (Brilliant Bookhouse, 2015), 23.

OCTOBER 2

ARMOR UP

Use all the armor and weaponry that God provides, so that you will be able to stand against the deceptive tactics of the Adversary....So take up every piece of war equipment God provides; so that when the evil day comes, you will be able to resist; and when the battle is won, you will still be standing. Therefore, stand! Have the belt of truth buckled around your waist, put on righteousness for a breastplate.

EPHESIANS 6:11, 13–14 CJB

Spiritual warfare isn't optional—it's inevitable. As believers, we are constantly engaged in a battle against the spiritual forces of darkness. Ephesians 6 reminds us that we're not defenseless in this battle. God provides us with spiritual armor to withstand the deceptive tactics of the Enemy.

The armor represents the power and authority we have in Christ. The *"belt of truth"* holds everything together, anchoring us in God's Word and the truth about who He is and who we are in Him. The *"breastplate of righteousness"* protects us from the Enemy's lies. In Christ, we are made righteous; this is our identity. We must declare and remember our righteousness in Christ to guard our hearts against Satan's lies taking root.

Each morning this month, pray through each piece of spiritual armor, putting it on in faith.

Today I…

OCTOBER 3

ADVANCE!

Wear on your feet the readiness that comes from the Good News of shalom. Always carry the shield of trust, with which you will be able to extinguish all the flaming arrows of the Evil One.

EPHESIANS 6:15–16 CJB

To stand firm in spiritual warfare, we must wear every piece of armor God provides. The Enemy is relentless, firing darts of doubt, fear, sickness, and financial calamity at us, but God equips us with everything we need. The shield of faith is crucial for extinguishing the Enemy's attacks before they take root in our hearts and minds. When faced with fear or struggle, we don't have to accept defeat. We can raise the shield of faith, trusting that God is who He says He is. Instead of being overwhelmed, we can remember that God is greater than the Enemy.

    Satan cannot do anything he hasn't been permitted to do—by God or by us. Faith empowers us to reject the attack and quench the Enemy's flaming darts. Just as shoes give us stability and allow us to move forward, being grounded in the gospel of peace provides the confidence to stand firm in God's love, hold our ground, and even advance to take new ground.

Listen to the song "No One" by Elevation Worship and make it your war cry.

Today I…

OCTOBER 4

EQUIPPED FOR VICTORY

Take the helmet of deliverance; along with the sword given by the Spirit, that is, the Word of God; as you pray at all times, with all kinds of prayers and requests, in the Spirit, vigilantly and persistently, for all God's people.

EPHESIANS 6:17–18 CJB

The helmet of salvation, or deliverance, protects our minds, shielding us from the lies and deceptions the Enemy tries to plant in our thoughts. It reminds us of the eternal security we have in Christ. No matter the accusations or attacks, we rest in the assurance that our salvation is secure, and this assurance should guard our minds from confusion and despair.

Alongside the helmet, we have the sword of the Spirit—God's Word. The Word is not just a defense but also an offensive weapon. When we declare Scripture, we cut through the Enemy's lies with God's truth. Jesus modeled this during His temptation in the wilderness (Matthew 4). God's Word is sharper than any sword (Hebrews 4:12), and when we speak it, we wield divine power. But none of this armor is complete without prayer. Through prayer, we activate the armor, staying in tune with God's voice and responding to His Spirit.

Declare Ephesians 6:10–18 over yourself today and put on each piece of armor with boldness.

Today I…

OCTOBER 5

WAIT ON THE LORD

They who wait for the Lord shall renew their strength; they shall mount up with wings like eagles; they shall run and not be weary; they shall walk and not faint.

ISAIAH 40:31 ESV

Patience is a rare virtue in a world demanding instant results. Yet waiting on the Lord is a powerful act of faith and trust. God promises that when we wait for His timing, profound transformation occurs that enables us to soar above our challenges. God's timing is different from ours (2 Peter 3:8–9). We are in God's river, and it has a flow even when we cannot perceive it. He is taking us somewhere specific, and we shouldn't swim ahead of Him or against the current.

Ultimately, we must surrender our impatience and allow God to work in His perfect time. Patience isn't just a virtue but also a weapon in spiritual warfare. When the Israelites faced Jericho, they waited on the Lord's instructions. Their patience and obedience led to a miraculous victory (Joshua 6).

If you find yourself in a season of waiting, ask God to renew your strength, and trust that He's at work. Embrace this period as a time of growth and preparation, knowing that God's timing is perfect and that His plans for you are good.

Today I…

OCTOBER 6

YOU ARE HIS TEMPLE

The cloud covered the tent of meeting, and the glory of the Lord filled the tabernacle. Moses could not enter the tent of meeting because the cloud had settled on it, and the glory of the Lord filled the tabernacle.

EXODUS 40:34–35 NIV

Exodus 40 details specific instructions Moses followed to make a temple worthy of God's presence. Isn't it astounding that Jesus' sacrifice on the cross and resurrection rendered us as temples worthy of God's indwelling presence? What brings me to absolute tears of adoration and praise is that the Bible says when we worship God, His presence fills the temple, and in the new covenant, we are the temple. When we worship, He comes and fills us, leaving no more room for sin, shame, or misplaced identity.

Jesus' response to the weight of sin on the cross was worship (Psalm 22). Worship as a response to trials is a powerful weapon against the Enemy. Instead of reacting with anger or fear, we can use worship to invite God's presence into our circumstances, making the Enemy tremble. God inhabits the praises of His people, driving out darkness and bringing light to every corner of our lives.

Listen to the song "Glory, Honor, Power" by Influence Music and consider that you are now the temple of the Holy Spirit.

Today I…

OCTOBER 7

CHRIST'S TRIUMPH

Stripping the rulers and authorities of their power, he made a public spectacle of them, triumphing over them by means of the stake.

COLOSSIANS 2:15 CJB

When Jesus died on the cross ("*the stake*"), He didn't just secure our salvation. He also disarmed the rulers and authorities of their power. The cross wasn't a moment of defeat but one of ultimate triumph. In Roman times, publicly parading defeated enemies symbolized complete victory, an image Paul used to describe Christ's triumph over evil. Christ's sacrifice stripped Satan and his minions of their authority, rendering their accusations powerless against those who are in Christ. The Enemy has been humiliated, exposed, and utterly defeated.

You are not striving to win this spiritual battle. You are standing firm in a victory that has already been secured through Christ. John Paul Jackson teaches that hell has only the authority we give it.[32] Christ gave us His authority (Luke 10:19) and stripped Satan of his power. Satan can only pick up what we set down. If we lay aside our God-given authority through fear, doubt, or sin, the Enemy seizes it. But when we stand firm in the authority Christ has given us, the Enemy remains powerless.

Today, declare Christ's victory over any area where the Enemy has tried to hold power.

Today I…

---

[32] John Paul Jackson, "Authority and Power—John Paul Jackson," posted August 19, 2020, by Frontline Church, YouTube, youtube.com.

OCTOBER 8

THE SWORD OF THE SPIRIT

Although we do live in the world, we do not wage war in a worldly way; because the weapons we use to wage war are not worldly. On the contrary, they have God's power for demolishing strongholds.

2 CORINTHIANS 10:3–4 CJB

In *Girls with Swords*, Lisa Bevere encouraged believers to wield the Word of God like a sword, using it to cut through deception and fear and break chains off captives. However, Bevere also emphasized that while the Word of God is a weapon, we must wield it with the purpose of setting captives free and speaking life—not to harm, condemn, or tear others down. When used carelessly or with wrong intentions, even the powerful truths of Scripture can be twisted to wound rather than heal.[33]

As we engage in spiritual warfare, it's vital to remember that the sword of the Spirit is given to us for healing and restoration, not for judgment or destruction. Our fight is not against people but against spiritual forces, and God has equipped us with powerful weapons that operate through His love, grace, and truth. Let's use His Word wisely, always seeking to bring life, healing, and freedom wherever we go.

Use your words today to speak life, truth, and freedom into someone's situation.

Today I…

---

33 Lisa Bevere, *Girls with Swords* (Waterbrook, 2013), 135.

OCTOBER 9

CAPTIVE THOUGHTS

We demolish arguments and every arrogance that raises itself up against the knowledge of God; we take every thought captive and make it obey the Messiah. And when you have become completely obedient, then we will be ready to punish every act of disobedience.

2 CORINTHIANS 10:4–6 CJB

Spiritual warfare often happens in our minds. We have divine power to tear down mental and spiritual barriers that hinder our ability to know and obey God. In Hebrew, a *stronghold* refers to fortified walls around cities. Similarly, we build emotional walls to "protect" ourselves, but they often trap us instead. Throughout *The Bait of Satan*, John Bevere described how emotional strongholds, like unforgiveness or bitterness, can hold us captive if we don't tear them down.[34]

Capturing every thought is crucial in spiritual warfare. The Enemy bombards our minds, and if we're not vigilant, those lies or offenses can take root and become strongholds. But in Christ, we have the authority to capture every thought that's contrary to God's truth and make it obedient to Him. You can actively choose to replace the Enemy's lies with God's Word, allowing truth to transform your thinking. Once you master this, you're ready for war.

Identify your strongholds. Capture thoughts that don't align with God's Word and replace them with His truth.

Today I…

---

[34] John Bevere, *The Bait of Satan: Living Free from the Deadly Trap of Offense* (Charisma House, 2014).

OCTOBER 10

MELT LIKE WAX

*The mountains melt like wax before the Lord,
before the Lord of all the earth.*

PSALM 97:5 ESV

In spiritual warfare, we must engage with God's kingdom, not with the Enemy. When we place too much attention on the schemes of the Enemy, we inadvertently make him appear larger and more powerful than he is. When we fix our eyes on the Lord instead, His power and majesty come into clear view. Psalm 97:5 reminds us that even the most insurmountable obstacles—the *"mountains"* in our lives—melt like wax in the presence of the Lord.

Whether it's fear, doubt, or spiritual attack, nothing can stand before God's greatness. Today's verse invites us to shift our focus away from the battle and onto the one who has already won the victory. When you engage God's kingdom by focusing on His power and glory, the mountains begin to dissolve, and you find peace in the presence of the Almighty. When we magnify God in our thoughts, prayers, and worship, the Enemy's influence diminishes. Worship becomes our weapon, and the more we exalt Jesus, the more the Enemy's tactics fade into insignificance.

**Listen to the song "What a Beautiful Name"
by Hillsong Worship.**

Today I...

OCTOBER 11

TEST THE SPIRITS

Dear friends, don't trust every spirit. On the contrary, test the spirits to see whether they are from God; because many false prophets have gone out into the world. Here is how you recognize the Spirit of God: every spirit which acknowledges that Yeshua the Messiah came as a human being is from God.

1 John 4:1–2 CJB

Discernment is crucial. Not every voice, teaching, or idea is from God. The Bible warns us that false prophets come as wolves in sheep's clothing (Matthew 7:15). This means that though they often present themselves as fellow believers or sources of truth, their subtle distortions of God's Word lead to destruction. Their teachings may seem right at first glance, but they ultimately lead to death.

First John 4 instructs us to test the spirits. A key test is whether a spirit or teaching acknowledges that Yeshua came in the flesh. Anyone who denies this central truth is aligned with the spirit of the anti-Messiah. The world is filled with voices that subtly twist Scripture, so we must be vigilant, ensuring we're not led astray by those who claim to speak for God but distort His message.

Ask the Holy Spirit to sharpen your discernment so that you can recognize truth and avoid the traps of false teachings disguised as truth.

Today I…

OCTOBER 12

SATAN'S LIMITATIONS

"Do not be afraid of those who kill the body but cannot kill the soul. Rather, be afraid of the One who can destroy both soul and body in hell."

MATTHEW 10:28 NIV

While Satan is real, his power is limited, and he operates under God's authority. Watchman Nee taught that unless a believer knows their work is complete, they should resist illness and death.[35] Throughout his book *Never Be Sick Again*, Chad Gonzales taught that while Satan may be permitted to bring sickness or adversity, you aren't obligated to accept it.[36]

Healing is always God's ultimate will. Jesus never turned away anyone who came to Him in faith, and He demonstrated God's heart by healing all who were oppressed by the Enemy (Acts 10:38). Yet in a fallen world, some experience delayed healing. This does not mean God is withholding healing—it means we must stand firm in faith, knowing that by Jesus' stripes, we are healed (Isaiah 53:5). As we trust God, we can boldly resist the Enemy and reject anything contrary to God's promises.

Declare God's promises over your life and resist anything contrary to His will.

Today I…

---

[35] Watchman Nee, "Death After the Completion of Our Work," Living Stream Ministry, ministrysamples.org.
[36] Chad Gonzales, *Never Be Sick Again: Access Supernatural Health Through Jesus' Resurrection Power* (Harrison House, 2024).

WORD CURSES

Those who guard their mouths preserve their lives, but those who speak rashly will come to ruin.

PROVERBS 13:3 NIV

Words have incredible power. God created the world through His spoken word, and in Numbers 14, we witness how the Israelites' own words sealed their fate. God was ready to bring them into the promised land, but their grumbling and disbelief led to their demise. In verse 28, God said to them, *"As surely as I live…I will do to you the very thing I heard you say"* (NIV). The Israelites declared defeat over themselves, and though it wasn't God's will that they die in the wilderness, they spoke it into existence.

This isn't just an Old Testament concept. In spiritual warfare, the words we speak have the power to either align us with God's promises or bring curses upon ourselves. As believers, we must be vigilant in guarding our mouths. Our words aren't neutral—they bring either life or death. The words we speak can either build up or tear down, bless or curse, align us with God's will or lead us away from it.

Stop putting word curses on yourself. Repent of the ones you've spoken and ask God that they be canceled. Speak life and watch things change.

Today I…

OCTOBER 14

LEGAL GROUND

Curses will not harm someone who is innocent; they are like sparrows or swallows that fly around and never land.

PROVERBS 26:2 NCV

I heard a powerful testimony from a former satanic high priest who revealed the persistence with which he cursed a praying church. Day after day, he hurled curses at them, knowing most couldn't land because they were yielded to Jesus and stood innocent before God. However, his strategy was to keep cursing them until he could find a foothold, an area they hadn't yielded to Jesus. He knew that even a small area of vulnerability—such as holding on to offense—would legally allow the curses to land.

Offense, unforgiveness, and hatred create fertile ground for curses to take root. Throughout *The Bait of Satan*, John Bevere warned that offense is one of the primary tools Satan uses to entrap believers.[37] When we hold on to offense, it can grow into bitterness or even hatred, creating a wide opening for the Enemy to move in. First John 4:20 says, *"If anyone says, 'I love God,' and hates his brother, he is a liar"* (CJB). We cannot walk in the fullness of God's love and authority while harboring bitterness toward others.

Invite the Holy Spirit to show you areas of spiritual vulnerability and surrender them to God.

Today I…

---

37 John Bevere, *Bait of Satan: Living Free from the Deadly Trap of Offense* (Charisma House, 2014).

A LITTLE SIN

Be careful! "Just a little yeast makes the whole batch of dough rise."

GALATIANS 5:9 NCV

In spiritual warfare, it's not just the big attacks we need to watch for but also the subtle, hidden influences that can infiltrate our lives. Galatians 5:9 warns us that even a little yeast can affect the entire batch of dough. Similarly, a small amount of unchecked sin can spread and impact every part of our lives, making us vulnerable to the Enemy's schemes.

Satan often gains access through seemingly insignificant compromises—just a bit of unrepented sin, bitterness, or neglect of our spiritual health. It doesn't take much for sin to grow and begin influencing our thoughts, actions, and even those around us. We need to remain vigilant, quick to identify and root out any "yeast" that could compromise our walk with Christ. Spiritual warfare begins by winning small victories, choosing repentance, and allowing the Holy Spirit to remove anything that threatens to spread and hinder our spiritual growth.

Ask the Holy Spirit to reveal any "yeast" in your life, and let God remove it before it affects every part of your life.

Today I…

OCTOBER 16

ULTIMATE AUTHORITY

At the name of Jesus every knee will bow, of those who are in heaven and on earth and under the earth, and that every tongue will confess that Jesus Christ is Lord, to the glory of God the Father.

PHILIPPIANS 2:10–11 NASB

Satan, his demons, and even death itself must bow in surrender to the lordship of Christ. Let this truth stir boldness in your spirit. As a child of God, you've been given the name of Jesus as a weapon. When you speak His name, chains break, mountains move, and heaven responds. Think of police officers arriving with a search warrant. The moment they arrive with the proper legal documentation, everyone in the building must submit and allow them to proceed, regardless of personal feelings or resistance. In the same way, when you invoke the name of Jesus, you carry the highest authority in the spiritual realm.

The forces of darkness have no choice but to submit and surrender to His authority. Jesus' name isn't just a phrase—it signals a power and authority that changes everything. Use it with confidence, knowing all of heaven stands behind you when you invoke His name.

Declare the name of Jesus over every situation in your life. Watch the atmosphere shift as His authority is released.

Today I…

OCTOBER 17

FEELINGS ASIDE

"He will yet fill your mouth with laughter and your lips with shouts of joy."

JOB 8:21 CJB

Kenneth Hagin shared a powerful testimony of how, during one of the darkest moments in his life, when he was experiencing great pain from an illness, the Holy Spirit instructed him to laugh. Feeling weighed down by the devil's taunts, Hagin couldn't at first. But the Holy Spirit persisted, urging him to laugh anyway. Hagin, barely able to muster the effort, began to pretend laugh: "Ha. Ha. Ha." He realized that the devil didn't know the difference between real and pretend laughter. Hagin then proclaimed 1 Peter 2:24—that Christ has already obtained healing for us all—and his symptoms immediately disappeared.[38]

The Enemy wants to paralyze us with fear, despair, and defeat. His goal is to keep us in a pit so deep that we can't think or move. But even when our emotions say otherwise, we can still speak life and declare God's authority and joy over our circumstances. Our words, empowered by faith, move things in the spirit realm. The Enemy doesn't care whether we feel powerful. He recognizes the authority of God's Word and the name of Jesus spoken in faith.

Even when your emotions tell you otherwise, speak life.

Today I…

---

[38] Kenneth Hagin, "Kenneth Hagin—Laughing at the Devil," posted November 29, 2023, by OnlyTheGodlySurvive, YouTube, youtube.com.

OCTOBER 18

FEARLESS

The LORD is my light and my salvation—whom shall I fear?
The LORD is the stronghold of my life—
of whom shall I be afraid?

PSALM 27:1 NIV

Fear is one of Satan's most powerful tools in spiritual warfare. It paralyzes, blinds, and hinders us from God's calling. When we give in to fear, we unwittingly give the Enemy access to our life and family. We also hand him permission to influence our thoughts, actions, and even our prayers. The Enemy uses fear to magnify obstacles, distort reality, and shift our focus from God's power to our problems.

Psalm 27:1 reminds us that God is our light and salvation. No matter how strong the Enemy's attacks may feel, God is stronger. He is the stronghold of your life—the one who holds you secure even in the midst of spiritual battles. When you focus on God, fear loses its power. The Enemy preys on fear because it's a distraction. But when you refuse to bow to fear, you strip the Enemy of one of his primary weapons. Fear cannot exist in God's presence. As you shift your gaze to Jesus, the light of His presence shines in the darkest places, scattering fear and restoring peace. Fear does not control your destiny—God does.

Reject the Enemy's attempts to intimidate you.

Today I…

CHOSEN

You are a chosen people, a royal priesthood, a holy nation, God's special possession, that you may declare the praises of him who called you out of darkness into his wonderful light.

1 Peter 2:9 NIV

Your identity in Christ is your greatest weapon in spiritual warfare. When you know who you are as a child of God, you don't react in fear, frustration, or doubt. You respond in faith and confidence. The Enemy's primary tactic is to make you forget your identity and authority, so he bombards you with lies and distractions. However, when you know that you're in Christ, you operate from a place of secured victory rather than trying to achieve it yourself.

The Enemy's goal is to get us to engage in battles with our emotions, flesh, or natural circumstances, but we fight true warfare in the Spirit with the weapons of God—His Word, faith, prayer, and our authority in Christ. The Enemy tries to keep us operating in our own strength, but the power of God is what destroys strongholds. It's only when we remain in Christ, declaring who He is and who we are in Him, that we can demolish the Enemy's schemes.

Declare your identity in Christ and walk in the authority He's given you.

Today I…

OCTOBER 20

PRAYING IN THE SPIRIT

You, dear friends, [build] yourselves up in your most holy faith and [pray] in the Holy Spirit.

JUDE 1:20 NIV

One of the most powerful tools in spiritual warfare is praying in the Spirit. Praying in the Spirit is essential to building ourselves up and drawing strength from God. When we pray in tongues, we're speaking mysteries to God, and though our minds may not understand, our spirits are being strengthened for battle (1 Corinthians 14:2–4). It allows us to pray God's perfect will even when we don't know what to pray ourselves (Romans 8:26).

If you haven't received the baptism of the Holy Spirit, ask God today. Luke 11:13 promises that God will give the Holy Spirit to those who ask. Invite Him to fill you, and surrender fully to Him. Don't worry if it feels unfamiliar—yielding is a step of faith. When you sense the Spirit's presence, speak out in faith, trusting He will provide the words (Acts 2:4).[39]

Pray in the Spirit or ask God to baptize you in the Holy Spirit and begin to pray in faith.

Today I…

---

39 For guidance, *The Holy Spirit and His Gifts* by Kenneth Hagin is a trusted resource on the baptism of the Holy Spirit and praying in tongues.

OCTOBER 21

WORSHIP AS A WEAPON

> About midnight Paul and Silas were praying and singing hymns to God, and the other prisoners were listening to them. Suddenly there was such a violent earthquake that the foundations of the prison were shaken. At once all the prison doors flew open, and everyone's chains came loose.
>
> ACTS 16:25–26 NIV

In one of their darkest moments, Paul and Silas didn't focus on their suffering. Instead, they worshiped God, and something incredible happened. As they sang, their praises shattered spiritual and physical barriers. The prison doors opened, and everyone's chains fell off. This is the power of praise in spiritual warfare. Worship is a weapon in the spiritual realm. When we lift our voices in praise, we align with heaven and bring God into our battles. Praise confuses the Enemy and shifts the atmosphere.

When we choose to worship in the face of opposition, we release God's power to break chains and open doors. It's important to remember that worship isn't about our feelings—it's about who God is. Even in times of fear, pain, or confusion, we can praise God for His goodness, faithfulness, and sovereignty. When we focus on His greatness rather than the battle we're facing, we allow His power to change everything.

Listen to the song "Surrounded" by UpperRoom.

Today I…

FASTING IN SPIRITUAL WARFARE

"Is not this the kind of fasting I have chosen: to loose the chains of injustice and untie the cords of the yoke, to set the oppressed free and break every yoke?"

ISAIAH 58:6 NIV

Fasting is a powerful yet often underutilized weapon in spiritual warfare. In Isaiah 58, God outlined the purpose of fasting. He showed that it's not an empty ritual but a path to spiritual breakthroughs. Lisa Bevere teaches that fasting isn't about changing our appearance but changing our perspective.[40] Denying ourselves food shifts our focus on physical needs to a deeper spiritual awareness, helping us perceive God's presence and align with His will.

Dan Mohler emphasizes that fasting humbles us, allowing God's strength to manifest in our weaknesses.[41] It heightens spiritual sensitivity, empowering us to discern and counter the Enemy's schemes. As we deny our flesh, we become attuned to the Spirit, enabling God to work deeply within us. Fasting liberates us from physical cravings and spiritual bondage. When we fast with the right heart, God promises to move mightily, breaking chains and setting captives free in our lives and communities.

Consider a fast to deepen your reliance on God and enhance your spiritual vision.

Today I…

---

40 Lisa Bevere, *Fast Forward: The Untapped Catalyst to Spiritual Growth*, (pub. by author), 86–87, PDF.
41 Dan Mohler, "HCSKL 2011 Day 32 Dan Mohler," posted January 14, 2014, by Harvest Chapel PA, YouTube, youtube.com.

OCTOBER 23

COVENANT PRAYER

> "Where two or three are gathered in my name, there am I among them."
>
> MATTHEW 18:20 ESV

Unity among believers is a formidable weapon in spiritual warfare. When we come together as one, our prayers and actions resonate with a power that can quickly dismantle the Enemy's strongholds. In Matthew 18:20, Jesus assured us of His presence whenever believers gather in His name. This emphasizes the strength of unity within the body of Christ, and covenant-prayer groups embody this principle. Unlike the perversion found in a "coven"—a term hijacked by those practicing witchcraft—*covenant* is a sacred agreement initiated by God. It embodies a divine commitment among His people to support, pray, and stand together against spiritual attacks.

John Bevere highlighted that covenant relationships reflect God's covenant with us, which is strong, unbreakable, and driven by mutual love and purpose.[42] By engaging in covenant prayer, believers access a deeper dimension of spiritual warfare, amplifying their authority in the spiritual realm with the support and strength of a committed community. This collective commitment fosters spiritual growth and resilience, creating an atmosphere where God's presence can move freely, breaking barriers and reinforcing unity.

Join or form a covenant prayer group. Commit to regular times of praying for each other and your community.

Today I…

---

42 John and Lisa Bevere, *The Story of Marriage* (Messenger International, 2014), 22–23.

OCTOBER 24

DIVINE ASSISTANCE

Are not all angels ministering spirits sent to serve those who will inherit salvation?

HEBREWS 1:14 NIV

In spiritual warfare, angels are mighty allies sent by God to protect and aid believers. Their presence reinforces our confidence in God's provision. One profound example of angelic assistance is found in 2 Kings 6. Elisha's servant was terrified when it seemed like it was just the two of them against an entire Aramean army. But when God opened the servant's eyes, the servant saw a mountain full of horses and chariots of fire—God's angelic forces ready to protect them. This illustrates that God's spiritual army surrounds us even when the odds seem overwhelming.

While acknowledging the angels' role, it is always crucial to keep a Christ-centered focus. Our eyes must remain on Jesus, the author and finisher of our faith. Angels work under His authority, executing His will. C. S. Lewis cautioned against an obsession with fallen angels.[43] The same should be said of an obsession with any angel. Our devotion should belong to Christ, through whom we have ultimate victory. Hebrews 1 emphasizes Christ's superiority over angels. Angelic support is part of God's provision, but our primary relationship must always be with Jesus.

Read 2 Kings 6 and notice how Elisha asked for and received God's protection through His angels.

Today I…

---

43 C. S. Lewis, *The Screwtape Letters* (HarperCollins, 2012), ix.

OCTOBER 25

OUTNUMBERED

He answered, "Don't be afraid—those who are with us outnumber those who are with them!"

2 KINGS 6:16 CJB

In 2 Kings 6:16, Elisha reassured his servant, whose eyes were opened to a spiritual reality: God's angelic forces vastly outnumber the Enemy's. This truth also applies to us in spiritual warfare. Scripture reveals that a third of the angels joined Satan's rebellion, leaving two-thirds faithful to God. In other words, even on a bad day, we still outnumber Satan's armies two to one. Additionally, it is crucial to remember that Satan is a created being, not an equally powerful counterpart to God. His power is limited, but God's authority is absolute and infinite.

This comparative strength reminds us of God's sovereign power and the assured victory we have in Christ. In every spiritual battle, we are supported not just by angels but by God's ultimate authority. We stand with confidence, knowing that God's forces are greater than any challenge we face. Elisha's words *"Don't be afraid"* urge us to trust in the invisible yet overwhelming support that God provides. When fear threatens to overtake us, remembering that we are not alone empowers us to face opposition with courage and faith.

Trust in God's overwhelming support, knowing that He is fighting on your behalf and that His power far surpasses any created being.

Today I…

OCTOBER 26

THE UNSTOPPABLE CHURCH

"I tell you, you are Peter, and on this rock I will build my church, and the gates of hell shall not prevail against it."

MATTHEW 16:18 ESV

In Matthew 16:18, Jesus made a powerful declaration that not even the gates of hell—the powers of death and darkness—would prevail against His church. In biblical times, gates symbolized authority and power, often representing the place where leaders made significant decisions. By stating that the gates of hell would not overcome the church, Jesus assured us that all the powers of darkness and death are ultimately impotent in the face of His authority and His gathered body of believers.

We are called to be active participants in God's mission, standing firm in the face of spiritual opposition, knowing that we are part of a victorious assembly. The Enemy's attempts to sow fear, discord, or destruction cannot succeed against us when we are rooted in Christ, our foundation and strength. Charles Spurgeon once said, "The church is not perfect, but woe to the man who finds pleasure in pointing out her imperfections. Christ loved His church, and let us do the same." Our role in spiritual warfare is to support and build up the church, advancing God's kingdom with the confidence that nothing can stop His purposes.

Pray for the strength and unity of the church.

Today I…

OCTOBER 27

RESISTANCE

Submit yourselves, then, to God. Resist the devil, and he will flee from you.

James 4:7 niv

Obedience to God is crucial in spiritual warfare, particularly in resisting temptation that can lead us into sin and conflict. James 4 warns us about entertaining internal desires that battle within us, giving birth to demonic strongholds. Submission to God is the first step in overcoming these temptations. Chad Gonzales teaches that when we choose obedience, we align ourselves with the flow of God's power. This alignment not only strengthens our defenses against the devil but also empowers us to break free from the cycles of sin. Gonzales emphasizes that resisting the Enemy is not just a defensive stance but also an offensive one where we stand firm in the strength of Christ, denying the Enemy any foothold in our lives.[44]

Resisting the devil isn't about our effort alone; it's about actively pursuing holiness and choosing God's truth over the Enemy's lies. James 4:7 promises that when we resist the devil, he will flee from us. Go ahead and laugh in victory at that visual.

Pray over 1 Corinthians 10:13, which assures us that God is faithful and will provide a way out of temptation. Align your desires with God's will, choosing obedience over sin, and tap into His victory.

Today I…

---

44 Chad Gonzales, "Never Get Sick! Stop Letting Satan Steal Your Health," Harrison House, December 3, 2024, harrisonhouse.com.

SPIRITUAL VIGILANCE

Stay sober, stay alert! Your enemy, the Adversary, stalks about like a roaring lion looking for someone to devour.

1 Peter 5:8 CJB

Staying vigilant in spiritual warfare requires us to *"stay sober"* and *"alert."* The Adversary, like a lion on the prowl, seeks moments of weakness to attack. Spiritual vigilance is crucial for maintaining our defense against the Enemy's schemes and involves more than mere awareness; it requires a proactive approach to fortifying our spiritual defenses. Engaging regularly in prayer and worship, immersing ourselves in Scripture, and committing to a lifestyle of holiness are foundational practices that sharpen our spiritual sensitivity. These disciplines equip us to discern truth from deception, ensuring that our minds remain clear and focused on Christ.

In today's world, discernment is especially critical as we consume media and news. John Bevere often emphasizes recognizing the subtle tactics the Enemy uses to incite fear and confusion through various agendas. By being discerning, we can identify ways the Enemy might exploit our distractions, and we can guard our thoughts against fear and remain steadfast in faith. When we maintain a sober and vigilant mind, we are less susceptible to the Enemy's attempts to divert our attention from God.

Stay vigilant against fear and confusion by evaluating, through the lens of God's truth, the media you consume.

Today I…

OCTOBER 29

OH, THE BLOOD

"They have conquered him by the blood of the Lamb and by the word of their testimony, for they loved not their lives even unto death."

REVELATION 12:11 ESV

The blood of Jesus is the cornerstone of victory in spiritual warfare. It signifies His triumph over sin and death, securing our redemption and equipping us with divine authority. When we declare Jesus' blood, we remind the Enemy of his defeat. Lester Sumrall taught extensively about pleading Jesus' blood for protection against Enemy attacks. Pleading the blood of Jesus isn't a ritualistic incantation but rather a profound declaration of faith in the completed work of Christ. As we testify to what Jesus has done for us, our words become powerful weapons that dismantle the strategies of the devil.

Dying to our flesh daily also strengthens our commitment to Christ, allowing us to embrace the spiritual life He offers over worldly desires. When we understand that physical death merely transports us to heaven, we are empowered to live boldly even amid persecution. As Paul stated in Philippians 1:21, *"For to me, to live is Christ and to die is gain"* (NIV). With this mindset, we stand firm in faith and live from a place of victory.

Praise Jesus for His blood. Plead His blood over yourself, your family, friends, and circumstances.

Today I…

OCTOBER 30

THE POWER OF HUMILITY

Humble yourselves before the Lord, and he will lift you up.
JAMES 4:10 NIV

Humility serves as a protective shield in spiritual warfare, allowing God's grace to permeate our lives and fortify us against pride. Pride is a primary tool the Enemy uses to draw us away from God's guidance. Proverbs 16:18 warns, *"Pride goes before destruction, and a haughty spirit before a fall"* (NIV), reflecting Lucifer's downfall when his pride led him to grasp at equality with God. In stark contrast, Philippians 2:6 illustrates Jesus' humility: *"Though he was in the form of God, he did not regard equality with God something to be possessed by force"* (CJB).

Other Bible translations highlight that Jesus did not view equality with God as something to be clung to for advantage, showing that His humility was a deliberate choice He made for our sake. Nineteenth-century evangelist Andrew Murray often emphasized that humility aligns our hearts with God's, fostering true fellowship with Christ and prompting divine upliftment even when we are at our lowest. Humility opens us to receive God's wisdom and strength amid challenges.

Approach your interactions with a servant's heart so that you reflect Christ's humility in your words and actions.

Today I…

OCTOBER 31

DIVORCE THE OCCULT

"Do not bow down before their gods or worship them or follow their practices. You must demolish them and break their sacred stones to pieces."

EXODUS 23:24 NIV

Halloween is associated with occult practices, drawing many into using tarot cards, playing with Ouija boards, and seeking psychics—tools that open doors to spiritual bondage and deception. Exodus 23:24 commands God's people not to engage in these kinds of dark practices. Instead, we are to demolish and break ties with any elements opposing God's authority. Participating in occult practices invites spiritual oppression and gives the Enemy a foothold in our lives.

True spiritual warfare involves actively removing occult influences and replacing them with God's truth and light. To walk in Christ's promises, we must intentionally reject and dispose of demonic things. Rabbi Jonathan Cahn urges believers to discern and renounce involvement with any form of idolatry or occultism. He teaches that embracing God's light and authority is the key to breaking free from the grip of darkness.[45] By removing these practices, we align ourselves more closely with God and His protective power, ensuring that our spiritual lives remain pure and untainted.

Examine your life for any practices or objects that do not honor God. Commit to removing them and invite God's truth and protection into your home and heart.

Today I…

---

45 Jonathan Cahn, *The Return of the Gods* (Charisma Media, 2022), 261–62.

NOVEMBER

Thanksgiving and a Cornucopia of Wisdom

NOVEMBER 1

NOVEMBER FOUNDATION

> Give thanks to the LORD, for he is good;
> his love endures forever.
>
> PSALM 107:1 NIV

Gratitude is a lifestyle and heart posture that radically transforms your life. Starting your day with thankfulness opens your heart to the fullness of God's goodness and relentless love. Gratitude shifts your perspective, lifting your eyes from your challenges to God's unwavering faithfulness. God is so good! He's always orchestrating your life according to His perfect plan. Gratitude helps you recognize blessings often taken for granted. As you list the things you're thankful for, you'll find that even in trials, God's presence and provision are present. There are close to a billion people without running water in their homes, for example. I think about this almost every time I shower, and I thank God for the blessing He's given.

It is important that you stop focusing on what you *don't* have and really think about all you *do* have. When you express thankfulness, you inspire those around you to reflect on their blessings. This creates an atmosphere of joy and appreciation. Your gratitude can draw others to God as they witness His goodness through your testimony. Every day this month, acknowledge God's fingerprints of grace that surround you and allow that recognition to deepen your relationship with Him.

List five things you're thankful for.

Today I…

NOVEMBER 2

GRATITUDE INTO GENEROSITY

You will be enriched in every way so that you can be generous on every occasion, and through us your generosity will result in thanksgiving to God.

2 CORINTHIANS 9:11 NIV

Gratitude naturally overflows into generosity, forming a beautiful cycle of blessings and giving. When you recognize the abundance of God's blessings in your life, you begin to want to share those blessings with others. This spirit of generosity isn't just an act of kindness; it's a reflection of God's heart. The parable of the Good Samaritan (Luke 10:25–37) illustrates this principle vividly. Through this parable, Jesus confronted the religious leaders to go beyond rituals and recognize who their true neighbor was. In stark contrast to the priest and the Levite, who ignored the injured traveler, it was the Samaritan—someone society deemed unworthy—who showed compassion and took action.

True followers of Christ reflect God's compassion and know that God enriches us so we can bless others on every occasion. When you act with compassion and generosity, you not only meet the needs of others but also fulfill God's purpose. God's generosity can't be outdone: The more you give, the more you experience His abundant blessings in return. Then your acts of love and service can inspire those around you to accept Jesus.

Let gratitude motivate an act of kindness today.

Today I…

NOVEMBER 3

WHY DOES EVIL EXIST?

Every good act of giving and every perfect gift is from above, coming down from the Father who made the heavenly lights; with him there is neither variation nor darkness caused by turning.

JAMES 1:17 CJB

Many people question how an all-powerful, loving God could allow evil and suffering. In his book *The Dragon's Prophecy,* Rabbi Jonathan Cahn asserted that God didn't create evil; God created free will. Satan, before he fell, was a perfectly created angel who sinned through his own free will (Isaiah 14; Ezekiel 28). Cahn wrote, "Free will is a necessity. If one does what is good because one has no choice in doing so, then it is not good.…To allow the choosing of good, one must allow the choosing of its opposite."[46]

Satan's existence serves as a reminder of the reality of choice. Evil doesn't negate the existence of God; instead, it affirms it. Cahn eloquently observed that evil must draw its existence from the good and cannot stand alone. For example, a marriage can exist without adultery, but adultery cannot exist without marriage. Good can flourish independently while evil relies on the framework that goodness provides.

Thank God for free will and the wisdom to answer this question: Why does evil exist?

Today I…

---

[46] Jonathan Cahn, *The Dragon's Prophecy: Israel, the Dark Resurrection, and the End of Days* (FrontLine, 2024), 10–11.

NOVEMBER 4

GRATITUDE SILENCES ANXIETY

Do not be anxious about anything, but in every situation, by prayer and petition, with thanksgiving, present your requests to God.

PHILIPPIANS 4:6 NIV

Thanksgiving in prayer transforms our petitions into profound expressions of trust. When you approach God with a thankful heart, you acknowledge His sovereignty and recognize that He's in control of every situation. This trust fosters peace that dispels anxiety, reminding you that your concerns are in the hands of a loving Father. Studies prove the truth of this verse, showing that fear and anxiety cannot coexist with gratitude. Focusing on what you're thankful for naturally pushes out feelings of fear and worry.

Dave Roberson emphasized that gratitude in prayer opens channels for God's grace.[47] It also aligns your heart with God's purposes and shifts your perspective toward His goodness, making your prayers effective. Being thankful in prayer cultivates intimacy and trust in your relationship with God. King David often began his prayers with gratitude, grounding himself in God's character and thus being reassured of His presence in times of trouble.

When you pray, start by thanking God for His past faithfulness before presenting your needs.

Today I…

---

47 Dave Roberson, *The Walk of the Spirit—The Walk of Power: The Vital Role of Praying in Tongues* (Dave Roberson Ministries, 1999), 339.

NOVEMBER 5

THE MONEY PIT

Keep your lives free from the love of money; and be satisfied with what you have; for God himself has said, "I will never fail you or abandon you."

HEBREWS 13:5 CJB

The world bombards us with desires, but Hebrews 13:5 reminds us not to fall into the trap of loving money. First Timothy 6:10 states,

> *The love of money is a root of all the evils; because of this craving, some people have wandered away from the faith and pierced themselves to the heart with many pains.*

This verse emphasizes the dangers of allowing materialism to take precedence over our relationship with God. God calls us to cultivate gratitude for what we have. Contentment doesn't mean complacency, though; rather, it means having a profound assurance that God's provisions are sufficient for our needs.

Remember that God *"will never fail you or abandon you"* and let go of the anxiety that comes from chasing wealth. When you prioritize relationships and experiences over material possessions, you create space for joy. This shift in focus helps you to see the countless blessings around you.

Evaluate your relationship with money and material possessions. Jesus said, *"You cannot serve both God and money"* (Matthew 6:24 NIV).

Today I…

NOVEMBER 6

ABUNDANT LIFE

"The thief comes only in order to steal, kill and destroy; I have come so that they may have life, life in its fullest measure."

JOHN 10:10 CJB

Many people reject belief in God, viewing it as a constraint on personal freedom. They often equate faith with restrictive rules and prefer to live according to their own standards. However, this perspective overlooks a profound truth: We are always enslaved to something—either to God or to sin (John 8:30–36; Romans 6:15–19; Matthew 6:24).

The concept of complete independence is an illusion. Sin leads to bondage and death (James 1:15; Romans 6:23). True freedom, however, is found in a relationship with God. Second Corinthians 3:17 says, *"Where the Spirit of the Lord is, there is freedom"* (NIV). The rules and ethical codes associated with faith are meant to guide us toward fulfillment, not constrain us. When we submit to God's authority, we discover purpose and belonging. After all, Jesus came to give us *"life in its fullest measure."* Choosing to follow Christ breaks the chains of sin, offering us genuine peace and freedom. In surrendering to Him, we're transformed into the people God created us to be.

Identify an area in your life where you seek independence apart from God and surrender it to Him for true freedom and fulfillment.

Today I…

NOVEMBER 7

COMMUNAL GRATITUDE

Let the shalom *which comes from the Messiah be your heart's decision-maker, for this is why you were called to be part of a single Body. And be thankful—let the Word of the Messiah, in all its richness, live in you, as you teach and counsel each other in all wisdom, and as you sing psalms, hymns and spiritual songs with gratitude to God in your hearts.*

COLOSSIANS 3:15–16 CJB

We are called to let Christ's peace guide our hearts and be our decision-maker. Remember, anxiety and gratitude cannot coexist. Thankfulness shared in a community acts as a catalyst for spiritual growth and unity. Embracing gratitude collectively helps dispel anxiety and fosters a deeper connection to God and each other. When believers gather to share stories of God's faithfulness, their testimonies strengthen the group's collective faith.

Graham Cooke teaches that gratitude is an act of worship that changes the atmosphere, inviting the Holy Spirit's transformative presence.[48] A church that stands in unity and gratitude creates a powerful force, disrupting the Enemy's plans and advancing God's kingdom by fostering a shared purpose and reminding us of our collective mission in Christ.

This week, share your testimony of God's goodness with your church group or a friend.

Today I…

---

48 Graham Cooke, "How You Can Shift an Atmosphere with Rest," Brilliant Perspectives, May 7, 2018, brilliantperspectives.com.

NOVEMBER 8

DAILY BREAD

"'Give us the food we need today.'"
MATTHEW 6:11 CJB

In the simplicity of the Lord's Prayer, the request for *"the food we need today"* acknowledges our daily reliance on God's provision. Being thankful for daily necessities shifts our perspective by reminding us that God is the ultimate source of everything we need. The Lord's Prayer invites us to focus on today's blessings, cultivate contentment, and resist the relentless pursuit for more that often leads to dissatisfaction. Jesus frequently taught about living in the present and trusting in God for our daily needs. In Matthew 6:34, He instructed us not to worry about tomorrow *"for each day has enough trouble of its own"* (NIV).

Gratitude for daily needs grounds us in God's sufficiency and enables us to trust in His provision instead of being consumed by worldly striving. Consider the Israelites in the wilderness, who received manna each day—just enough for their needs. This daily reliance taught them trust and dependence on God's faithfulness. Similarly, acknowledging your daily provisions nurtures a deep trust in God, reminding you that His faithfulness is renewed with each sunrise.

Today, thank God for both the big and small provisions in your life. Reflect on His sustaining power and how His faithfulness meets your needs each day. If you're lacking something, simply ask Him in faith for what you need.

Today I…

NOVEMBER 9

FRIENDSHIP WITH GOD

His clothes became dazzling white, whiter than anyone in the world could bleach them. And there appeared before them Elijah and Moses, who were talking with Jesus.

MARK 9:3-4 NIV

I'm incredibly humbled and grateful when I think of how deeply God desires friendship with us. In Mark 9, Jesus was transfigured, and both Moses and Elijah appeared to consult with Him. Consider this: They didn't need to speak to Jesus because they had direct access to the Father. It was Jesus who chose to consult with them. God desires intimacy and friendship with humanity.

The creator of the universe wants to include us in His plans and counsel. However, friendship with God comes at a cost. Moses exemplified this when he left everything behind to pursue God's calling. As a former prince of Egypt, Moses had wealth and control, yet he abandoned those comforts for a life of service. Despite isolation and misunderstanding while leading the Israelites through wilderness hardships, he relied on God for direction. Similarly, Elijah faced loneliness and persecution in his prophetic mission. Though both men encountered significant challenges, they clung to their relationship with God, demonstrating what it means to be a friend of the Almighty.

Ask God to reveal His heart to you and show you how to be a better friend to Him.

Today I…

NOVEMBER 10

OVERFLOWING WITH HOPE

May the God of hope fill you with all joy and peace as you trust in him, so that you may overflow with hope by the power of the Holy Spirit.

ROMANS 15:13 NIV

Trust is the foundation of thanksgiving, joy, hope, peace, faith, and righteousness. Thankfulness is an expression of trust. When we acknowledge the blessings in our lives, we recognize God's hand at work. In turn, as we trust in His faithfulness, He fills us with joy and peace, transforming our hearts and minds.

Gratitude applies to every circumstance. By choosing to focus on what God has given us, we enable His joy and peace to overflow in our lives. When we're grateful even in trials, the Holy Spirit empowers us to be testimonies of hope for those around us. When others observe our calmness amid chaos and our joy during hardship, they can't help but wonder about the source of our strength, which creates fertile ground to sow seeds of faith and hopefully lead others to salvation.

List at least five things you are grateful for that you already have and five things you're grateful for that you don't have yet but that you're hoping and trusting Him for.

Today I…

NOVEMBER 11

GREAT DEBT

"Two people owed money to a certain moneylender. One owed him five hundred denarii, and the other fifty. Neither of them had the money to pay him back, so he forgave the debts of both. Now which of them will love him more?" Simon replied, "I suppose the one who had the bigger debt forgiven." "You have judged correctly," Jesus said.

LUKE 7:41–43 NIV

Our capacity for love is directly influenced by how well we understand the magnitude of God's forgiveness for us. When we truly comprehend our shortcomings—the depths of our sin, guilt, and shame—we can easily be overwhelmed with tears of gratitude for Christ's sacrifice and God's forgiveness. The sinful woman who wept at Jesus' feet recognized her debt, so her love for Jesus overflowed.

Conversely, those who believe they've been forgiven *"only a little"* often love *"only a little"* (v. 47 CJB) because they underestimate their need for grace. They may see their sins as minor compared to others, which leads to a diluted appreciation for redemption. They miss the truth that every sin, regardless of size, separates us from God. When we acknowledge our brokenness and the abundant grace, love, forgiveness, and redemption Jesus provides, we naturally respond with unrestrained love and adoration, just as the woman did.

Listen to the song "Pour My Oil" by Legacy Nashville and thank God for His forgiveness.

Today I…

NOVEMBER 12

BROKEN AND ACCEPTED

"Therefore, I tell you, her many sins have been forgiven—as her great love has shown. But whoever has been forgiven little loves little."

LUKE 7:47 NIV

Have you ever felt crushed by the weight of your sins? Yet when you finally surrender them to Christ, His forgiveness washes over you, perhaps leaving you in tears of gratitude. The sinful woman in the Pharisee's house embodied this experience. Despite her brokenness, she boldly approached Jesus, pouring out her love and gratitude for the one who could redeem and heal her.

We can be broken and still find acceptance at Jesus' feet. He welcomes us regardless of our past, cleanses us of our guilt, and empowers us to walk out our deliverance. No human can offer such profound forgiveness or transform our mistakes into testimonies of hope—only Jesus can. Shame and fear often hinder us from embracing His forgiveness, but being at the feet of Jesus is the safest place to be. When the woman poured out her devotion, Jesus defended and validated her love. His yoke is light, and our gratitude for how He pulls us out of our pits should far outweigh the burden of guilt for having fallen in.

Pour out your gratitude to Jesus. Release any lingering shame and embrace His forgiveness, knowing that you're fully accepted and loved.

Today I…

NOVEMBER 13

THE BRIDGE

He has made everything beautiful in its time. He has also set eternity in the human heart; yet no one can fathom what God has done from beginning to end. I know that there is nothing better for people than to be happy and to do good while they live.

ECCLESIASTES 3:11–12 NIV

Gratitude is a bridge between our present reality and the eternal hope we have in Christ. God's timing and works are beyond our understanding, yet He's woven beauty into every moment of our lives, placing eternity in our hearts—a sense of His divine work throughout our story. In seasons of waiting or hardship, we often struggle to see beauty. But thanksgiving isn't about perfect circumstances. It's about trusting that God is always working. Even when we can't see the full picture, we can choose to be thankful, knowing He's crafting something good and eternal.

Solomon also spoke to the joy in the present: *"There is nothing better for people than to be happy and to do good"* (v. 12). True thanksgiving recognizes the goodness in each day, whether it is mundane or extraordinary. Though we may not fully understand God's plan, we can trust His goodness.

Take time to notice the beauty around you and thank God for His promises and plans.

Today I…

NOVEMBER 14

WATCHFUL IN PRAYER

Continue steadfastly in prayer, being watchful in it with thanksgiving.

COLOSSIANS 4:2 ESV

Prayer is an open dialogue with God, a constant communion that we are invited to engage in daily. But here in Colossians, Paul called us not only to persist in prayer but to do so with a posture of watchfulness and thanksgiving. Why thanksgiving? Because God, as our infinitely loving benefactor, deserves it and because it shifts our focus. Even in times of waiting or uncertainty, gratitude anchors us in the faithfulness of God.

When we pray with thanksgiving, we're acknowledging that God is already at work even if we can't see it yet. We're not just offering requests but affirming our trust in His sovereignty and goodness. Thanksgiving is an act of worship, turning our hearts toward God's unchanging nature and thanking Him for His past, present, and future provision. In moments when prayers seem unanswered or the future looks unclear, let thanksgiving be your steady companion. It will remind you of the many ways God has been faithful and open your eyes to see His hand in the smallest details of your life.

Today, as you pray, make a list of things you're thankful for. Let gratitude shape your prayers and trust that God hears you and is working behind the scenes.

Today I…

NOVEMBER 15

ONE WAY

Yeshua said, "I AM the Way—and the Truth and the Life; no one comes to the Father except through me."

JOHN 14:6 CJB

Unbelievers often question how any single religious belief can be true amid so many differing views, leading some to conclude that if not all are true, then perhaps none are. However, this perspective undermines the fundamental nature of truth. Just as a good counterfeit resembles the real thing, many belief systems may appear valid on the surface, yet anything that deviates from Jesus leads to destruction. Satan often hides deception within partial truths, making it essential for us to skillfully discern what aligns with the teachings of Christ.

As believers, it's vital to strengthen our knowledge of the gospel. While understanding other worldviews can help us share our faith effectively, we must remain unwavering in the truth that Jesus is the only path to the Father. This truth is not only evident in Scripture but also affirmed in real-life testimonies. In his book *Imagine Heaven*, John Burke shared remarkable accounts of individuals who went through near-death experiences. Many of these individuals were not Christians, yet their encounters lined up with the biblical Jesus and His teachings, further affirming that He alone is the way, the truth, and the life.[49]

Ask the Holy Spirit for more wisdom and discernment.

Today I…

---

49 Burke, *Imagine Heaven*, 18.

NOVEMBER 16

GRATITUDE'S PROTECTION

Although they know who God is, they do not glorify him as God or thank him. On the contrary, they have become futile in their thinking; and their undiscerning hearts have become darkened.

ROMANS 1:21 CJB

Romans 1:21 gives a sobering reminder of what happens when we fail to honor and thank God. It tells the story of hearts that once knew God but drifted into darkness because they chose not to give Him the glory or gratitude He deserves. This is a warning for us today. Gratitude is not just a feeling; it's a safeguard for our hearts. When we stop thanking God, we lose sight of His presence and begin relying on our limited understanding. Our thoughts become clouded, and we start to trust in our own reasoning.

Thanksgiving is what keeps our hearts humble, soft, and connected to God. It pulls us out of the trap of pride and entitlement, keeping us grounded in His grace. Paul highlighted how this lack of honor and gratitude led to darkened hearts and futile thinking. But when we choose to honor God and cultivate gratitude, we open ourselves up to wisdom, clarity, and a renewed sense of His presence in our lives.

Take time to honor God today not just with your words but with a heart full of gratitude. Reflect on areas where you've neglected to thank Him and then bring those areas before Him in prayer.

Today I…

NOVEMBER 17

GOD'S CHARACTER

Adonai is merciful and compassionate, slow to anger and great in grace. Adonai is good to all; his compassion rests on all his creatures. All your creatures will thank you, Adonai, and your faithful servants will bless you.

PSALM 145:8–10 CJB

Psalm 145 paints a beautiful picture of God's character—merciful, compassionate, and full of grace. He's patient, slow to anger, and extends His goodness to all of creation. God's kindness is a breath of fresh air in a harsh world. When we meditate on God's mercy and compassion, it stirs our hearts to gratitude. It's impossible to encounter His love and not be moved to give thanks.

God's grace isn't just for a select few but for all His people. It is a reflection of His infinite goodness. This realization calls us into deeper worship where we acknowledge that we are recipients of His unending grace and love. Gratitude isn't just a human response; it's the song of all creation. Every creature and every faithful heart will one day acknowledge and praise the goodness of God.

As you go through today, take moments to thank God for His compassion, grace, and mercy in your life. Let His goodness toward you stir your heart to worship and then join with all creation in blessing His name.

Today I…

NOVEMBER 18

EQUIPPED TO DEFEND

In your hearts honor Christ the Lord as holy, always being prepared to make a defense to anyone who asks you for a reason for the hope that is in you; yet do it with gentleness and respect.

1 Peter 3:15 ESV

As believers, we're called to stand firm against deceptive ideologies that seek to undermine our faith (Colossians 2:8). To do this, we must be ready to defend our beliefs. After all, faith and reason are not mutually exclusive. Many renowned philosophers, scientists, and theologians throughout history have engaged deeply with questions about the existence of God and the nature of reality.

C. S. Lewis, once an atheist, articulated his spiritual journey from skepticism to faith in *Mere Christianity*. His arguments provide a robust foundation for belief, demonstrating that intellectual inquiry can lead to a deeper understanding of God rather than guide thinkers away from Him. As you engage in apologetics and witness to unbelievers, remember the significance of approaching these discussions with gentleness and respect so that you reflect the love of Christ in every interaction.

Study God's Word and embody Christ's love and gentleness as you share your faith.

Today I…

NOVEMBER 19

INCOMPARABLE

How much you have done, ADONAI my God! Your wonders and your thoughts toward us—none can compare with you! I would proclaim them, I would speak about them; but there's too much to tell!

PSALM 40:6(5) CJB

As you ponder God's works and the magnitude of His thoughts toward you, realize the impossibility of fully comprehending His magnificence and love. Yet each day, He wants to encounter you and reveal aspects of His character that fill your heart with awe and gratitude. God's wonders aren't just historical events; they're still present in your life today. From a gentle whisper of encouragement in moments of despair to the overwhelming grace that meets you in your failures, His love is ever present.

There's no one like our God. His wisdom is unmatched, and His thoughts toward you are filled with purpose and affection. Have you encountered God in a way that leaves you speechless? If not, start to worship and thank Him for the many things He's done and who He is, and let His Holy Spirit envelop you as He inhabits your praises.

Take a moment to reflect on a time when God was particularly faithful to you. This is your testimony—an organic witness to those around you, a witness that overcomes the Enemy (Revelation 12:11), softens hearts, and leads others to Jesus.

Today I…

NOVEMBER 20

OUR COMFORTER

Then you will say on that day, "I will give thanks to You, Lord; for although You were angry with me, Your anger is turned away, and You comfort me."

ISAIAH 12:1 NASB

God's anger isn't punitive but corrective. He doesn't want to punish you but to guide you back to Him and lead you away from harm and toward wholeness. Just as a loving parent disciplines a child out of care and protection, God's corrections are rooted in His profound love for you. He wants you to experience the fullness of life that comes from walking with Him. God's corrections aren't meant to cause fear but to draw you closer to Him so He can comfort and heal you. God's anger is an expression of His holiness, and it's aimed at restoring your relationship with Him.

God's anger is ultimately a catalyst for your spiritual growth. In acknowledging your failings, you open the door to God's grace, love, and healing. When you feel the weight of His conviction, take a moment to reflect on His unwavering love. You're never beyond the reach of His grace. Understanding this allows your heart to overflow with gratitude, turning struggles into opportunities for deepening your relationship with God.

Ask the Holy Spirit to expose areas of your life that you need to surrender to Him.

Today I…

NOVEMBER 21

ETERNAL THANKS

Ever since I heard about your trust in the Lord Yeshua and your love for all God's people, I have not stopped giving thanks for you.

EPHESIANS 1:15–16 CJB

Witnessing the transformation in someone's life when they come to know Jesus is exhilarating! The moment you lead someone to the Lord, you're witnessing the greatest miracle: They're raising from spiritual death to life. Like Paul, I thank God every time I think about someone I led to Jesus and the ripple effect they're now having that I got to help start.

As you reflect on the people in your life, consider those who don't yet know Jesus, especially those struggling with their purpose. Each represents a unique opportunity for you to be the light of Christ. Imagine the joy of seeing someone you care about embrace the gospel! It's a reward that far surpasses earthly treasures. Your prayers and your willingness to share the love of Christ can lead to transformative encounters that change thousands of lives for eternity.

Take a moment today to think of those in your circle who need the hope of Jesus. Pray boldly for them and be prepared to share your story. Commit to spreading the light of Christ and watching as He transforms hearts.

Today I…

NOVEMBER 22

UNDONE

I planted the seed, Apollos watered it, but God has been making it grow.…The one who plants and the one who waters have one purpose, and they will each be rewarded according to their own labor.

1 Corinthians 3:6, 8 NIV

Growing up, I dreamed of being a missionary, but God called me to Hollywood instead. I often envied those preaching the gospel in remote mission fields. Anytime I questioned why I couldn't serve in that way, God reminded me that my job was to fund their missions. Honestly, that disappointed me. It didn't feel as meaningful—until He opened my eyes. Jesus said,

> *The reaper and the sower may be glad together.…I sent you to reap what you haven't worked for. Others have done the hard labor, and you have benefited from their work.* (John 4:36, 38 CJB)

When I connected this with 1 Corinthians 3:6–8, I wept. Our job is to be obedient to the Great Commission, not to measure results. Whether we plant seeds, water them, or witness the harvest, each role matters because God is the one who makes the fruit grow. God's economy wrecks me! Through Jesus, He paid a debt we could never repay. Moreover, when we sow into ministries, He also credits their labor and the souls they win to our accounts. Hallelujah!

Marvel at God's generosity.

Today I…

NOVEMBER 23

GRATITUDE TRANSFORMS

Everything created by God is good, and nothing received with thanksgiving needs to be rejected, because the word of God and prayer make it holy.

1 Timothy 4:4-5 CJB

Everything God has created is inherently good, but it's our response to His gifts that transforms them into blessings. When we receive His gifts with hearts of gratitude, we honor Him as the source of all good things. Prayer plays a vital role in this process, not only aligning us with God's will but also consecrating the things we enjoy.

Dan Mohler teaches that when we approach the things in life with thanksgiving and prayer, we actively engage with God's intent for them. Through prayer, we acknowledge His provision and set apart those things as holy, whether it be food, relationships, or opportunities.[50] Chad Gonzales often emphasizes that thanksgiving is more than a ritual—it's a powerful act of faith. When we thank God, we position ourselves to receive more and to enjoy the fullness of what He's already given us. Prayer then becomes the act that purifies and perfects these gifts, elevating them from mere material blessings to holy encounters with God's grace.

Pray over the things you enjoy, asking God to sanctify them and make them holy in your life.

Today I…

---

50 Dan Mohler, "Being Thankful Changes Everything—Dan Mohler," posted September 16, 2023, by Dan Mohler, YouTube, youtube.com.

NOVEMBER 24

SCIENCE CONFIRMS GOD

Since the creation of the world God's invisible qualities—his eternal power and divine nature—have been clearly seen, being understood from what has been made, so that people are without excuse.

ROMANS 1:20 NIV

Some argue that there is insufficient proof of God's existence. However, this perspective ignores the abundant evidence nature provides. Consider the universe's fine-tuning: A slight alteration in the gravitational constant would prevent our universe from existing. If we were closer to the sun, we'd face extreme heat; farther away, a freezing ice age. These precise conditions indicate intentional design.

Studies examining the conditions necessary for life reveal that the mathematical odds of these conditions occurring by chance are astronomically low. In fact, astrophysicist Fred Hoyle estimated the odds to be one in ten to the forty-thousandth power.[51] This is a number so staggeringly small that it underscores intentional design. Science, rather than contradicting faith, points us back to the Creator, revealing His wisdom and power in every detail. When we open our eyes to the intricacies of the universe, we see not chance but a divine invitation to know and trust the one who set it all in motion.

Praise God that science only confirms His existence.

Today I…

---

51 John W. Oller, "Not According to Hoyle," Institute for Creation Research, December 1, 1984, icr.org.

NOVEMBER 25

I AM

"About the resurrection of the dead—have you not read what God said to you, 'I am the God of Abraham, the God of Isaac, and the God of Jacob'? He is not the God of the dead but of the living."

MATTHEW 22:31–32 NIV

Here, God used the present tense intentionally, illustrating that His relationship with these patriarchs is active and ongoing. Abraham, Isaac, and Jacob are still alive; they're just unbound by their earthly bodies. God is unbound by death or time. In declaring, *"I AM,"* He established Himself as the one who simply *is*—transcending time and space, fully capable of interacting with us in every moment, and continually fulfilling His promises.

If we truly believe that God is the God of the living and not of the dead, we must recognize that His power and promises are as real today as they were thousands of years ago. He is alive in every situation we face, available to bring resurrection and restoration to every broken area of our lives. This revelation should fill us with immense gratitude and confidence. God's promises to you are as active today as they were for the heroes of the faith.

Ask God to reveal areas where you need His "I AM" power. Allow Him to breathe life into those places.

Today I…

NOVEMBER 26

DON'T PANIC, PRAISE

I will keep on trusting even when I say, "I am utterly miserable," even when, in my panic, I declare, "Everything human is deceptive."…I will offer a sacrifice of thanks to you and will call on the name of Adonai.

PSALM 116:10–11, 17 CJB

The psalmist's candid admission of misery and doubt is relatable. We often find ourselves in situations that provoke fear and panic. But when we panic, we're reacting in the flesh. Remember, anything not based on trust is sin (Romans 14:23). Instead of panicking, we should pause and try "moving in the opposite spirit."[52] We should thank God that He is with us even in the moments of uncertainty. Gratitude is a gateway back into the spirit that gives us a heavenly perspective, shifting our focus from our circumstances back to God's faithfulness. By offering a sacrifice of thanks when our flesh wants to panic, we acknowledge that God is still present and invite Him to intervene in our circumstances.

Choosing to call on the name of Adonai in your darkest moments doesn't dismiss your feelings, but it opens the door for God to turn your struggles into testimonies. Consider Jesus: He wept when Lazarus died, but He still gave thanks to God before the miracle of Lazarus' resurrection happened (John 11).

Next time you feel panic coming on, praise instead.

Today I…

---

52 Graham Cooke and Gary Goodell, *Permission Granted to Do Church Differently in the 21st Century* (Destiny Image, 2011), 197.

NOVEMBER 27

OVERCOMING DOUBT IN PAIN

A father to the fatherless, a defender of widows, is God in his holy dwelling.

PSALM 68:5 NIV

Many reject belief in God due to personal traumas and feelings of abandonment. Those who pray fervently but feel no response or face tragedy often struggle with disbelief and doubt about His existence. Life can be filled with great pain and heartache, but it's crucial to remember that God is not the source of suffering. He's a good Father who cares deeply for His children. While we often associate pain with God's will, most of the suffering we experience is a result of sin and our fallen world. God is present in our suffering even when He feels distant.

In a message titled "Healing, the Bible Way," Dan Mohler recounted how he dealt with his wife's medical crisis by trusting in God's power, eventually leading to her miraculous recovery.[53] This testimony illustrates the importance of faith and surrender in the healing process. When we lay our burdens at God's feet, just as the woman did when she poured out her tears at Jesus' feet (Luke 7:37–38), we open ourselves to transformation and restoration.

When facing doubts from emotional pain, bring those feelings to God for healing and restoration.

Today I…

---

53 Dan Mohler, "Healing, the Bible Way—Dan Mohler," posted October 5, 2013, by fortygreen, YouTube, youtube.com.

NOVEMBER 28

GRATITUDE BEFORE MIRACLES

Taking the five loaves and the two fish and looking up to heaven, he gave thanks and broke the loaves.

MARK 6:41 NIV

Giving thanks, especially in times of scarcity, is powerful. Before the miracle of the multiplication of the loaves and fishes even occurred, Jesus gave thanks for the small provision that would end up feeding thousands. Gratitude often precedes miracles because it creates fertile ground in our hearts for God's work. Gratitude stirs up our faith. Through thanksgiving, we ready our hearts to witness and receive the miracles God is eager to perform.

God delights in providing for His children. He's a good Father (James 1:17; Matthew 7:11). Often, we lack because we don't ask or because we approach Him with doubt, forgetting that He's both willing and able to provide (James 4:2–3; Matthew 21:22). However, our gratitude must be sincere, not just lip service. We cannot lie to the Holy Spirit (Acts 5:3–4). We shouldn't expect God to move because we've demanded it like a spoiled child. True gratitude is a heart posture (Psalm 9:1). When we're truly thankful, God delights in blessing us abundantly.

Thank God for what you have and trust that He is able and willing to provide for all your needs.

Today I…

NOVEMBER 29

PRAISE BEFORE BREAKTHROUGH

*After consulting the people, Jehoshaphat appointed men to sing to the L*ORD *and to praise him for the splendor of his holiness as they went out at the head of the army, saying: "Give thanks to the L*ORD*, for his love endures forever." As they began to sing and praise, the L*ORD *set ambushes against the men of Ammon and Moab and Mount Seir who were invading Judah, and they were defeated.*

2 CHRONICLES 20:21–22 NIV

The Israelites understood that praise and thanksgiving precede breakthrough. When King Jehoshaphat faced an overwhelming army, he didn't rally the strongest fighters or strategize a military plan. Instead, he appointed singers to lead his people in worship, declaring God's greatness and thanking Him for His enduring love even before the battle began. His thankfulness to God in the face of adversity demonstrated profound faith.

Worship invites God into our situations, shifts our focus from overwhelming circumstances to His power and majesty, and strengthens our relationship with Him. As the musicians began to sing, God intervened, sending confusion among the enemy ranks and granting the Israelites victory. When we choose praise and thanksgiving instead of complaint and doubt, we confuse the enemy and partner with God as He moves and takes ground.

Listen to the song "Praise Before My Breakthrough" by Bryan and Katie Torwalt.

Today I…

NOVEMBER 30

IT'S EASY

"Now bring me a harpist." While the harpist was playing, the hand of the Lord came on Elisha and he said, "This is what the Lord says:…You will see neither wind nor rain, yet this valley will be filled with water, and you, your cattle and your other animals will drink. This is an easy thing in the eyes of the Lord; he will also deliver Moab into your hands."

2 Kings 3:15–18 NIV

In 2 Kings 3, the Israelite armies were parched in a dry valley with no water or rain cloud in sight. Needing divine intervention, they consulted the prophet Elisha. Elisha requested a harpist to create an atmosphere of worship, enabling him to receive a word from God. I love how God called the miracle easy and how His miraculous provision not only quenched their thirst but also led to their enemy's demise.

Again, worship proceeded God's provision. Worship shifted the atmosphere, inviting God's presence and reminding everyone of His power. When we praise God for what hasn't happened yet, we wake up our faith. Praising God in advance isn't wishful thinking—it's an act of trust that declares He is already at work.

Create a list of needs, and as you bring them before the Lord, thank Him for His provision even before it manifests.

Today I…

DECEMBER

Miracles Aren't Just for Christmas

DECEMBER 1

RELATIONSHIP OVER AUTHORITY

"Lord, even the demons submit to us in your name." He replied, "I…have given you authority…to overcome all the power of the enemy.…However, do not rejoice that the spirits submit to you, but rejoice that your names are written in heaven."

LUKE 10:17–20 NIV

This month, we're discussing how God still performs miracles, but our focus must remain on Jesus, not on the excitement of signs. We can operate in signs and wonders yet still not enter heaven (Matthew 7:21–23). While God can use us through His authority, we mustn't be deceived into thinking that our ability to operate in His authority equates to a true relationship with Him.

During my battle with bulimia, I loved God but also had an idol in my heart (Ezekiel 14:3). Although I had a genuine heart for Jesus and sought to share Him with others, I'm not sure I was still saved (Hebrews 10:26). I believed that God's grace would cover my sinful condition. After all, God sometimes moved in miracles and prophetic moments through me, yet many could claim the same without true connection and submission to Jesus. It's imperative to celebrate that it's our names—not the miracles God performs through us—that are written in heaven.

Be excited that God still moves but stay focused on Jesus.

Today I…

DECEMBER 2

THE BASICS

> He said to them, "Go into all the world and proclaim the gospel to the whole creation.…And these signs will accompany those who believe: in my name they will cast out demons; they will speak in new tongues;…they will lay their hands on the sick, and they will recover."
>
> MARK 16:15, 17–18 ESV

In November, we learned that gratitude often precedes miracles, and now that we've prioritized our relationship with Jesus over signs, let's talk miracles. The Great Commission wasn't a suggestion—it was a commandment. Jesus said signs would follow not just the apostles but *"those who believe."*. Yet we've drifted from expecting miracles as "normal" and now consider them paranormal.

Faith is spelled R-I-S-K.[54] The first disciples understood this. They took bold steps of faith to heal the sick, cast out demons, and spread the gospel. When they stepped out, God stepped in. We are called to live with that same expectation. If God says believers will lay hands on the sick and see them recover, why don't we act in faith? The problem isn't with God's promise—it's with our willingness to take risks and step out in faith.

This month, choose faith over fear. Expect miracles!

Today I…

---

[54] John Wimber, *The Way in Is the Way On: John Wimber's Teachings and Writings on Christ* (Ampelon, 2006), 171.

DECEMBER 3

THE GREATEST MIRACLE

He has rescued us from the dominion of darkness and brought us into the kingdom of the Son he loves, in whom we have redemption, the forgiveness of sins.

COLOSSIANS 1:13–14 NIV

If you believe in salvation, you already have the faith for miracles. Think about it: Trusting that your sins are forgiven, that you've been eternally redeemed, and that you've been spiritually transferred from Satan's kingdom into God's kingdom—where life is breathed into your once-dead spirit—is far greater than believing in any other miracle. Yet we often accept this truth without hesitation. The same faith that brought you into salvation is the faith that can move mountains, heal the sick, and cast out demons.

The issue isn't whether we have faith but where we've chosen to apply it. In many ways, we've sidelined the parts of the Great Commission—such as healing the sick and casting out demons—while holding tightly to the promise of eternal life. But *"these signs will accompany those who believe"* (Mark 16:17 NIV). If you've believed in the miracle of salvation, don't stop there. You have the faith to perform other miracles through the power of Jesus. Salvation wasn't meant to be the only miracle—it was the first of many.

If you believe in the miracle of salvation, start believing in other miracles.

Today I…

CRUCIFIED WITH CHRIST

"I have been crucified with Christ and I no longer live, but Christ lives in me. The life I now live in the body, I live by faith in the Son of God, who loved me and gave himself for me."

GALATIANS 2:20 NIV

Many times, when we witness miracles and healings, we mistakenly think the believer commanding the miracles is the one performing them. However, the miracles don't come from the person—they come from Jesus working through that person. Galatians 2:20 reminds us that we have been crucified with Christ and that now it's Christ living in us. The power behind miracles isn't human; it's the presence of Christ dwelling in us. We're merely vessels that God uses for His glory and kingdom.

Don't get caught up in glorifying the individual. Focus on the one who lives within them—Jesus, who deserves all the glory. The person praying for people and seeing healings or exorcisms has great faith, and we should honor that. But we should also never lose sight of the actual miracle worker, Jesus. It's His power flowing through us that brings about healing and deliverance. He alone deserves the praise for every miracle, and it's our privilege to be used by Him as instruments of His will.

Praise Jesus for every miracle, recognizing that He's the one working through believers to perform His will.

Today I…

DECEMBER 5

DON'T ASK, COMMAND

The tongue has the power of life and death, and those who love it will eat its fruit.

PROVERBS 18:21 NIV

As believers, we often overlook the power of our words, yet Scripture tells us that life and death are in the power of the tongue. When it comes to healing, we need to realize that we're not meant to beg or plead for it—we're called to command it. Jesus didn't ask sickness to leave. He commanded it. He spoke with authority to the lame, the blind, and the possessed, and the natural world responded to His words. We have that same authority as believers. We're meant to speak in faith, to command healing in Jesus' name, and to trust that God will do the supernatural when we do the natural.

It's not about asking God to heal. He's already provided healing through the finished work of Jesus. Our role is to take authority and declare it over ourselves and others. After all, faith requires action. When we speak life and healing, we align ourselves with God's promises. So when you're praying for healing, remember to declare it boldly, knowing that God is faithful to do what He promised.

Today, when you encounter sickness or need healing, don't ask—command. Speak life over the situation, knowing that God's power works through faith.

Today I…

THE POWER OF LIFE

The light shines in the darkness, and the darkness can never extinguish it.

JOHN 1:5 NLT

We carry the light of Christ within us—a light that no amount of darkness can extinguish. This is the reality for every believer: Wherever we go, the light of Jesus goes with us. But it doesn't just illuminate; it has the power to expel darkness entirely. When Jesus walked the earth, demons trembled at His presence, and they also should tremble when we enter a room not because of who we are but because of who lives in us.

We are vessels of the Holy Spirit, and the same power that resurrected Jesus is at work in us. The key is to understand and walk in that authority—but with humility. It's not our authority but Christ's. The darkness will never overpower the light of Jesus, but we must boldly let His light shine through us. Instead of fearing darkness, we should recognize that through Christ, we are the ones who bring the breakthrough.

Walk in the boldness of Christ's authority and remember that His power is what brings healing and freedom. Declare the victory He's already won and watch the darkness flee.

Today I…

DECEMBER 7

STAY FREE

He said to her, "Daughter, your faith has healed you.
Go in peace and be freed from your suffering."

MARK 5:34 NIV

When Jesus told the woman with the issue of blood to *"go in peace,"* He was telling her to continue walking in the healing she had just received. Healing and deliverance don't end with the miracle. We must keep walking in faith and continue claiming the healing. There are countless testimonies of addicts becoming *instantly* sober at an altar call, only to return to addiction soon after. God opens the door to your prison cell instantly, but you must choose to walk out of it.

Repentance and deliverance are not one-time events; they involve a daily walk with the Holy Spirit. God's grace is more than undeserved favor. It's God's empowerment to stay free from addiction, sickness, and every other form of bondage. When you experience healing or freedom, be ready—temptation will come. The Enemy will try to convince you that the pain is returning or that you still need the addictive substance. But remember, sin is simply trusting in anything more than you trust in God (Romans 14:23). In moments of temptation, ask yourself, *What am I trusting more than God?*

In the face of temptation and fear, ask yourself, *What am I trusting most right now?*

Today I…

DECEMBER 8

SHORT AND SWEET

"When you pray, don't babble on and on like the pagans, who think God will hear them better if they talk a lot. Don't be like them, because your Father knows what you need before you ask him."

MATTHEW 6:7–8 CJB

When it comes to prayer, especially prayer for healing, we don't need to prattle on or try to convince God. Healing isn't something we have to beg for. God has already paid for and provided it through the finished work of Christ. When we pray for healing, we don't have to convince God or earn His favor. Jesus took our sickness, pain, and suffering upon Himself at Calvary. The healing we seek is part of the atonement, part of the victory Jesus already secured.

Instead of praying with desperation or uncertainty, we can approach God with confidence, knowing that He already knows what we need and has made provision for it through His Son. The Father does not withhold from us. He's waiting for us to receive what's already been given through Christ. So when you pray for healing, stand in faith, knowing that Jesus has finished the work. You don't need to strive. Just believe and receive.

When you doubt, pray like the father in Mark 9:24: *"Lord, I believe; help my unbelief!"* (NKJV).

Today I…

DECEMBER 9

PRAYER AND FASTING

He said to them, "This kind can come out by nothing but prayer and fasting."

MARK 9:29 NKJV

In Mark 9:29, Jesus explained to His disciples why they struggled to cast out a particular demon. Even though they used Jesus' name, the demon didn't immediately surrender. Many assume Jesus was referring to a stronger kind of demon, but in context, He was addressing His disciples' unbelief (Mark 9:19, 23–24). The issue wasn't the demon's power; it was the disciples' lack of faith. Jesus had already given them authority over demons (Mark 6:7), yet in this moment, their hearts wavered unknowingly. The afflicted boy's father recognized the real problem and cried, *"Lord, I believe; help my unbelief!"* (Mark 9:24).

Jesus was teaching that some breakthroughs require prayer and fasting not because His name is weak but because fasting removes hidden unbelief. Fasting heightens our discernment so that when we speak in Jesus' name, we do so with unwavering faith and full authority. The name of Jesus is never insufficient, but we must be spiritually prepared to exercise the authority we've been given.

If you're facing a situation that seems unbreakable, take time to fast and pray.

Today I…

DECEMBER 10

THE GREAT DECEPTION

Jews demand signs and Greeks look for wisdom, but we preach Christ crucified.

1 CORINTHIANS 1:22–23 NIV

Miracles are powerful displays of God's compassion and love, but they shouldn't be the foundation of our faith. We shouldn't chase after signs as reasons to believe. Instead, our faith must rest on Christ crucified and resurrected, the ultimate miracle and wisdom of God. Many don't realize that the Enemy is capable of performing deceptive signs to distract people from the truth. Consider the story of Pharaoh's magicians, who were able to replicate some of Moses' miracles through sorcery. They turned their staffs into snakes and mimicked the first two plagues—turning water into blood and summoning frogs (Exodus 7:8–22; 8:1–7). However, their power was limited, and eventually they had to admit defeat and declare, *"This is the finger of God"* (v. 19 NIV).

Satan's goal is to keep people from the truth even if it means using counterfeit miracles. While Satan's power is nowhere near God's, he can deceive through signs and wonders. For example, Revelation 13:3 speaks of the beast who performed signs to lead people astray. So don't base your assurance of salvation on miracles. Instead, anchor your faith in the finished work of Christ, the greatest miracle of all.

Thank God for His miracles but place your trust in Christ, the greatest miracle of all.

Today I…

DECEMBER 11

THE POWER OF DISCERNMENT

Paul was filled with the Holy Spirit, and he looked the sorcerer in the eye. Then he said, "You son of the devil, full of every sort of deceit and fraud, and enemy of all that is good! Will you never stop perverting the true ways of the Lord?"

ACTS 13:9–10 NLT

In Acts 13, Paul confronted Elymas the sorcerer, who was trying to influence the governor and distort the gospel message. This illustrates how Satan often targets those in power, seeking to manipulate authority—a reality we see in today's world. Paul, filled with the Holy Spirit, boldly discerned the deception and called out Elymas, quoting Proverbs 10:9: *"Whoever walks in integrity walks securely, but whoever takes crooked paths will be found out"* (NIV). Paul's authority didn't stop with words. He commanded Elymas to be struck blind, and immediately the sorcerer was rendered powerless. This miraculous sign led the governor to faith in Jesus.

Paul's boldness and discernment shifted the spiritual atmosphere and broke the Enemy's grip on the governor so his heart could receive Jesus. Discernment makes us more sensitive to the Spirit and better equipped to confront spiritual deception. Satan targets leaders and influencers, but as believers, we cannot afford to be passive in a world of spiritual manipulation.

Ask the Holy Spirit for boldness and discernment.

Today I…

DECEMBER 12

PROCLAIM HIS PROMISES

With the heart one goes on trusting and thus continues toward righteousness, while with the mouth one keeps on making public acknowledgement and thus continues toward deliverance.

ROMANS 10:10 CJB

Trusting with our hearts leads us toward righteousness (Hebrews 11), but it's the spoken declaration of that faith that brings breakthrough and deliverance into our lives. This aligns with Revelation 12:11, which declares that believers overcome Satan by the blood of the Lamb and the word of their testimony. Trusting in Jesus' sacrifice makes us righteous, but it is the continual speaking of our testimony that solidifies our deliverance and allows us to take ground spiritually.

In Romans 10:11, Paul quoted Isaiah 28:16, reminding us that those who trust in God will never be put to shame. This truth applies to everyone—Jew and Gentile alike. Romans 10:17 says, *"Trust comes from what is heard, and what is heard comes through a word proclaimed about the Messiah."* Faith comes by hearing, and deliverance comes not just through belief but also through the spoken Word. Deliverance is activated by speaking God's Word and promises into the atmosphere. Declare your healing out loud as often as needed.

Proclaim God's promises out loud today.

Today I...

DECEMBER 13

DECLARING LIFE

Seated in a window was a young man named Eutychus, who was sinking into a deep sleep as Paul talked on and on. When he was sound asleep, he fell to the ground from the third story and was picked up dead. Paul went down, threw himself on the young man and put his arms around him. "Don't be alarmed," he said. "He's alive!"

ACTS 20:9–10 NIV

I love how Paul didn't panic or hesitate when the boy died. Instead, he immediately went to him and declared, *"He's alive!"* Paul didn't beg or plead with God; instead, he declared life over Eutychus. He didn't let the circumstances or emotions dictate his faith but trusted in the resurrection power of Jesus working through him.

This moment is a powerful reminder of the authority believers have in Christ. Paul didn't pray for hours or engage in complicated rituals; he simply used bold faith to declare the young man alive. Remember, the authority to command healing or life doesn't come from us—it comes from Jesus. Our words, when aligned with His power, can move mountains. Just like Paul, we must confidently speak God's truth, trusting in His power to bring life where there seems to be death.

Next time something scary happens to you or someone you love, try to speak life instead of panicking.

Today I…

DECEMBER 14

HOLY SPIRIT POWER

"You will receive power when the Holy Spirit comes on you."
Acts 1:8 NIV

Being filled with the Holy Spirit brings about a radical transformation, not just a quiet, internal change. This is a transformation that fills us with divine power, courage, and authority. When the Holy Spirit comes upon us, we're no longer operating in our own strength but in God's power. This empowerment doesn't just shake the physical world; it shakes spiritual strongholds, breaking the chains that bind people and opening doors for the advancement of God's kingdom.

The early disciples didn't timidly go out after receiving the Holy Spirit. They were bold, courageous, and unstoppable. The same Spirit that filled them is available to us today, equipping us for every spiritual battle and calling we face. The Holy Spirit empowers us to do what we could never accomplish in our own strength: heal the sick, cast out demons, and proclaim the gospel with power. He is the divine empowerment we need to live out our faith boldly, moving in the miraculous and advancing God's kingdom wherever we go.

Ask the Holy Spirit to fill you afresh today. Step out in boldness, knowing His power equips you for the impossible.

Today I…

DECEMBER 15

OUR MISSION FIELD

Jesus said to them, "It is not the healthy who need a doctor, but the sick. I have not come to call the righteous, but sinners."

MARK 2:17 NIV

Jesus didn't come for those who thought they were righteous but for those who knew they were in need. This verse reminds us that the world is our mission field. We are called to step out of our comfort zones, go beyond the walls of the church, and engage those who are hurting, broken, and spiritually sick. Every environment—whether it's your workplace, neighborhood, or even your family—is a mission field. Those you encounter daily may not seem lost, but everyone needs Jesus. The mission field isn't far away—it's right in front of us.

Like Jesus, we are called to see those around us with eyes of compassion, reaching out to offer hope, healing, and salvation. Remember, just as Jesus didn't wait for people to come to Him, we can't wait for others to seek God on their own. We are called to bring the gospel to the hurting, knowing that God's love is the ultimate cure.

Pray today for God to open your eyes to the mission field around you.

Today I…

DECEMBER 16

SHUT UP

> They brought to him all who were sick or oppressed by demons.…And he healed many who were sick with various diseases, and cast out many demons. And he would not permit the demons to speak, because they knew him.
>
> MARK 1:32, 34 ESV

I love how Jesus didn't allow the demons to speak. He commanded the demons to leave, and they obeyed. This is a crucial lesson for us as believers—we don't need to engage in conversations with the Enemy during deliverance. Jesus' sacrifice on the cross canceled every spiritual debt and voided all legal claims the Enemy had over us (Colossians 2:14–15). If the person is a believer, the devil has no right to stay! He is a liar (John 8:44), so why would we let him have a voice? Jesus didn't, and neither should we.

We're called to walk in the same authority, silencing the Enemy's attempts to deceive and distract. When faced with opposition, we don't negotiate—we command it to leave in Jesus' name. No long-winded interactions. No back-and-forth. Just a declaration of the truth and a firm stand on the authority Christ has given.

When confronting spiritual opposition, don't engage the Enemy in conversation. Silence the lies and speak the name of Jesus with authority.

Today I…

DECEMBER 17

MOVED WITH COMPASSION

A leper came to Jesus. He knelt down and begged him, "If you are willing, you can make me clean." Moved with compassion, Jesus stretched out his hand and touched him. "I am willing," he told him. "Be clean." Immediately the leprosy left him, and he was healed.

MARK 1:40–42 EHV

Jesus was and is always willing to heal. His compassion moved Him to act, and the healing was immediate. Compassion always precedes miracles. Jesus wasn't simply exercising His authority; He was moved by love and pity for those suffering. Compassion is the key to releasing the power of God. We can't have true authority over things we aren't compassionate about. Jesus' heart was deeply stirred by the brokenness of others, and that love empowered Him to heal.

Today we do not need to beg for healing. Christ has already paid for it through His sacrifice. But it's through love that faith is activated. *"Faith working through love"* is the only thing that matters (Galatians 5:6 ESV). When we, like Jesus, allow our hearts to be moved by compassion, we are positioned to operate in the authority God has given us to bring healing and restoration.

Ask God to fill your heart with love for those in need, knowing that through love, you can operate in His authority to release healing and miracles.

Today I…

DECEMBER 18

SPIRITUAL AFFLICTIONS

A demon-oppressed man who was blind and mute was brought to him, and he healed him, so that the man spoke and saw.

MATTHEW 12:22 ESV

Some illnesses have spiritual roots. Scripture shows multiple accounts of spirits causing afflictions (Matthew 9:32; Mark 9:17; Luke 9:39; Luke 11:14). Jesus didn't just heal physical ailments. He also confronted spiritual oppression. While not all sickness is demonic, we're called to walk in discernment and authority just as Jesus did. The power He carried over sickness and demons is the same power He has given us.

Sometimes, unforgiveness can be the root cause of a demonic foothold. Ephesians 4:26–27 warns us not to give the devil a foothold through unresolved anger, and Hebrews 12:15 cautions us against allowing bitterness to take root, which can defile many and cause trouble. Unforgiveness opens doors that allow the Enemy to operate, creating spiritual strongholds that may manifest in various forms, including sickness. But walking in forgiveness frees us from the Enemy's grip and closes doors to spiritual oppression. Jesus empowers us not only to confront physical sickness but to walk in spiritual authority, closing the doors that give the Enemy access.

Ask the Holy Spirit to reveal any areas of unforgiveness in your heart. Release them to Him and declare freedom over yourself.

Today I…

DECEMBER 19

UNLOCKING THE IMPOSSIBLE

During the night, an angel of ADONAI opened the doors of the prison, led them out and said, "Go, stand in the Temple court and keep telling the people all about this new life!"

ACTS 5:19–20 CJB

The apostles were imprisoned for preaching the gospel, but God had other plans. An angel miraculously opened the prison doors and led them to freedom. Yet the next morning, the guards found the prison *"securely locked and the guards standing at the doors"* (v. 23 ESV). The apostles had been miraculously translated out of the prison without the guards realizing it.

And this isn't the only biblical account of translation. God often moves people supernaturally, showing He isn't limited by physical barriers. He can break through impossibilities to fulfill His purposes. The apostles' escape wasn't just for freedom; it was to continue proclaiming new life in Jesus. God's power is always for the advancement of His kingdom. Like the apostles, we may face impossible situations, but God can unlock any door and move us beyond barriers. He's still the God of miracles.

If you feel trapped in an impossible situation, trust God to work supernaturally in your life and make a way. Be bold in proclaiming the new life you have in Christ.

Today I…

DECEMBER 20

LIVING IN YOU

If the Spirit of the One who raised Yeshua from the dead is living in you, then the One who raised the Messiah Yeshua from the dead will also give life to your mortal bodies through his Spirit living in you.

ROMANS 8:11 CJB

The same Spirit that raised Jesus from the dead is alive in you! Think about that: The resurrection power of the Holy Spirit—the same force that broke the grip of death and raised Jesus from the grave—is in *you*. So often, we live as though we're powerless, weighed down by sickness, sin, or fear. But Romans 8:11 reminds us that the very source of life and power resides within us. It's this Spirit that gives life to our mortal bodies not just for eternal life but for healing, renewal, and strength here and now.

When sickness or weakness attacks your body, remember that the Holy Spirit is already at work within you, ready to quicken and revive your physical body. You aren't left to battle alone. You carry within you the Spirit that conquered death itself.

Today, declare that the same Spirit who raised Jesus from the dead is alive and active in you. Speak life over any area of your body that needs healing, and trust in God's resurrection power.

Today I…

DECEMBER 21

BREAD OF LIFE

They took up twelve baskets full of broken pieces and of the fish.... For they did not understand about the loaves, but their hearts were hardened.

MARK 6:43, 52 ESV

After the miraculous feeding of the five thousand, the disciples collected twelve baskets of leftover bread and fish. This wasn't a coincidence—it was a prophetic picture of the abundance found in Jesus and a foreshadowing of the work each disciple would do. The bread represents His body, which would soon be broken for all, while the twelve baskets point to the harvest each disciple would be a part of, bringing the gospel to countless souls.

But what's striking is that even after witnessing this incredible miracle, the disciples didn't fully understand its significance because their hearts were hardened. Sometimes, we can be right in the middle of God's miraculous provision and still miss the deeper meaning. The abundance was more than physical bread—it was the overflowing, spiritual nourishment Jesus offers because He is the Bread of Life. He's more than enough, and He equips us to share His abundance with the world.

Ask God to open your eyes and soften your heart to His provision and the deeper truths in the miracles you see.

Today I…

DECEMBER 22

GREATER THAN GOLD

Peter said, "I have no silver and gold, but what I do have I give to you. In the name of Jesus Christ of Nazareth, rise up and walk!" And he took him by the right hand and raised him up, and immediately his feet and ankles were made strong. And leaping up, he stood and began to walk, and entered the temple with them, walking and leaping and praising God.

ACTS 3:6–8 ESV

Peter and John didn't offer the lame man money, but they gave him something far more valuable: healing in Jesus' name. What we carry in Christ is more powerful and valuable than any material possession. After the miracle, Peter made it clear that it wasn't by his own power that the man was healed but by faith in Jesus' name (Acts 3:12, 16).

This miracle went beyond Peter; it was about the power of Jesus, who's still healing today. We're called to walk in that same boldness, trusting in the name of Jesus to work through us. The lame man's healing became a testimony of God's power and goodness to all who witnessed it. When God moves in our lives, it's not just for us but also for the world to see His glory and believe.

Ask God to increase your faith in the power of Jesus' name.

Today I…

DECEMBER 23

CONFIDENT AUTHORITY

Jesus called his twelve disciples to him and gave them authority to drive out impure spirits and to heal every disease and sickness.

MATTHEW 10:1 NIV

John Paul Jackson emphasized that when a judge issues a ruling in court, they don't need to raise their voice or shout to establish their authority. The power is not in the volume of their speech but in the position they hold.[55] When a judge delivers a sentence or a verdict, it is final. They can calmly say, "You owe $1,000" or "Case dismissed," and the ruling is binding because of their authority. We don't need to scream or shout at demons or sickness for them to obey. It's not the loudness of our voice but the authority of Jesus that commands results.

Just as a judge's words carry weight due to their position, our words carry weight because we are seated with Christ (Ephesians 2:6). When you command sickness or darkness to leave in Jesus' name, it's a statement of authority, not a battle of strength. Demons tremble and sickness flees because of who stands behind your words: Jesus Christ. Authority is something that must be understood and embraced, not fought for.

As you pray for healing or deliverance, remember that you don't need to shout or struggle. Speak with Christ's authority.

Today I…

---

[55] John Paul Jackson, "How to Use Your Authority and Power as a Believer," posted August 16, 2022, by Advancing the Kingdom of Jesus, YouTube, youtube.com.

DECEMBER 24

THE MESSIAH

The angel answered, "The Holy Spirit will come on you, and the power of the Most High will overshadow you. So the holy one to be born will be called the Son of God."

LUKE 1:35 NIV

The conception of Jesus was one of the most miraculous events in history. Mary's response of humble submission, *"I am the Lord's servant"* (v. 38 NIV), shows her incredible faith and willingness to be part of God's divine plan despite the impossible circumstances. The virgin birth is a powerful reminder that God's ways transcend our understanding. The conception of Jesus wasn't the result of human will or ability but a direct act of God. It fulfilled centuries of prophecy and made way for the Messiah, the savior of the world, to enter humanity.

God has limitless power to bring about the impossible. God is not bound by natural laws or human limitations. In fact, this divine miracle was essential for our salvation. Jesus had to be fully divine and fully human, born without sin, so He could live a perfect life and become the spotless Lamb sacrificed for our redemption.

Is God calling you to surrender and trust Him for a miracle? Ask for the same faith and humility Mary displayed.

Today I…

DECEMBER 25

THE BEST CHRISTMAS GIFT

He chose us in him before the creation of the world to be holy and blameless in his sight. In love, he predestined us for adoption to sonship through Jesus Christ, in accordance with his pleasure and will.

EPHESIANS 1:4–5 NIV

On Christmas Day, we celebrate the ultimate gift—God's plan of redemption and adoption, set in motion before the creation of the universe. God always planned that the Lamb would be slain so that all nations—Jews and gentiles alike—could worship Him and have an intimate relationship with Him (Revelation 13:8).

As an adoptive mom, I don't see any difference between my adopted and biological children, and neither does God with us. The Greek word for "adoption" used in Ephesians refers to the full legal standing of an adopted heir. Through Jesus, we now share in His inheritance. Romans 8:17 confirms this: *"Now if we are children, then we are heirs—heirs of God and co-heirs with Christ"* (NIV). That means we have the same legal standing as Jesus in God's family. This is the greatest Christmas gift of all: God's intentional, sacrificial love for us. Because of Jesus, we are forever God's children, and we have the same legal standing and inheritance.

Reflect on God's deep love for you. It made a way for you to be part of His family forever.

Today I…

DECEMBER 26

STAND FIRM

"Behold, I have given you authority to tread on serpents and scorpions, and over all the power of the enemy, and nothing shall hurt you."

LUKE 10:19 ESV

The authority of Christ is not something we eventually earn—it's something we receive at salvation. The same authority Jesus demonstrated when casting out demons or healing the sick is available to us today. Yet many believers don't fully understand or walk in this authority, leaving them vulnerable to the Enemy's attacks. Satan's forces operate by deception, always trying to convince us that they are stronger. But when we stand firm in Jesus' power, even the most stubborn demonic forces must flee.

Faith isn't a feeling or a mental ascent. It's a bold trust in what Christ has already accomplished and the authority He's given us. Lester Sumrall learned this firsthand. While preaching at a church in Indonesia, he unexpectedly found himself faced with a demon-possessed person. Instead of backing down, he took God at His word, commanded the demon to leave in Jesus' name, and saw the power of Christ at work. That moment ignited Sumrall's lifelong ministry in deliverance from demonic forces.[56] Authority isn't about our strength—it's about standing firm in Christ's victory.

Watch some Lester Sumrall on YouTube.

Today I…

---

56 Lester Sumrall, *Alien Entities: A Look Behind the Door to the Spirit Realm* (Sumrall Pub, 1983), 152–55.

DECEMBER 27

WE ARE HEALED

He was pierced for our transgressions, he was crushed for our iniquities; the punishment that brought us peace was on him, and by his wounds we are healed.

Isaiah 53:5 NIV

Jesus' sacrifice saved us from sin, but it also brought complete healing and restoration. This healing isn't limited to physical ailments; it extends to freedom from shame, guilt, and emotional wounds. Isaiah 53:5 uniquely uses the present tense—*"By his wounds we are healed"*—emphasizing that healing is not a future promise but a present reality. Healing has already been accomplished through Jesus' *finished* work on the cross.

The blood of Jesus can break any stronghold. Stan Lovins teaches that strongholds include generational curses, deep-rooted bitterness, and regret or shame. Jesus' blood is sufficient to bring freedom and wholeness—it's already been provided. But Lovins often teaches that true deliverance and healing require not just belief but action, stepping into the authority Christ gave us. He reminds us of Jesus' command to *"heal the sick, raise the dead, cleanse those who have leprosy, drive out demons"* (Matthew 10:8 NIV). We're called to step boldly into that same God-given authority and bring healing to others in Jesus' name.

Remember, faith is spelled R-I-S-K.[57] Take risks in praying for people and trust God to work through you.

Today I…

---

57 John Wimber, *The Way in Is the Way On: John Wimber's Teachings and Writings on Christ* (Ampelon, 2006), 171.

DECEMBER 28

LOVE MOTIVATES MIRACLES

Jesus stopped and called them. "What do you want me to do for you?" he asked. "Lord," they answered, "we want our sight."

MATTHEW 20:32–33 NIV

Missionary Heidi Baker once shared about a day when she was running late for a meeting but encountered a blind woman sitting in the scorching sun. The Holy Spirit prompted her to stop. The woman had no name, and her community believed she was cursed. Heidi didn't perform any formal prayer or ask for a miracle. Instead, she simply led the woman to shade, hugged her, gave her a name, and showed her the love of Jesus. Miraculously, the woman received her sight. Heidi said she didn't even ask God to heal the woman, but the overwhelming love of Christ that was poured out in that simple gesture was enough to bring about the miracle.[58]

Miracles are often birthed from love. Sometimes we get so busy with our own agendas that we overlook those around us who desperately need a touch of God's love and power. But when we allow Christ's love to flow through us, we create an atmosphere where the impossible becomes possible.

The next time you're busy with your own plans, stop, die to yourself, and ask if there's someone nearby who needs to experience God's love.

Today I…

---

[58] Heidi Baker, *Birthing the Miraculous: The Power of Personal Encounters with God to Change Your Life and the World* (Charisma House, 2014), 29–30.

DECEMBER 29

YIELDED VESSELS

"'Not by might nor by power, but by my Spirit,' says the Lord Almighty."

Zechariah 4:6 NIV

Kathryn Kuhlman was a remarkable woman of God, known for the miracles that happened during her meetings. She always emphasized that the miracles weren't because of her but because of the Holy Spirit working through her. She continually reminded people that it was not by might nor by power but by the spirit of God that healings and transformations occurred. Kuhlman often said that God isn't looking for golden vessels or silver vessels; He's looking for *yielded* vessels.[59] Kuhlman believed that miracles happen when we fully surrender our will to God and allow His Spirit to move. This doesn't require formula, technique, or special prayer but only the deep, total surrender to the Holy Spirit.

In her ministry, Kuhlman would often ask, "Are you willing to die?" She meant, "Are you willing to die to your own will, your own pride, and your own agenda so that God's power can flow through you unhindered?" The miracles we long to see aren't from our efforts or strength but through complete reliance on the Holy Spirit. When we surrender to God's will and allow His Spirit to work through us, we position ourselves to be conduits of His miraculous power.

Be a yielded vessel.

Today I…

---

[59] Kathryn Kuhlman, "Yielded Vessel," posted March 9, 2024, by Maths Made Simple, YouTube, youtube.com.

MOVE!

"Truly I tell you, if you have faith as small as a mustard seed, you can say to this mountain, 'Move from here to there,' and it will move. Nothing will be impossible for you."

MATTHEW 17:20 NIV

The name of Jesus carries unparalleled power, and we're called to wield it with bold authority. Healing, deliverance, and miraculous signs are for every believer. Smith Wigglesworth, known for his extraordinary healing ministry, didn't approach healing or deliverance with hesitation. He was fully convinced that the name of Jesus had the power to change any situation, no matter how dire.

Similarly, Reinhard Bonnke, who saw millions come to Christ, said "The less Holy Spirit operation we have, the more cake and coffee we need to keep the church going."[60] He recognized that the church must rely on the power of the Holy Spirit to reach the lost. We must be fully convinced that God will back His Word. Mountains don't move because of our emotions or efforts—they move because of faith in the unshakable power of Jesus' name. When we speak with confidence in His authority, heaven responds, demons tremble, and impossible situations must yield.

Speak in faith to the "mountain" in your life, trusting that God will move it.

Today I…

---

[60] Reinhard Bonnke, *Holy Spirit: Are We Flammable or Fireproof?* (Christ for All Nations, 2017), 34.

DECEMBER 31

WAKE UP YOUR FAITH!

Besides all this, you know at what point of history we stand; so it is high time for you to rouse yourselves from sleep; for the final deliverance is nearer than when we first came to trust.

ROMANS 13:11 CJB

This verse is a wake-up call for every believer. We are living in a pivotal time in history, and spiritual complacency is no longer an option. The final deliverance—our ultimate salvation in Christ—is closer now than ever before. If there was ever a time to rise from spiritual slumber, it's now. The Enemy would love nothing more than for believers to stay in a state of sleep—passive, unaware, and ineffective. But today's verse urges us to wake up! God is calling us to stand, fight, and take back the ground the Enemy has stolen.

The time for passive faith is over. This is the hour to rouse yourself, shake off the distractions, and walk fully in the purpose God has for your life. Don't hit the spiritual snooze button any longer. Now is the time to wake up your faith, engage in spiritual warfare, and pursue Jesus with everything you have. Don't let distractions or the cares of this world lull you into spiritual slumber. God has called you for this very moment in history.

Spend time reflecting on your faith journey this year and continue to wake up your faith!

Today I…

ABOUT THE AUTHOR

Jen Lilley is an award-winning actress, producer, singer, and now author. She is recognized for her vibrant and heartfelt performances in the Academy Award–winning film *The Artist*, NBC's *Days of Our Lives*, and ABC's *General Hospital* and for her appearances as a leading lady on Hallmark and Great American Family.

Beyond her work on screen, Jen is an entrepreneur whose businesses provide creative and philanthropic solutions to problems. As a musician, she gives 100 percent of her profits to charity. Her Christmas album, *Tinsel Time*, topped Amazon's jazz charts, and her debut original album *Hindsight* directly supports foster care initiatives and even provided lifesaving heart surgery to a child in Africa.

Inspired by her experiences as a foster mom and advocate, she helped start Tulsa Girls' Home and continues to advocate for children in need across the world. With *Wake Up Your Faith: 365 Daily Encounters with Jesus*, she seeks to rouse a spiritually sleeping church and encourage believers to set their eyes on Jesus, become His hands and feet, and boldly advance the kingdom of heaven.